The Do It Yourself Show
Book of
HOME
IMPROVEMENTS

The Do It Yourself Show Book of
HOME IMPROVEMENTS

Robert Roskind   •   Do It Yourself, inc.

ADDISON-WESLEY PUBLISHING COMPANY, INC.

READING, MASSACHUSETTS • MENLO PARK, CALIFORNIA
DON MILLS, ONTARIO • WOKINGHAM, ENGLAND • AMSTERDAM
SYDNEY • SINGAPORE • TOKYO • MEXICO CITY • BOGOTA
SANTIAGO • SAN JUAN

Library of Congress Cataloging in Publication Data

Roskind, Robert.
The Do-it-yourself show book of home improvements.

1. Dwellings — Remodeling — Amateurs' manuals.
I. Do-it-yourself show (Television program) II. Title.
TH4816.R67   1985   643'.7   84–29991
ISBN 0–201–06573–8
ISBN 0–201–06574–6 (pbk.)

Photographs in the color section appear courtesy of: *page 1*: copyright Michael Skott, 1985; *pages 2, 4 (top) 5 (bottom)*: courtesy of Armstrong World Industries, copyright Armstrong World Industries; *pages 3, 5 (top), 6, 7 (bottom)*: courtesy of Armstrong World Industries; *page 4 (bottom)*: reprinted with permission from Appropriate Technology Corporation; *page 7 (top)*: reprinted with permission from FPG International/Alan McGee; *page 8*: reprinted with permission from California Redwood Association. Cover photograph and photographs on pages xvi, 44, 100, and 150 by Fred Lyon © 1985. All other photographs reprinted with permission from Robert Roskind Associates and DIY, Incorporated.

Illustrations by Bill Schaeffer, Schaeffer Associates.

Copyright © 1985 by Robert Roskind/Do It Yourself, inc.

A Note to Do-it-yourselfers

The author and publisher have made every effort to make sure that the information in this book ensures safety as well as efficiency. Because the specifics of each environment, the design, materials, and even the uses of each project vary greatly, the author or the publisher cannot be held responsible for injuries that might result from the use of this book.

Cover design by Carson Designs
Text design by Carson Designs
Set in 10 point Korinna Roman by Compset Inc., Beverly, MA

ISBN 0-201-06574 P
0-201-06573 H

Acknowledgments

Many authors, when they write their acknowledgment page, say that there are many people to thank. With this book there are many, many people to thank. More than I could possibly list in the space allotted. A book is a combination of many people's energies merging together. A book like this, with its diagrams and photos, its need for vast technical input, requires more people than do most books. I was only the glue that held the people (and pieces) in place.

This book was an easy birth, given the size of the undertaking. Everyone put their heart into it. To the many people I've worked with on this project, to the many I've met personally, and to those I've not yet had an opportunity to meet, I offer my heartfelt thanks. In particular:

To Julia Holiman — for research, support, pressing details, and hours of listening to me talk

To Marnie Poirier — writer, compiler, organizer, and the person who kept expanding to hold it all

To Bill Schaeffer — his beautiful diagrams speak for themselves

To Robert Lavelle, Harlyn Aizley, and the staff of Addison-Wesley who believed in the book

To David Brayton and the members of the production crew at Calvin David Media, Inc., who created some fine videos on which this book is based

To Bill Diers for the photos

To Blair Abee for the friendship

A special thanks to Roger Albertson and Patrick Kocian authors of *The Woodstripper's Handbook*, for their help with Chapter Eight.

And, of course, to the following companies, all of which took a big gamble and are firmly committed to quality education for the do-it-yourselfer:

THE SKIL CORPORATION
THE COOPER GROUP
3M
DAP
INGERSOLL-RAND AIR COMPRESSORS
SCHLAGE LOCK COMPANY
OLYMPIC STAINS
CALIFORNIA REDWOOD ASSOCIATION
SILVER METAL FASTENERS
SPEED QUEEN
THOMPSON WATERSEAL
ARMSTRONG WORLD INDUSTRIES
EZ PAINTER
CHAMBERLAIN CONSUMER PRODUCTS
LUCITE PAINT

I would like to give a special thanks to the following companies which graciously provided us with many of the finished-room photographs that appear in this book: Armstrong World Industries, Appropriate Technology Corporation, California Redwood Association, EZ Painter and FPG International, and the Michael Skott Studio.

Thank you one and all.

Dedication

*To "the other" Robert Roskind — thanks for being
there when we needed you.*

And to the light that shines within us all.

Contents

Preface

I never really intended to devote so much of my life to teaching people to re-model and build their own homes. It just happened that way. I'm thankful that it did, because it brought me many friends, a lot of work, and even more satisfaction.

In 1978 I co-founded a do-it-yourself school with a good friend, Blair Abee. The school, The Owner Builder Center, located in Berkeley, California, is dedicated to teaching people how to build and remodel their own homes through live classes and summer camps. During my time at the Center I dealt directly with thousands of novice and would-be remodelers, sometimes, at our summer camps, living with them for three months at a time. I learned a tremendous amount from them about their hopes, their fears, and what they needed in the form of education.

In 1983 we started a new company, Do It Yourself, inc. Its purpose was to offer quality instruction in yet another format — video. We chose our two best teachers, Avion Rogers and Curt Burbick, to star in the show. Our taped series, "The Do It Yourself Show," has appeared on over 288 PBS stations, setting a new PBS record.

Recently we installed Do It Yourself Video Learning Systems in hardware and home center stores across the country. At these stores customers can borrow or rent our videos, to learn how to do the projects themselves at home. It is from this material that the book is drawn.

In gathering the material we dedicated ourselves to its detail, accuracy, and completeness. We wanted to be sure that the information was not regimentally based on one contractor's point of view. In compiling our informational base, we drew from over 100 years of experience. The foundation has been well laid.

How To Use This Book

In writing and compiling this book, I did not intend a thorough examination of each subject. My intention was rather to distill the information into concise, step-by-step construction processes, understandable and doable to the novice do-it-yourselfer.

Each chapter is detailed enough to guide you through each process. The actual designs you use and the specific problems (or challenges) you may face will vary according to your taste, the tools you have to work with, and the money you have to spend. What is presented here, in a manner I've not seen elsewhere, is a usable guide to the construction process. Read each chapter and decide whether the process as shown applies to your project. If not, you may want to consult other do-it-yourself books, local professionals, or knowledgeable salespeople at your hardware or home center store.

Be sure to consult too with your local code enforcement department. I often indicate where a local code may apply; but check with your local office for all possible codes before you begin. Also, be sure to follow all safety guidelines as outlined by O.S.H.A. (Occupational Safety and Health Administration). Remodeling, by its very nature, is a somewhat dangerous business.

At the beginning of each project I've listed the most common mistakes to avoid. (Unless the mistakes and project are too complicated, in which case I've listed the most common mistakes before each relevant step.) Study these carefully. They are an accumulation of mistakes made by many people over many years. You can learn from the mistakes of others, but don't be lulled into thinking that therefore your project will proceed without any mistakes or problems. It won't. Most novices — and professionals, too — underestimate the time, energy, hassle, and money that projects demand. Add 30–50 percent onto your present estimates in each area.

Be sure to read the entire project's chapter before you begin the work. Throughout the book I've made very effort to tell you what you will be doing, what you'll need, and what problems to watch out for; but, to really prepare for a project, you'll need to understand the construction process as a whole before proceeding step by step.

Finally, enjoy yourself. The experience of doing your own work offers not only financial benefits but also a potential for self growth and enjoyment rarely found in other endeavors. It will push you to new limits, until they are no longer limits, and, in the end, you will have a house that feels more like a home because you took an active part in the creation process.

The Do It Yourself Show Book of
HOME IMPROVEMENTS

CHAPTER ONE

Tools
Getting Down to Basics

WHAT YOU WILL BE DOING

In this chapter I talk about building your tool inventory, the distinction of quality when purchasing, and the appropriate use and care of your tools and work area.

The various types of tools I discuss are those for measuring and leveling, those for cutting and drilling, tools to help you attach and assemble or dismantle, and tools you will use for finishing. There is also a section on pneumatic tools; that is, air compressors and accessories.

In addition, I will pass along to you many time- and effort-saving tips from the professionals.

BEFORE YOU BEGIN

One recommendation I like to make to those of you who will be taking on projects in and around the house from time to time is that you first acquire a copy of the local building code from the office of your county or city building inspector. Keep a copy of this on hand so you will know when your project requires a permit of any kind. Although tools can be fun, and can open doors to new and interesting do-it-yourself projects, always keep in mind that they should never be treated as toys. If you have small children, it's a good idea to keep your tools where they will be inaccessible to curious young hands.

A workshop is a very personal thing. It should be geared to an individual's own needs, extent of do-it-yourself involvement, and space available. As your inventory of tools grows, you will want to set aside a special workplace. You will find that organized workspace makes for an organized, smoother-flowing project, because you will always know where to find that special tool when you need it. If you are unable to designate a separate room for your tools and projects, at least have a closet or locking toolbox that will secure your tools when not in use.

SAFETY

Anytime you work with tools safety must be your primary concern. A few general rules to keep in mind are:

1. Protective glasses or goggles should be worn whenever power tools are in use; and when chiseling, sanding, scraping, or hammering overhead, especially if you wear contact lenses.

2. Wear ear protectors when using power tools, since some operate at noise levels that damage hearing.

3. Be careful of loose hair and clothing, so they don't get caught in tools.

4. The proper respirator or face mask should be worn when sanding or sawing or using substances with toxic fumes.

5. Keep blades sharp. A dull blade requires excessive force, can slip, and cause accidents.

6. Always use the appropriate tool for the job.

7. Repair or discard tools with cracks in the wooden handles, or chips in the metal parts, that could fail and cause injury.

8. Don't drill, shape, or saw anything that isn't firmly and properly secured.

9. Take care in storing oily rags, which can spontaneously combust.

10. Don't abuse your tools.

11. Keep a first aid kit on hand.

12. Don't work with tools if you are tired. That's when most accidents occur.

13. Read the owner's manual for all tools and know the proper use of each.

14. Keep all tools out of reach of small children.

15. Unplug all power tools when changing settings or parts.

PURCHASING YOUR TOOLS

Give enough care and thought to the purchase of your tools. Conscientious investment should carry you through years of enjoyable projects.

1. Acquire tools as you need them; avoid buying unnecessary tools or tools you will never use.

2. Always purchase the best tool you can afford. Cheap tools are never a bargain.

3. Purchase from reputable dealers and manufacturers.

4. Choose the tool for the most comfortable fit and weight for your hand.

5. Examine tools carefully for their sturdiness and smooth finish.

6. Check all moving parts for smoothness and freedom from play.

CARING FOR TOOLS

Caring for your tools is also extremely important, if they are to do the jobs for which they are intended.

1. Keep your tools properly cleaned and lubricated.

2. Keep your tools out of the weather and store them out of the way when not in use.

3. If the storage area is damp (in the basement, for example), install a dehumidifier and keep tools covered with a film of rust-inhibiting oil.

4. Never throw tools into the toolbox. Handle them carefully to avoid dulling edges and nicking surfaces.

5. Whenever possible, hang tools with cutting edges separately to keep them from getting nicked or dulled.

6. Purchase carrying cases for your power tools to protect them and to store their accessories.

SECTION ONE

TOOLS TO MEASURE AND LEVEL

MOST COMMON MISTAKE

1. Not measuring more than once. A good carpenter measures three times and cuts once.

Accuracy and care in measuring are all important. They can mean the difference between a well-put-together project and a sloppy one.

Carpenter's pencil. This is flat, to prevent its rolling away, and encases a large lead for drawing broad, easy-to-see lines.

Steel tape measure. (Figure 1.) 16′ to 33′ in length, this tool belongs in every home. A blade that is 1″ (or more) wide will be stiffer and easier to use. Those with cushioned bumpers protect the hook of the tape from damage — likely to occur when the tape retracts back into the case. The play in the hook allows you to make either inside or outside measurements without having to compensate for the hook. Its flexibility allows it to measure round, contours, and other odd-shapes. When making inside measurements, add the measurement of the tape case, usually marked on the case.

Squares. Squares are used for laying out work, checking for squareness during assembly, and marking angles. The **carpenter's square**, also called a **framing square**, is used for marking true perpendicular lines to be cut on boards and for squaring some corners, among other things. One leg is 24″ long and 2″ wide, the other, 16″ long and 1½″ or 2″ wide. The better types have a number of tables, conversions, and formulas stamped on the side to simplify many woodworking tasks.

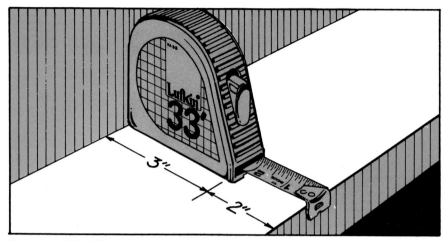

Figure 1. A 25′–33′ steel tape measure with a 1″ blade is recommended.

The **combination square** is a most versatile tool. (Figure 2.) It has a movable handle which can lock in place on the 12″ steel rule. It is used to square the end of a board, mark a 45-degree angle for mitering, and even make quick level checks with the built-in spirit level. It can also be used as a scribing tool to mark a constant distance along the length of a board.

Levels. Levels are used to make sure your work is true horizontal (level) or true vertical (plumb). The trick is to always use the longest level possible. The **torpedo level** is 8″ or 9″ in length, with vials that read level, plumb, and 45 degrees. It is used for small pieces of work. A **two-to-four-foot level** is a must for any home woodworking project, like building shelves or structural carpentry.

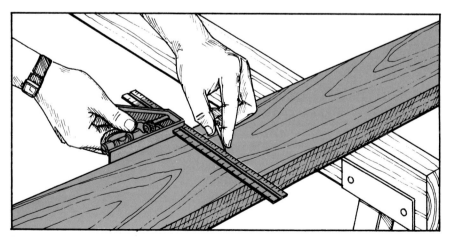

Figure 2. Using a combination square to prepare for a crosscut.

Plumb bob. This is a heavy, balanced weight on a string, which you drop from a specific point to locate another point exactly below it, or to determine true vertical (Figure 3).

Chalkline. This is a string or line coated with colored chalk, used to transfer a straight line to a working surface easily and accurately. Pull the line out and hold it tight between the two points of measurement. Then snap it to leave a mark. Some have a pointed case to double as a plumb bob.

Tips on Measuring

1. When many pieces need to be cut and/or drilled the same, use one accurately cut or drilled piece as a template to mark all the others. However, for greatest accuracy, always rely on your tape measure.

2. Remember the old maxim: "A good carpenter measures three times and cuts once."

Figure 3. A plumb bob always hangs true vertical (plumb).

SECTION TWO

CUTTING AND DRILLING TOOLS

MOST COMMON MISTAKES

1. Setting a board to be cut between two supports. Instead, cantilever the board over the outside of one support to avoid binding the saw blade when the board drops. This method will avoid "kick back."

2. Neglecting to choose the appropriate saw blade for the material being cut. Always use the proper cutting edge for the job you are doing. That means one that is sharp as well as made for a given material.

For sawing and assembling, one of the most useful accessories is a pair of **sawhorses**. They can mean the difference between an easy, comfortable task and a difficult one. Sawhorses support both ends of your work while allowing room for the saw.

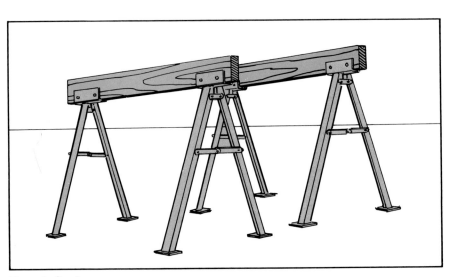
Figure 4. Saw horses.

POWER TOOLS

Circular saw. (Figure 5.) This saw is one of the most common and most popular tools. It consists of a replaceable blade; a blade guard, part of which is spring loaded to move out the way as you saw; a sole plate, which may or may not be attached to a ripping fence; a cutting guide; and knobs to adjust the cutting angle and depth of the blade. Set the cutting depth to $1/8''$ more than the thickness of the board. Avoid binding by keeping the sole plate flat on the surface of the wood. There are two basic kinds of circular saws. The **worm drive saw** is used for heavy-duty framing-type work. The **side winder** is used for lightweight jobs and finishing work.

Jig saw or **saber saw.** (Figure 6.) This saw is used to cut curving lines or make detailed cuts. When starting your cut from inside a piece of wood, you can drill a starting hole to cut openings in paneling, drywall, or counter tops. Most models can accommodate a circle guide and angle cutting and ripping accessories.

Reciprocating saw. This is generally used to cut openings in existing walls. It is ideal for remodeling or demolition work. It can rough-cut green wood, metal, leather, rubber, cloth, linoleum, and plastic.

Figure 5.   The circular saw is a popular tool for homeowners.

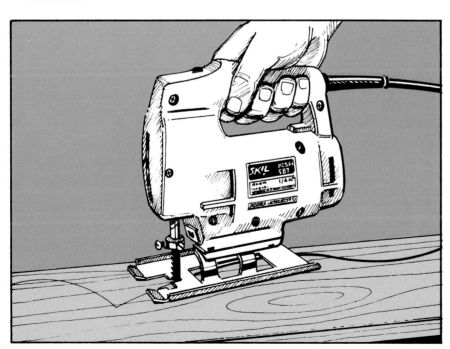

Figure 6.   A saber saw allows you to make fine cuts in curved and detailed patterns.

Figure 7. A small table or hand saw allows flexibility for trim, cabinets, and other flushing work.

Figure 8. Using a radial arm saw.

Table saw. (Figure 7.) Sometimes called a **bench saw**, it can crosscut, rip, miter, groove, and bevel. With a 7½″ to 12″ blade, this saw can cut depths of 1½″ to 3⅜″. With accessories, it will cut dadoes, make moldings, and sand stock. Smaller table saws are good for general hobby and repair work.

Radial arm saw. This saw makes all the cuts a table saw makes but is used for heavier stock. The board is usually held stationary for crosscutting, with the saw blade bearing down across the board. This tool is usually used by professionals.

Band saw. A small band saw can be useful for more creative wood cutting where complex shapes, curves, and precision cutting is needed.

Most do-it-yourselfers end up with a good ⅜″ **electric** or **power drill** because of its versatility. If it has a variable-speed trigger, as well as a reversing switch, the utility of the drill is greatly increased. A **cordless drill** (Figure 9) eliminates the need for cumbersome extension cords and can be used where power is not available.

You'll need **drill bits** of carbon steel for soft materials like wood and plastic. High-speed steel bits work well on metals, and carbide-tipped bits are used for concrete or masonry.

Other useful **attachments** include hole saw blades, spade bits, buffing disks and depth stops, screwdriving bits, sanding disks, or even a power grinder. You can add a paint mixer, right-angle drive, wire brushes, wood countersinks, and even saws, lathes, and rotary rasps and files.

The **router** is used to cut contours in wood for edgings and moldings or for more complex relief panels and inlay work, dovetails, and mortises.

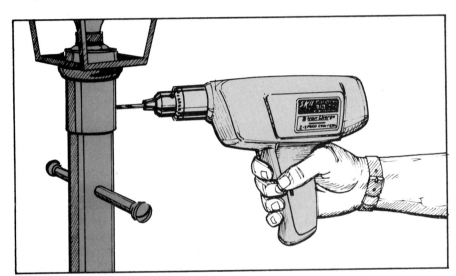

Tips on Cutting and Drilling

1. When rip cutting, use a rip guide, or tack down a straightedge to use as a cutting guide.

2. Always secure your stock before cutting or drilling.

3. Use caution when ripping small, narrow pieces. Use a push stick with the radial arm saw or table saw, and always keep hands clear of blades.

4. When drilling into metal, squirt a lightweight oil onto the drill bit and into the hole to cool the bit.

5. Predrilling a "Pilot hole" with a smaller drill bit makes nailing into hardwood, as well as screwing into all types of wood, easier, and lessens the chance the wood will split.

6. Always unplug your power tools when adjusting or changing accessories.

7. Keep any tool adjustment keys taped to the cord near the plug. This will remind you to unplug the tool, as well as keep you from losing the key.

8. Be sure your tools are properly grounded. Unless a tool is double insulated, it should be plugged into a three-hole grounded outlet.

9. Watch cord placement so it does not interfere with the tool's operation.

10. Never use a power tool in wet or damp conditions, no matter how well grounded. Moisture readily conducts electricity.

11. Be sure both ends of a board are well supported, and don't cut between the supports; cantilever the scrap end instead.

12. When using a table saw, choose the guide that allows the longest edge of the stock to be used against the guide.

Figure 9. Cordless drills offer the advantage of working where no power is available or where power cords are inconvenient.

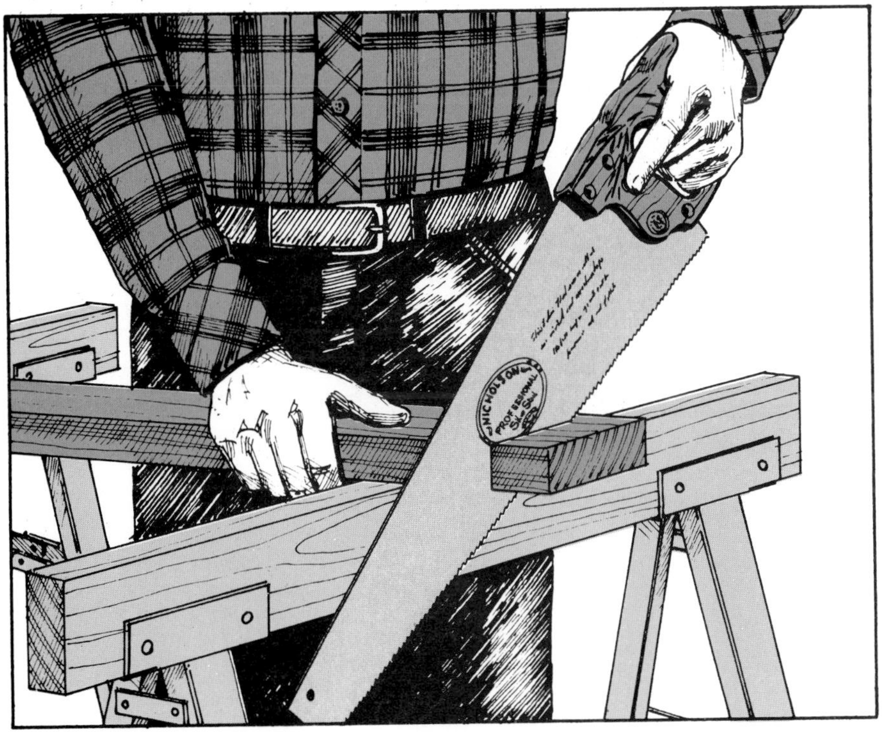

HAND TOOLS

Hand tools are as essential as the power tools.

Crosscut saw. This is used to cut across the grain of wood. It has smaller, offset teeth. An 8-point saw is best for general use.

Rip saw. A rip saw cuts with the grain, and has much larger teeth.

Combination saw. This cuts both across and with the grain. (Figure 10.)

Hacksaw. This tool is used on metal, plastic, and electrical conduit.

Backsaw. This saw is used in conjunction with a miter box to cut a perfectly straight line across a piece of wood. The steel backing keeps it aligned. (Figure 11.)

Keyhole saw. This has a blade that is narrower at the tip than at the heel or handle. It is used for cutting openings in drywall or paneling or for curved cuts.

Figure 10. A combination handsaw can saw both across and with the grain.

Figure 11. A miter box and saw are used to make accurate cuts for trim and molding.

Tips on Chiseling

1. Start your blade digging into the wood, slightly inside your guideline mark.

2. Do not cut too deeply. Chisels are meant to chip and shave away. The beveled edge goes into the work so that it constantly directs the chisel out of the wood for better control.

3. Keep the cutting edge directed away from your body and hands.

Coping saw. A coping saw is needed to follow an irregular, delicate, or intricate cut in wood. The blade is thin, fine toothed, and removable.

Tips on Sawing

1. Do not store saws in toolboxes or where the teeth will get damaged. Hang your saws if possible. If not, buy a plastic tooth guard or make one out of cardboard.

2. Keep saw blades sharp. Keep them out of contact with metal or concrete and stone. Remove any nails from wood before sawing.

3. Protect your saw blades by coating them with paste wax or a lighter grade of machine oil. Keep them in a cardboard sheath.

Chisels are wood-cutting tools. It is best to purchase a set of chisels ranging from ¼″ to 1½″ in widths for general use. Socket chisels are meant to be used with a mallet. (I recommend not using a hammer to strike a chisel.) Tang chisels are for working with the weight of the hand only. For more specialized use, purchase a good beveled-edge cabinetmaker's chisel for finish work. The square edge of a framing chisel is best for forming work, while the narrow mortise chisel serves to break waste away.

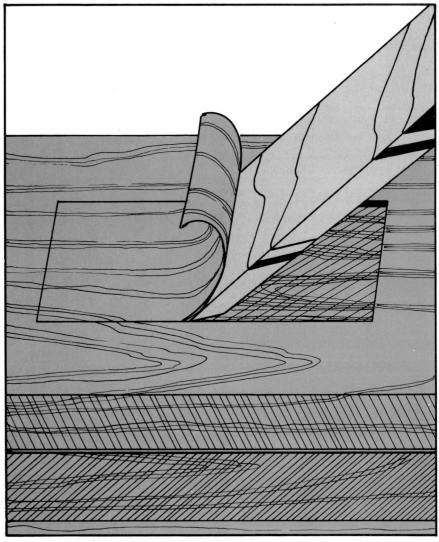

Figure 12. A good set of chisels completes a homeowner's tool shop.

SECTION THREE

TOOLS FOR ATTACHING, ASSEMBLING, AND DISMANTLING

MOST COMMON MISTAKES

1. "Choking up" on the hammer handle. This reduces leverage and usually disables the head from striking flat against the surface being struck.

2. Not predrilling a pilot hole before nailing or screwing into hardwoods or near the ends of boards.

3. Using extra-leverage items to tighten clamps.

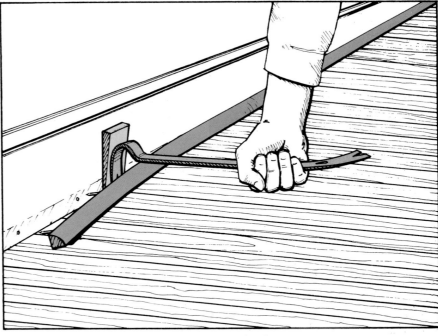
Figure 13. Removing shoe molding with a pry bar and wedge.

At some point in any project you will be attaching, dismantling, or assembling what you have been measuring and sawing. These operations can be done in a variety of ways.

Most people need a **pry bar** around the house. This demolition tool is useful where pulling nails, ripping wood, and prying molding from walls needs to be done. A pry bar offers more leverage than a hammer. (Figure 13.)

Another special item useful around the house is a **com-a-long**. This device has a cable and a ratcheting handle used to pull things together. It is useful for anything from making framing sections square and plumb to pulling a car out of a ditch.

Figure 14. Use a soft mallet to avoid marring wood.

9

HAMMERS

The **carpenter's hammer** is available in two patterns. The **claw hammer** is made with a curved claw, better suited to pulling nails. But for those who will also be ripping boards out, the **ripping hammer** with its straight claw will more easily fit between boards. Both are used to drive or remove nails. They come with wood (usually hickory), steel, or fiberglass handles and in a variety of face styles and weights. A 12 to 16 oz. **finishing hammer** is recommended for small workshop projects and general use; 18 to 24 oz. for heavier framing work. Finishing hammers are those with smooth faces.

You will also be using the following:

Tack hammer. This is useful for driving tacks and brads. Some have magnetic heads.

Ball peen hammer. The face of this hammer is rounded, with beveled edges. The other end is a ball-shaped peen for metal working.

Mallets. These tools are used primarily for striking other objects, notably chisels, or to form sheet metal. A soft-faced mallet is used with wood- and plastic-handled chisels. (Figure 14.)

Sledge hammer. This is necessary for heavy work on concrete, or for wood splitting in conjunction with a wedge.

Nailset. This device, used with a hammer, is for pushing the nail below the surface of the wood when you don't want it to show.

Nails. Nails range from the smallest, thinnest brads to large, weighty spikes. Just be sure you are using the correct nail for the job at hand.

Figure 15. Use a block of wood to avoid marring wood while pulling nails.

Tips on Hammering

1. To withdraw a long nail, place a block of wood under the hammerhead for extra leverage and to avoid marring the wood. (Figure 15.)

2. Use safety goggles when hammering metals. Too often chips fly from steel chisels, or nailheads break off.

3. Whenever possible, drive the nail through the thinner piece of wood into the thicker one. Use a nail that is at least twice in length the thickness of the thinner piece of wood.

4. Predrilling a pilot hole, slightly smaller than the nail thickness you will be using, prevents splitting the wood and is recommended for hardwoods (oak, maple, etc.) or near the ends of boards.

5. Blunting the point of the nail with your hammer before driving it also prevents splitting. Do this by tapping the end of the nail while the head rests on a solid surface.

SCREWDRIVERS AND SCREWS

Screwdrivers are self-explanatory. They are used to drive in and remove screws. Too often they are wrongly used — for chipping, punching holes, scraping, prying, and so forth. The **Phillips head** is a common screw and screwdriver. Its design reduces blade slippage from the cross-shaped slot and lends itself to driving with a power bit. The **conventional screwdriver** has a single blade and is used with screws of matching heads. **Battery-powered cordless screwdrivers** are now on the market and are a very helpful tool.

Screw heads are usually flat, oval, or round, and each has a specific purpose for final seating and appearance. **Flat heads** are always countersunk or rest flush with the surface. **Oval heads** permit countersinking, but the head protrudes somewhat. **Round-headed screws** rest on top of the material and are easiest to remove.

Screw types include the **wood screw** for when stronger joining than a nail is

Tools

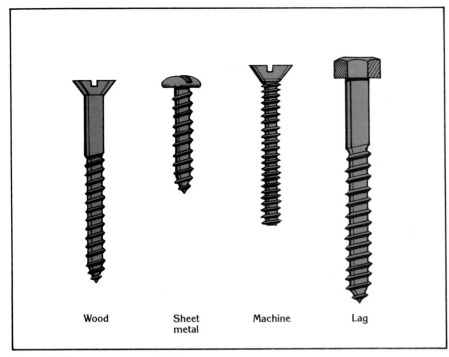

Figure 16. **Common screws and bolts.**

needed, or for when other materials must be fastened to wood. This screw is tapered to help draw the wood together as the screw is inserted. A **sheet metal screw** can also be used to fasten metal to wood, as well as metal to metal, plastic, or other materials. Sheet metal screws are threaded completely from the point to the head, and the threads are sharper than those of wood screws. **Machine screws** are for joining metal parts, such as hinges to metal door jambs. Machine screws are inserted into tapped (prethreaded) holes and are sometimes used with washers and nuts. **Lag screws**, or square-headed bolts with screw heads, are for heavy holding and are driven in with a wrench rather than a screwdriver.

Remember, when choosing screw length, that the screw should penetrate 2/3 of the combined thickness of the materials being joined. Consider as well moisture conditions and the makeup of the materials being fastened, to avoid corrosion. Use galvanized or other rust-resistant screws where rust could be a problem.

Tips on Screwdriving

1. Lubricate screws with soap or wax for easier installation.

2. Whenever possible, hold the work in a vise or clamp when inserting a screw. If this is not possible, keep your hands and other parts of the body away from the tip of the driver.

3. To remove a screw with a damaged slot, another slot can be cut with a hacksaw blade if the head is exposed enough.

4. A pilot hole (usually 2 sizes smaller than the shank of the screw) should always be made before driving a screw. This is especially crucial in hardwoods or when driving a screw near the end of the board. When working with screws of larger diameter, a pilot hole of the same diameter as the shank of the screw should be drilled into the wood to a depth of 1/3 the length of the screw.

5. Always keep the screwdriver shank in line with the screw shank. This will avoid damaging the screw slot and pushing the screw out of line.

Figure 17. **Using an adjustable wrench.**

11

WRENCHES AND PLIERS

A wide variety of **wrenches** or **pliers** are not necessary for woodworking, but some of the more common ones have their place around the house.

An adjustable **open-end wrench** will fit any size nut within its opening capacity. The best choice for the homeowner is one that opens to $^{15}\!/_{16}''$.

The **box** or **socket wrenches** are used for removing nuts and bolts and are fitted to the size of the fastener.

Allen wrench. These are useful for recessed screws and setscrews.

Pipe wrenches. Pipe wrenches are necessary to tighten (or loosen) plumbing pipes. Use two wrenches (especially when working on existing pipe) — one to keep the pipe in place, the other to turn the pipe or fitting out.

Locking wrench. This wrench works like a clamp for holding pipes and other objects in place.

Strap wrench. Primarily for chrome-plated fittings, this wrench prevents marring the chrome-plated finish.

Slip joint pliers. These pliers have jaws that lock into normal and wide opening positions, for use in holding.

Lineman's pliers. These are useful in electrical work. They have side cutters for heavy-duty wire cutting and splicing.

Channel lock pliers. These pliers, with multi-position pivots, adjust for openings up to 2″.

Long-nosed pliers. Sometimes called "needle-nosed pliers," these get into hard-to-reach places and are used to shape wire and thin metal.

End-cutting nippers. Use these to snip wire, small nails, and brads.

Tip on Wrenching and Plying

1. Make sure the jaws of the wrench or pliers are snug in position before you manipulate the handle, to avoid slippage or scraped knuckles.

Figure 18. C-clamps are available with different size openings.

Bar clamp using wood scraps for padding

Figure 19. Large items can be clamped with bar clamps.

CLAMPS

Clamps are for holding objects together while they are being worked on, or while various adhesives are drying.

C-clamp. This clamp is the most common. So named because of its shape, it has a swivel head that makes the clamp self-aligning for odd-shaped pieces. (Figure 18.)

Bar clamp. This is useful for clamping extra-wide work. (Figure 19.)

Vise. The vise is a workbench tool and should be firmly secured before being used. It is used for holding work being sawed, bored, glued, or formed in some way.

Handscrew. This has hardwood jaws which move in opposite directions due to the threading of the screws. The smooth wood and broad jaws protect the surface of the work being clamped. This is used for cabinet and furniture work. (Figure 20.)

Spring clamps. These clamps are for smaller bonding uses. They are also used when slow removal of pressure is needed.

Tips on Clamping

1. Use padding or scraps of wood between clamps and the work, to avoid any pressure damage to the surface.

2. Never tighten a clamp or vise with extra leverage items such as a wrench or pipe. Nor should you pound on the handle to obtain extra leverage.

ADHESIVES

The best joining is accomplished with **adhesives**, in conjunction with screws, nails, or other fasteners. A few of the more common types include:

Polyvinyl (carpenter's wood glue). This is a white, creamy glue, usually available in convenient plastic bottles. Mainly used for furniture, craft, or woodworking projects, polyvinyl sets in an hour, dries clear, and won't stain. However, it is vulnerable to moisture.

Resorcinol and **formaldehyde.** These are mixed just prior to using, can be used two to four hours after mixing, but must be used at temperatures over 70 degrees F. Both the resin (powdered resorcinol) and the powdered formaldehyde that you mix with water are brown and will stain light wood. Follow the manufacturer's instructions carefully.

Contact cements. These are used to bond veneers or to bond plastic laminates to wood for table tops and counters. Coat both surfaces thinly and allow to dry somewhat before bonding. Align the surfaces perfectly before pressing together, since this adhesive does not pull apart. Use in a well-ventilated area.

Epoxy. Epoxy is the only adhesive with a strength greater than the material it bonds. It resists almost anything from water to solvents. Epoxy can be used to fill cavities that would otherwise be difficult to bond. Use it in warm temperatures but read the manufacturer's instructions carefully, since drying times vary and mixing the resin and hardener must be exact.

Tips on Bonding

1. With the exception of epoxy, too much adhesive will weaken the hold of the materials you are bonding.

2. Rough up smooth surfaces slightly before applying adhesives so they will grip more securely.

3. Apply a thin coat of glue, clamp securely, and allow to dry the recommended amount of time.

4. Wipe away excess glue immediately after clamping.

Figure 20. A handscrew won't mar the wood and can be adjusted to various angles.

FASTENERS AND CONNECTORS

Ready-made fasteners and connectors are now on the market for just about any job you may need to do, whether it's building a fence, a deck, or a house. They can be used where wood meets wood, concrete, or brick, and most are approved by the Uniform Building Code requirements. However, you should always consult your local building code before using. These connectors can oftentimes save you money, labor, materials, and time when constructing a project.

Safety plates. These prevent accidental nailing into utility wires or pipes that pass through framing.

Nail plates and **plate straps.** These work well as mending plates or for light-duty wood-to-wood splices.

Fence brackets. These simplify fence construction and allow for easy disassembly when necessary.

Sawhorse brackets. These turn a 2 × 4 or 2 × 6 into a necessary support tool in just one step.

Stud shoe. This will reinforce a joist, stud, or rafter that may have been drilled or notched during construction.

Drywall clips. These can be used for wallboard or paneling.

Foundation and **masonry connections.** These include foundation anchors, brick wall ties, and floor jacks, among others.

Post anchors. These are designed to support a post from the ground up. These eliminate deep post holes and prevent wood rot or termite damage.

Post caps and **plates.** These are used for a strong support where one or more beams must be connected.

Joist hangers. These aid in accurate, uniform connections and allow a structure to hold greater loads than do other techniques.

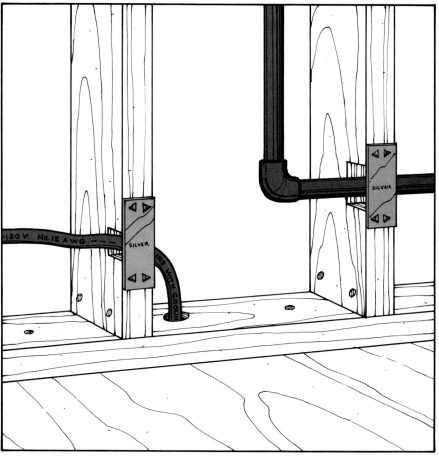

Figure 21. Nail guards protect wires and pipes from drywall nails.

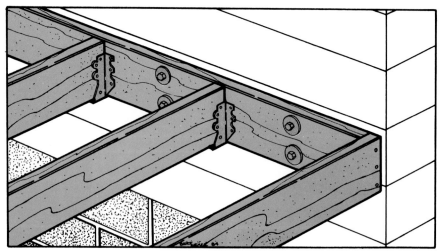

Figure 22. Joist installed and nailed to joist hangers.

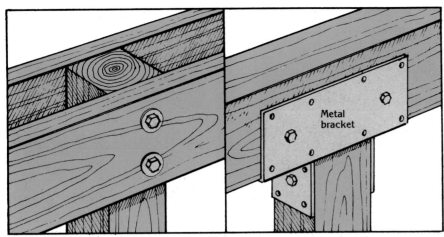

Figure 23. Two types of girders using 2″ and 4″ stock.

Belt sander. The belt sander is designed for quickly sanding rough work on large areas, or wherever heavy-duty sanding is needed.

Disk sander. The disk sander is useful for fast removal of wood on uneven surfaces. Disk sanding attachments can be purchased as a drill accessory.

Sandpapers. Sandpapers run from very coarse (20 to 40 grits per inch) all the way up to the very fine (600 grits per inch). The materials range from flint and garnet emory to aluminum oxide and silicon carbide. **Flint** is best for hand sanding painted or pitchy surfaces which can clog the paper. **Garnet emory** is for hand sanding clean wood. **Aluminum oxide** is fast and longer lasting when power sanding wood. It can also be used on plastics and fiberglass and for polishing stainless steel, high carbon steel, or bronze. **Silicon**

SECTION FOUR

FINISHING TOOLS

MOST COMMON MISTAKES

1. Allowing a power sander to dig into the wood being finished. To avoid this, keep the sanding machine always moving over the wood.

2. Putting the belt on a belt sander backward. This tears the seams.

3. Using an inappropriate grit of sanding paper for the desired effect.

Finishing is usually the last step in building a project. The finishing tools are designed to smooth something to its desired finished state.

SANDING TOOLS

Sanding block or **block sander.** This is wrapped with the appropriate sandpaper and hand rubbed across the surface. (Figure 24.)

Sanding cloth. This is essential for curved or round objects. It's easier on you and gives a much more even finish.

Power orbital sander. This power tool is found in most workshops. Sometimes called a **pad sander**, it is the ideal all-around sanding tool. Use it for rough or finish work on walls, ceilings, floors, furniture, or other woodwork. (Figure 25.)

Figure 24. Using a hand-held sanding block for sanding.

Figure 25. Using an orbital sander to sand a large patch. For larger jobs use proper dust mask.

Figure 26. Using a belt sander for larger sanding jobs.

carbide is harder than aluminum oxide and is best used for hard plastics, glass, and ceramics, or grinding and finishing brass, copper, and aluminum.

Emory cloth. This is another option for metal polishing.

Steel wool. Steel wool is available in #3 coarse to #0000, which is very fine.

For a glassy finish, use pumice or rottenstone (decomposed limestone).

Generally, you will want to start with a coarse paper and work to a fine paper for the smoothest finish. Whenever possible, sand with the grain.

Tips on Sanding

1. When using a power sander, do not press down on the machine. Let its own weight do the sanding. Pressing down inhibits the natural action of the machine.

2. Whenever operating any power sander, engage and disengage the machine from the material being sanded while the belt or disk is still in motion to avoid gouging the wood.

3. Wrap a padding material around a stick or dowel, then wrap sandpaper over it to use on inward curves.

4. When sanding wood, seal any heating and air-conditioning ducts and electrical outlets with plastic sheets and/or duct tape. Wood dust can ignite.

PLANES

Planes are for removing very thin layers of wood, for trimming and smoothing, for straightening edges or beveling them, and even for adding a groove.

Block plane. This plane is about 6″ long and is used for small smoothing and fitting jobs.

Trimming plane. Use a trimming plane for more delicate work. These are only 3½″ in length and have a 1″ blade.

Jack plane. At 12″ to 15″ this plane smooths rough surfaces with its 2″ blade.

Smooth plane. This smaller plane runs from 7″ to 10″ long with a 1¾″ blade. It is also used to smooth rough surfaces.

Scrub plane. If you desire a hand-hewn effect, a scrub plane, about the same length but with a blade of 1¼″, works fast for those rough cuts.

Fore and **joiner planes.** At 18″ to 24″ in length, these are your best bet for straightening edges.

Rabbit plane. This will cut recessed grooves along an edge.

Grooving plane. This plane will cut a long slot.

Tips on Proper Planing

1. Plane with the grain of the wood whenever possible, to avoid catching and lifting chips of wood.

2. Prevent splitting the corners on material you are planing by clamping scraps of wood on either side of the corner and at the same level.

3. Always keep blades razor sharp.

4. When it's not in use, rest your plane on its side to avoid dulling the blade.

5. When starting cuts, apply more pressure to the front of the tool; when completing, apply more pressure to the rear.

FILES AND RASPS

Files are used for shaping. You will find files that are round, half-round, flat, square, and even triangular. Single-cut file teeth run in one direction; double-cut teeth run in opposing directions. The latter will cut more coarsely, but quicker. **Rasps** differ from files in that the teeth are formed individually, not connected to one another. In general, a longer file or rasp will have somewhat coarser teeth than a shorter one. Files will cut smoother than rasps, but, when used on wood, will work much slower and are susceptible to clogging.

Tips on Filing

1. Files are easier to use with an attachable handle.

2. Secure your work with a vise or clamps: at elbow height for general filing, lower for heavier filing, and nearer to eye level for delicate work.

3. Keep files clean with a file brush.

4. Store files in a rack or protective sleeves to keep from dulling the teeth.

SECTION FIVE

PNEUMATIC TOOLS

Pneumatic tools are fast becoming recognized as both affordable and indispensable to the home do-it-yourselfer. Pneumatic means containing air. Specifically, pneumatic tools include an air compressor and a variety of tool attachments. This may sound somewhat intimidating to a newcomer in the do-it-yourself field. However, although pneumatic tools may take some special handling, they actually save a great deal of working time and effort and are relatively easy to use. They also afford professional results.

MOST COMMON MISTAKES

1. Not reading the instruction manual and safety labels.

2. Using an improper length or gauge of extention cord. A long extension cord will reduce the power and efficiency of the motor. Use extension air hose rather than cord for distance work.

3. Using an incorrect pressure for the tool and the task.

4. Not changing the oil every 250 hours of use or every six months.

5. Neglecting to locate the working air compressor on a clean, dry, level site.

6. Neglecting to keep the compressor properly lubricated.

SAFETY

1. Many tasks for which an air compressor is used require safety glasses or goggles, protective clothing and a dust- or paint-filtering mask.

2. Make sure the pressure of the compressor has been completely relieved through the line to the tool before changing to another, except where a quick connection is being used.

3. Make sure any tool has completely stopped before changing or disconnecting.

4. Never point the blow gun toward your eyes or any other part of your body.

5. Never exceed recommended pressure for the tool being used or the job being done.

6. Never alter the three prong plug to fit an outlet other than the one it is designed for.

7. Always unplug the cord from the receptable before disengaging it from the compressor.

8. Test safety relief valves periodically.

9. Open the tank valve after every use.

10. Never allow children around the compressor whether it is in operation or stored.

11. Never operate the compressor without the belt guard in place.

12. Always read the owner's manual completely and read all safety oriented labels on the unit before using.

Air Compressor

An **air compressor** is the central power source and your major investment. Air compressors are available in horsepowers of ¾ to 5, or even larger, with a variety of tank sizes up to 80 gallons. The capacity and the frequency and duration of use will determine the horsepower and tank size you'll need for your own projects. A 2 hp or smaller will be adequate for most tanks around the house. Typically these size units will have tanks from 7½ to 20 gallons. Choose an air compressor for quality and protective features. Certification by ASME — the American Society of Mechanical Engineers — is the only guarantee of quality in workmanship and materials, and is a main measure of quality. The ASME label will appear on the tank. All compressors do not have ASME certification. Only ASME certified compressors can be sold in some states.

Other features that will be found in a quality compressor include:

An ASME certified **safety relief valve** which will allow air to escape automatically if pressure in the tank should ever exceed the maximum. This valve will have a pull ring attached to it to allow you to check the valve to make certain the valve is not clogged or corroded.

An oil level **sight glass**, a tank **pressure gauge** and, of course, a **pressure regulator** and gauge are important, as each tool and job has a specific pressure requirement. The tank maintains air at maximum pressure from 100 to 125 pounds of pressure per square inch. PSI is the force of the pressurized air delivered to the tool. Projects and tools have both pressure and volume requirements. Volume is measured in cubic feet per minute (CFM) or standard cubic feet per minute (SCFM). When selecting and using a compressor, it is the relationship of CFM (volume of air) and PSI (force or pressure of air) that is important.

A manual **thermal overload button** is important in case of overloads or if the motor overheats. If the motor overheats, it automatically shuts off. This protective **control button** must be pushed for the compressor to run once the motor has cooled down, preventing a sudden and unexpected restart. The best air intake **filtration system** will be enclosed and mounted on the side of the compressor. This does more to protect the filtering foam, inside the housing, keeping the compressor cleaner, longer.

A **belt guard** is indispensable protection and the compressor should never be turned on without the guard in place.

A **hose rack** is desirable for convenience and for protecting the air hose when not in use.

One other feature, most desirable to the do it yourselfer, is a toll free number to call should a question or problem arise.

There are five basic steps in the operation of an air compressor.

1. Check the oil level to make sure the compressor is properly lubricated.

Figure 27. An air compressor can be used to apply caulking or adhesive.

Goggles

Figure 28. Using an air stapler.

2. Plug the unit into the correct grounded, 3-pronged outlet. Turn the pressure switch on and close the tank drain valve.

3. Adjust the pressure for the tool you will be using and the job you will be doing. Never exceed recommended pressure for the tool or the job.

4. When finished, shut off the motor, unplug the unit, and turn off the regulator valve. Then bleed the air out of the hose, remove the tool and open the regulator to bleed the air in the tank. If you have a quick connect, you must either remove the hose to bleed off the air from the tank or bleed the air through the drain cocks.

5. After storing the hose, open the drain cock to release any accumulated moisture. Leave it open until the next time the compressor is used.

Attachments

Now let's talk about the available tool **attachments**. If kept properly cleaned and lubricated, air tools are virtually indestructible. With few actual moving parts, maintenance is minimal. They run cool, since their power source is the compressor.

Perhaps two of the most obvious and useful tools are an **inflation kit** and **quick connect couplers**. The quick connect couplers make it fast and simple to change tools. The inflation kit attachments allow you to inflate everything from beach balls to automobile tires.

Blo-gun. This attachment is great for blasting away dirt, grease, and dust from hard-to-reach areas. Never point the gun at the eyes or other parts of the body.

Nail gun. Always be sure the gun is flat against the surface being nailed and know what is on the other side, so you won't cause damage or injury with the high pressure of the gun.

Air stapler. Again, be sure the stapler is flat against the surface being stapled. Larger staplers are available for attaching roofing shingles and so forth.

Air sander. The dual-action air sander should always be touching the surface when it is turned on. This type sander is frequently used in automotive work but many other uses around the house, such as rust removal or paint preparation, make it a handy tool to have.

Spray gun. This speeds up paint application and gives a smooth finish. There are a variety of spray gun designs on the market for various types of painting. Many times you can reduce the time required to do a job by 50% or more.

Sandblaster. This works well for removing rust and old paint and for preparing surfaces for painting. This same equipment can be adapted for use with soap and water for pressure cleaning such as degreasing auto engines and lawn and garden equipment.

Caulking gun. This tool takes the toil out of caulking, by giving a fast, uniform bead. Uniform and consistant pressure makes for a stronger bead. This tool can be used for any tube material such as adhesive or grease.

Air ratchet wrench. This is great for tightening bolts, whether building a deck, working on an automobile engine or installing a muffler.

Air hammer/chisel. The masters jobs from masonry to tailpipe removal. It must be up against the surface when started.

Air drill. An air drill makes drilling into any surface an effortless task.

Impact wrench. This is used in automotive and assembly work.

Most air tools are available at hardware stores and home centers. Specialty air tools can be rented. Instructions for each tool attachment are included with the purchase or rental. Read these instructions carefully before attempting to use the tool.

19

TOOLS FOR TODAY'S DO-IT-YOURSELFER

Tools for Measuring and Leveling

Steel tape measure	Torpedo level
Carpenter's square	2' to 4' level
Combination square	Plumb bob
	Chalkline

Power Tools for Cutting and Drilling

Circular saw	Band saw
Jig saw	⅜" variable-speed drill
Reciprocating saw	Cordless drill
Table saw (Bench saw)	Router
Radial-arm saw	

Hand Tools for Sawing and Chiseling

Crosscut saw	Chisel set ¼" to 1½" in widths
Rip saw	Cabinetmaker's chisel
Combination saw	Framing chisel
Hacksaw	Mortise chisel
Back saw and miter box	Mallet
Keyhole saw	
Coping saw	

Tools for Attaching, Assembling, and Dismantling

Hammers	*Screwdrivers*
Claw hammer	Conventional screwdrivers
Ripping hammer	Phillips-head screwdrivers
Tack hammer	Cordless screwdriver
Ball peen hammer	Wood screws
Sledge hammer	Sheet metal screws
Nailset	Machine screws
Pry bar	
Brads, nails, and spikes	

Figure 29. An air compressor can be used for sanding, painting and fastening.

Figure 30. Using an air compressor to paint.

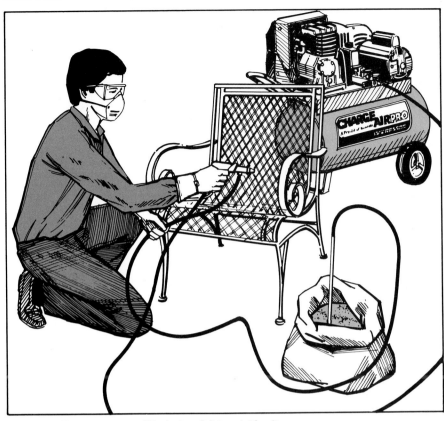

Figure 31. You can use a sandblaster to refinish metal furniture.

Wrenches
Open-end wrench
Box or socket
    wrench
Allen wrench
Pipe wrenches (2)
Locking wrench
Strap wrench
Lag screws
Bolts

Clamps
C-clamp
Bar clamp
Spring clamp
Handscrew
Vise

Pliers
Slip joint pliers
Lineman's pliers
Channel lock
    pliers
Long-nosed pliers
End-cutting
    nippers

Adhesives
Polyvinyl
Resorcinol and
    formaldehyde
Contact cement
Epoxy

Tools for Finishing Work

Power Sanders
Orbital sander
Belt sander
Disk sander

Hand Sanders
Sanding block
Sanding cloth
Sandpapers
Steel wool

Files
Single cut
Double cut
Rasp

Planes
Block plane
Trimming plane
Smooth plane
Scrub plane
Jack plane
Fore and joiner
    planes
Rabbit plane
Grooving plane

Pneumatic Tools

Air compressor
Spray gun
Air drill
Air ratchet
Air sander
Air hammer/chisel
Impact wrench

Quick-connect
    couplers
Blo-gun
Caulking gun
Stapler
Nail gun
Sandblaster

Miscellaneous Tools

Sawhorses

Shop vac

Figure 32. Using an air compressor to fasten bolts.

CHAPTER TWO

Interior Painting and Wallpapering
Easy Methods for Professional Results

WHAT YOU WILL BE DOING

This chapter will assist you in doing your own painting and wallpapering. Both of these are rather simple projects, and by following the advice presented here you will find them to be enjoyable and effective as well. You'll learn how to prepare a wall, estimate materials, and use your tools correctly. Pay particular attention to the section on wall preparation and repair. It will guide you through this most neglected step for a final result that is more attractive and longer lasting.

Neither painting nor wallpapering demand a lot of you physically. The toughest part will be painting or papering the ceilings. Mentally, as well, they are rather simple, except for planning your paper application. The key thing is proper prep. You may want to take shortcuts here. Don't.

BEFORE YOU BEGIN

SAFETY

Always understand, develop, and adhere to proper safety practices for each project. For both painting and wallpapering, these include:

1. Always use the appropriate tool for the job.

2. Keep blades sharp. A dull blade requires excessive force and can slip.

3. Safety goggles or glasses should be worn when using power tools, especially if you wear contacts.

4. Always unplug your power tools when making adjustments or changing attachments.

5. Be sure your tools are properly grounded.

6. Watch power cord placement so that it does not interfere with the operation of the tool.

7. The proper respirator or face mask should be used when sanding or working with chemicals.

8. Wear ear protection when operating power tools, because some operate at a noise level that can damage hearing.

9. Be careful of loose hair and clothing so that they don't get caught in power tools.

10. Wipe up spills immediately.

11. Don't smoke or allow open flames, such as a pilot light, around solvents or solvent-based paints.

12. Dispose of rags carefully to avoid spontaneous combustion.

13. When using a stepladder, have both pairs of legs fully open and the spread bars locked in place. Never climb higher than the second step from the top. When bracing a ladder against the wall, a safe distance between the feet and the wall is one quarter the height of the ladder. Don't use an aluminum ladder when working near electrical wires.

USEFUL TERMS

Booking the wallpaper. Loosely folding presoaked wallpaper pasted side to pasted side to allow a few minutes for curing (or expansion of the adhesive) before applying to the wall.

Cutting in. Using a 3″ or 4″ brush to paint corners and edges where wall meets wall and wall meets ceiling and next to the trim. These places cannot be covered by a roller.

Feathering. A series of light strokes with brush or roller, lifting the applicator lightly at the end of the stroke to blend in the paint.

Sash brush. A 1½″ angled brush made for detail painting of windows and narrow trim pieces.

Sizing. A liquid to be painted on the wall prior to papering. Sizing dries to a tacky feel, assuring proper adhesion of wallpaper and allows for easy removal of wallpaper at some future time.

Trim brush. A 2″ brush for painting door trim and other wide moldings.
TSP. Trisodiumphosphate, an industrial cleaner.

WHAT YOU WILL NEED

Because the requirements for painting and wallpapering are so different, you will find descriptions of what you will need presented separately for each project.

PERMITS AND CODES

Some areas require permits whenever you are spending over a certain amount of money on any repairs or remodeling. Sometimes this figure is as low as $100. Check with your local municipalities to see if you need a permit. Usually only a small fee is required, and often this ordinance is not enforced. Other than this, no permits or inspections apply in either painting or wallpapering projects.

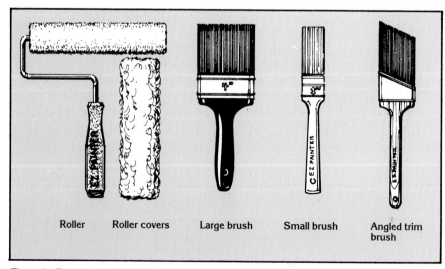

Roller   Roller covers   Large brush   Small brush   Angled trim brush

Figure 1. Tools needed for a typical painting project.

PAINTING

WHAT YOU WILL NEED

Time. Preparation time will depend on the extent of the problems encountered. Painting (including cutting-in) will take approximately 30 to 60 minutes per 100 square feet.

Tools for Painting. The tools you will need for your painting project are listed in the Tools and Materials Checklist at the end of the chapter. But let's discuss some things you will need to know when purchasing these tools.

For the most part, it is wise to use paint rollers for the large areas, brushes for smaller areas, and specialized tools for corners, trim, and so on. For tight maneuvering in areas like small bathrooms and closets where there may be lots of trim and little room to exploit the speed of a roller, consider using a paint pad instead. Always purchase high-quality tools, or you will regret it later. Cheap rollers, pads, and brushes can cause a poor application.

With rollers, purchase a handle with nylon bearings, a comfortable grip, a threaded hole for an extension, and a beveled end. Usually a good synthetic roller cover will work as well as a lambswool roller. Also note that rollers come in many different types. Their naps differ according to their use. Read the package and be sure you buy the proper ones for your application. Also, purchase a metal or plastic grid, called a screen, to go in your pan. This assures that the roller is properly loaded.

Pads should have beveled edges and a curled rear edge.

When purchasing brushes, buy either synthetic or natural bristles. Natural bristles are recommended for oil-based paints but not water-based paints. Synthetic filament brushes (nylon or polyester) must be used for water-thinned paint, although they work in solvent coatings as well. Polyester brushes should not be used with shellacs and lacquers. Always purchase high-quality brushes. Most jobs require a 4″ brush for "cutting in," a 2″ brush for baseboards and trim, and a 1½″ to 2″ angled sash brush for windows and smaller trim. Also, several specialty tools, such as those shown in Figure 2, may be required for your application. Refer to the checklist to see if any apply to your job.

Materials for Painting. There are two types of paint: alkyd-base, called oil-based paint, and latex, or water-based paint. Latex paints are generally used in areas where there is little need for frequent washing. Clean-up with these paints requires only water and is much easier than with oil-based paints, which require a solvent.

Oil-based paints are applied where washing may be needed frequently. They are also often applied over metal or wood, since they are more resistant to damage.

Paints also come in several finishes: primers, gloss, and flat. Primers (undercoats; sealers) are used as bases or undercoats for the finish coat of paint. Flat paints with no gloss are frequently used on walls and ceilings. Gloss finishes (from low to high gloss) are used on woodwork and in bathrooms and kitchens.

Estimating paint. Multiply the perimeter of the room by the height of the walls. This will give you the square-foot area of the walls. For ceilings, multiply the length by the width. A gallon of base coat will cover 350 to 450 square feet. If you figure the square footage and add a little more for touch up, that should do. Always purchase all you need in one order to avoid mismatching colors.

MOST COMMON MISTAKES

The single most common mistake in any project is failure to read and follow manufacturer's instructions for tools and materials being used. In regard to painting, the most common mistakes are:

1. Not preparing a clean, sanded, and primed (if needed) surface.

2. Failure to mix the paints properly.

3. Applying too much paint to the applicator.

4. Using water-logged applicators.

5. Not solving dampness problems in the walls or ceilings.

6. Not roughing up enamel paint before painting over it.

STEP ONE

PREPARING THE WALL

Margin of Error: Not applicable

Most of us believe we know everything we need to know about painting, an assumption that often leads to poor quality work. This applies to both the preparation and the actual paint application. Be sure that you understand, and use, the proper procedures to assure a quality paint or papering job.

If it's worth doing, it's worth doing right the first time. And proper preparation is the key. Few of us really realize this, or even like to admit it, since it leads to more work. It is a step that is all too often left out, and the final job reflects its omission. It is too easy just to start painting or papering and not go through the necessary prep steps. Indeed, for a while the paint job may even look pretty good. But sooner or later the poor quality will show up.

Prepping the wall for a new covering is much the same whether you are papering or painting. Prepping the wall for papering may involve a few more steps. However, there are several basic things to do to prep for either papering or painting. These include:

1. Turn the electricity off and remove everything from the walls and ceilings, including electrical wall and ceiling light fixtures, switch plates, and outlet plates. After you have safely wrapped all disconnected light fixture wires, you can turn the electricity back on.

2. Use a drop cloth to cover the floor. Place any objects you are not removing from the room in the center and cover them with a drop cloth.

3. Remove all trim pieces using a pry bar and wooden shims so as not to damage the trim or the wall.

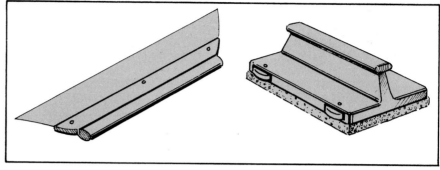

Figure 2. Specialty tools needed: a paint guide and a paint edger. Both can be used for "cutting in."

4. Once the surfaces to be covered are repaired, the walls and room must be thoroughly cleaned. The walls and ceilings should be washed with trisodium-phosphate (TSP) and a large sponge. Use rubber gloves when working with TSP. Rinse the walls with plain water before painting. Also vacuum and/or mop the floors and all ledges to remove all dust and debris.

5. A primer coat of paint is recommended in many instances, painted on prior to the color coat. Also, you can apply an adhesive "pad" to the wall. This is a liquid just like a primer, but it dries with a tacky feel to it. Ask your paint supplier which is recommended for your application.

6. Always apply a coat of liquid sizing to your surfaces before hanging wallpaper. The sizing gives a better adhesive to the wallpaper and also makes removal easier years later.

7. Mask off the woodwork, trim, and windows with newspaper and 2"-wide masking tape. Wider masking tape, 3"–12", can also be used.

8. Although I do not recommend it, it is possible to paint and paper over old wallpaper if it is well bonded and not vinyl, embossed, or textured. It is best to test a small section and allow it to dry. Sand any raised lap seams in the old wallpaper. If you are papering, plan your application to be sure the new paper seams do not fall in the same location as the old seams. Removing old wallpaper is covered under the section on wallpapering below.

9. Assemble ladders, buckets, materials, and so on in the room before beginning.

Aside from the above-mentioned prep steps, you may need to repair other problems with your walls or ceilings. No matter what repairs you make, be sure to apply your primers or sizings *after* the repairs are done. Let's take a look at several common conditions that require special prepping.

Peeling, Flaking, or Bubbling Paint

Most of these problems are caused by lack of proper preparation when the previous coat was applied. Perhaps oil-based paint was applied over new plaster, or enamel surfaces were not roughed up first. Or perhaps the coat of paint was not compatible with the one it was applied over. Also, dampness and leaks in the wall cause many of these problems. If these conditions exist on the wall, use a quality paint scraper and sandpaper. Rub the scraper back and forth across the problem areas until they are relatively flush with the wall. Then follow up with a fine-grit sandpaper (100-grit silicon carbide) to smooth out the areas and wipe with a tack cloth to remove all dust. If you leave ridges or dips, they will be visible once the wall is painted. If the dip or indentation is too great, you will need to fill it with drywall compound and sand. Be sure to prime or size any newly applied drywall compound before painting or papering.

Large Holes

Large holes in the wall will need special attention. The repair procedures differ depending on whether it is an older wall with lath and plaster, or a newer wall using gypsum wallboard (drywall).

Repairing holes in lath and plaster usually involves several steps. First, clean the hole and the edges of the hole of any debris. The sharp end of a can opener comes in handy here. If the lath is still intact, you can start to fill the hole with compound. If the lath is missing or badly damaged, you will need to stuff something into the hole to serve as a backing for the drywall compound that will fill the hole. You can either use steel wool or a wad of newspaper (sports page preferred). Also, a wire mesh held in place with a piece of string, attached through the mesh and around a pencil, on the outside of the wall will work (see Figure 4). Place the newspaper or steel wool so that it is recessed about 1″ from the finished surface of the wall.

Moisten the edges of the hole with a little water. Using a drywall knife that is at least 1″ wider than the hole, spread the compound over the hole. Do this until the compound is about ¼″ recessed from the finished surface of the wall. Allow this coat to dry until it is tacky. Score this tacky compound with a nail to rough it up so that it will receive the second layer. Let this scored layer dry, then moisten and repeat the process, filling to within ⅛″ of the finished surface. (Two coats can be used if the hole is less than 4″.) Sand this coat and apply the final coat, sanding this smooth with steel wool or a fine-grit sandpaper (100-grit silicon carbide). Use an orbital sander if you have one. To quicken the drying time between coats, direct a fan at the patch. Also, fast-drying compounds are available. Always clean your tools immediately after using this type of compound. And be sure to prime any fresh compound after repairing, but before painting.

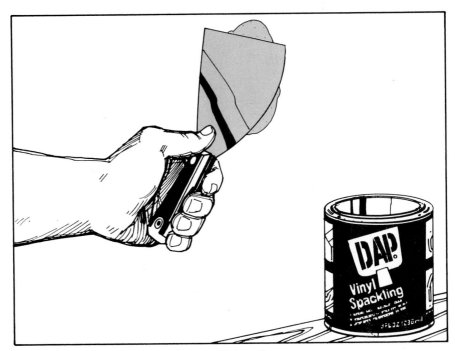

Figure 3. Use a putty knife and spackle to patch the wall.

Figure 4. Using a pencil to hold wire mesh in place as a support where lath is missing.

Figure 5. Using an orbital sander to smooth a patch. Use a mask if doing large areas.

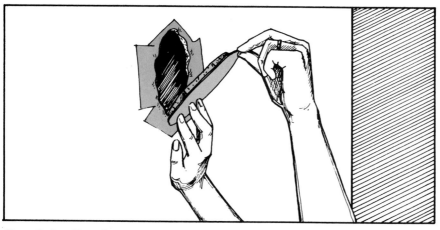

Figure 6. Installing a "hat patch." Note that the paper on the drywall has also been removed around the hole for a flush finish.

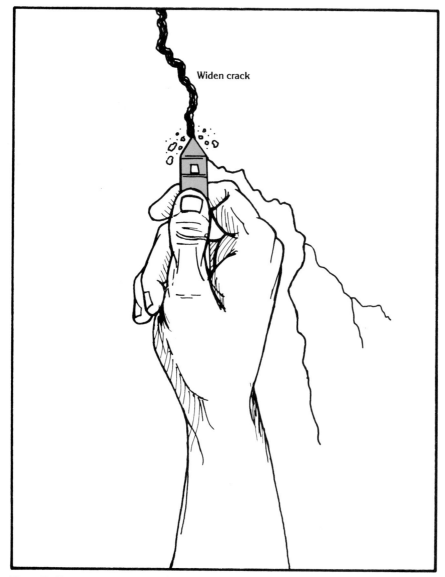

Widen crack

Figure 7. You can use a can opener to widen, clean, and undercut a crack. Widening tools are also available.

An alternate method of repairing large holes in either lath and plaster or drywall is to use the "hat patch" method, as shown in Figure 6. This involves cutting a patch that will fit over the hole. First undercut the edges around the hole so that you have a good clean hole. Again, you can use the sharp end of a can opener. Around the perimeter of the hole tear away a 1″ strip of drywall paper so that only the bare gypsum is showing. Use a utility knife to score the drywall paper around the diameter of the cut. This will assure that the hat patch will lie flat with no raised edges.

Cut a piece of drywall to the exact shape and dimensions as the total area defined by the bare gypsum. Remove enough of the gypsum from this piece so that you are left with a plug the size of the hole and a paper brim that will cover the bare gypsum. Apply compound around the hole and insert the patch. Cover the patch with compound, allow it to dry, and sand it smooth after drying. Apply a second coat (and third coat if needed), sanding after each coat. Paint the fresh compound with primer before painting or papering.

Repairing Cracks

Cracks are usually rather simple to repair. Small hairline cracks can be repaired by simply spreading compound over them and sanding them smooth. Larger cracks need more attention.

To repair larger cracks, you first need to scrape and widen them. Also you need to undercut the edges. This can be done with a widening tool or the sharp edge of a can opener, as shown in Figure 7. Be sure all the debris is cleaned away. You may want to vacuum out all the dust as dust can cause adhering problems. After you have prepared the crack, dampen the edges before applying spackling or drywall compound. If the crack is large enough, over ⅛″–¼″, you should apply a self-adhering fiberglass drywall tape directly to the wall before applying the compound, but after filling the crack with compound. This will assure that the crack does not reappear. Apply two coats of compound with a putty knife, allowing the first coat to dry, then sand and apply the second coat, feathering the edges.

Prepping the Trim and Woodwork

You will be painting your woodwork and trim last, but you need to prep it before beginning to paint, or else the debris from prepping will settle on the new paint. Usually woodwork and trim are painted with an enamel or glossy paint, which will have to be roughed up so that the new paint will adhere properly. You can use a chemical deglossing agent or lightly sand with steel wool or fine-grit sandpaper. If you are using a chemical, avoid those containing ethyl alcohol, which can make you sick.

Often you need to scrape off old deteriorating paint. If it's in bad condition you may even need to use a water-soluble gel remover. Also, fill all dents and gouges with wood putty or patching compound. Avoid fast-drying compound; it is hard to sand. If the gouge is over 1/8″, use two layers. Always sand where the old paint is breaking away from the underlying surface.

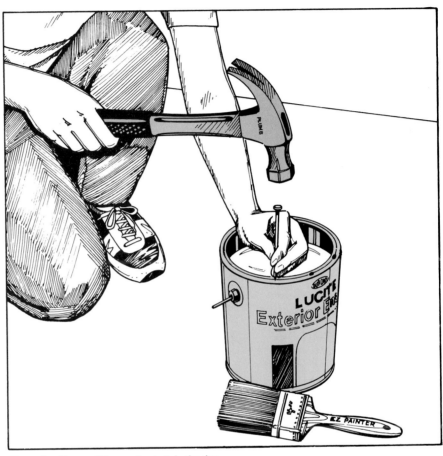

Figure 8.   Use a nail to punch a hole in the rim.

Applying the Paint

Properly applying the paint is your final step toward a professional-looking paint job. You have prepped the surfaces and chosen the right paint and applicators and now the fun starts.

Before applying paint, be sure that it is properly mixed. Professionals use a system called "boxing." This process assures that there are no mismatches among different cans of paints. Mix all your paint into one large container until the paint's color and consistency are uniform. It is important to prepare enough paint to cover all surfaces with this mix, since matching can be difficult if you run out.

Air often causes a scum on oil-based paints. In this case you will need to strain it through a nylon stocking to separate this "skin." Also, if you are thinning paint with either a thinner for oil-based paints or water for water based, thin slowly so as not to over-thin and thereby require adding more paint. Finally, use a nail and hammer to punch a hole in the rim of the can so that ex-

cess paint will drip back in (see Figure 8).

There is a sequence often used in painting which I recommend:

1. Ceilings

2. Walls

3. Trim (windows, door, then baseboard)

By painting the ceilings first you can be sure that any drips falling on the walls will be covered. When painting the walls, always paint from the top down, again to be sure drips are covered. And, finally, do the trim so that any paint that accidentally gets on the trim can be covered.

Needless to say, wear old clothes. A hat and scarf or hooded sweatshirt is recommended while doing the ceilings (unless you want to try some unusual hair coloring combinations). Again, be sure that everything is properly prepped and covered.

Figure 9. Areas to be "cut in" before painting large surfaces.

STEP TWO

CUTTING IN

Margin of Error: Not applicable

"Cutting in" is a process of applying paint at all corners where ceilings meet walls or where walls intersect. Also, paint is applied next to all molding, trim, and baseboards. Since these are areas rollers or sprayers cannot neatly reach, use a 3"–4" brush, painting all these edges before doing the large surfaces. You can use a paint edger, as shown in Figure 11. This sponge-type brush has a small set of wheels on the side that enable it to make an even close cut. A paint edger or straightedge can be used next to trim or baseboard to be sure that no paint gets onto the wood. Cut in around all appropriate areas before painting the large surfaces.

TIP: Use nail and hammer to punch holes in the rim of the can so that excess paint will drip back in.

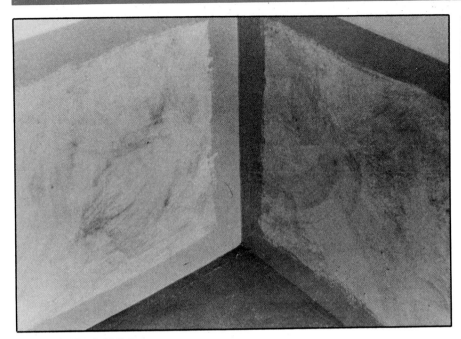

Figure 10. "Cutting in" at corners.

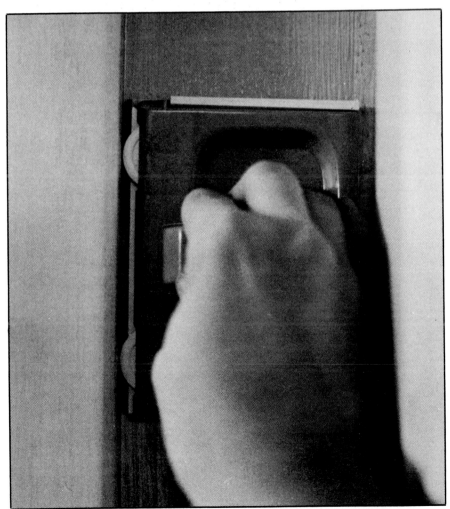

Figure 11. Use a paint edger to "cut in." The wheels allow the edger to paint right next to the trim.

STEP THREE

PAINTING THE LARGE SURFACES

Margin of Error: Not applicable

After cutting in all areas, you are ready to paint your ceiling and then your walls. Be sure the area is well lighted so you can see any ridges or drips. The ceilings will be some of your toughest painting. It is physically difficult: painting overhead can cause back or neck strain and an occasional eye full of paint. Because of this, safety goggles (and yoga) are a must during this process. When painting ceilings, use a high-quality roller with an extension so that you can easily reach all areas of the ceiling without strain. In this way ladders will not be needed except for touch-up and cutting in. These same extensions are used for the high areas of the walls. You may want to erect some low scaffolding, using sawhorses or ladders with a 2 × 12 between them for high ceilings.

To properly use a roller, pour the paint into the roller tray or paint pan so that ½″ of the paint is in the reservoir. This will enable you to fully load the roller without underloading or overloading. Also, you can save on clean-up time by lining your tray with heavy-duty aluminum foil before loading. A new option on the market is the electric roller. It supplies rollers with a continuous supply of paint. Another time saving device is the air compressor with a painting attachment (see Chapter One).

Roll or dip your roller into the paint reservoir. Roll it around in the paint until the paint has thoroughly covered the roller. Then run the roller a couple of times over the washboard area of the

31

tray. This will remove excess paint so that the roller will not drip. Often too much paint on the roller drips. You will be surprised at how much paint rollers hold, so don't be concerned about thoroughly saturating the roller.

To avoid splattering, distribute the paint *slowly* on the ceiling and walls. In the beginning, use overlapping "V"-shaped strokes, as shown in Figure 12. Begin at a corner and work across the wall or ceiling. Cover about three square feet at a time. After you have made your "V"-shaped zig-zag patterns, fill in the unpainted areas with parallel strokes without lifting the roller from the surface. Increase the pressure on the roller as you work to deliver the paint smoothly.

When you are rolling into unpainted or previously painted areas, feather the paint in, in a series of light strokes, and lift the roller at the end of each stroke. When you need to remove the roller to reload, begin the next section, rolling in a zig-zag into the outer border of the area you just completed. Then lightly roll the area between the two sections. Paint the entire surface. Do not stop and allow the paint to dry on part of the wall or ceiling.

STEP FOUR

PAINTING THE TRIM AND WOODWORK

Margin of Error: Exact

After you have finished all the large surfaces, you are ready to paint the trim and woodwork. In order to do this successfully, you need to change your mental set about painting. Up until now most of your work has been on large surfaces, and detailing was not important. Now, you are changing from rough work to finishing work. Attention to detail and care at this stage will mean the difference between a professional-looking job and a sloppy one.

Your tools will also be different. During this stage you will be using the smaller angled brushes and metal paint guide. A 1½" angled sash brush is often used for narrow molding and a 2" trim brush on wider trim. As you apply the paint to the trim and woodwork,

keep a supply of clean rags near you to immediately wipe off any excess paint that gets on the previously painted surfaces. With oil-based paints, use a little mineral spirits or paint thinner. With water-based paints, a mild detergent and water will work fine. For a more durable finish, oil-based paints are most often used on trim. With these enamel paints, fingerprints are more easily removed. On trim that has been previously stained, bleeding may occur. In this case two coats of shellac will be needed first.

Always paint horizontal surfaces first and then vertical surfaces. Begin with the trim closest to the ceiling and work down. Do baseboards last. When doing baseboards, paint the top edge first, then the floor edge, and finally the large center area last with a larger brush. Be sure to cover the edge of the floor with a paint guide or masking tape.

Paint inner sections of doors and windows before the outer portions. Windows especially require great care. Because of their many small areas, infinite patience is required. Apply the paint right down to the glass. The paint will thereby create a seal between the wood and the glass. You can either tape the glass or remove the excess paint later with a razor-blade knife. If you are applying masking tape to the panes, leave a hairline crack of glass exposed between the tape and the wood to be sure you have a good paint seal between the wood and glass. As soon as the paint is dry, remove the tape.

TIP: To help a window move more smoothly rub a candle or bar of soap over the wood jambs.

Figure 12. Spread your zig-zag "V" patterns first.

When painting double-paned windows, a certain order is followed. You will need to raise and lower the sashes to be able to reach all areas. Begin by painting the exterior sash. Paint the horizontal side pieces, then the vertical, and then the muttins (the pieces that divide the window into small sections). Paint the lower part of their sash first, then raise the window and do the upper part. Next, repeat this process with the interior sash. Afterward, paint the frame and trim, first the top sides and finally the sill.

Raise and lower the sashes a few times while the paint is drying to be sure they do not dry stuck. I recommend not painting the jambs (the area where the window slides) unless absolutely necessary. After the window is dry, rub a candle over any wood jamb to create easy window movement.

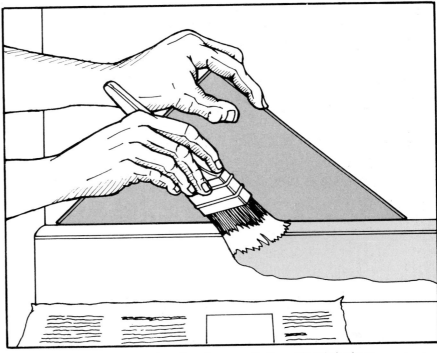

Figure 13. Use a paint guide on the walls and paper on the floor while painting baseboards.

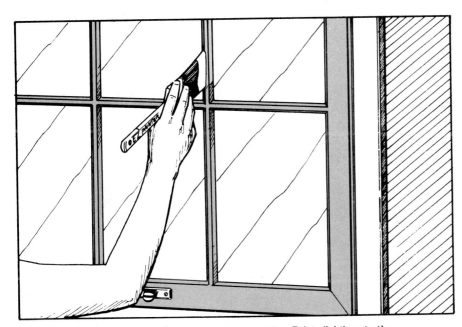

Figure 14. Use an angled trim brush to paint the muttins. Paint slightly onto the glass.

Doors are best painted removed from their hinges and set on sawhorses. Flat doors are easily painted with rollers. Panel doors take much greater care. First remove all hardware. With panel doors, first paint the molding and the inside edges of the panel cavities. Then the panels. Finally, paint all the horizontal and vertical pieces around the panels. If the door opens into the room, paint the door's latch edge, the jamb, and the door side of the door stop as well. Once the door is dry, replace the hardware and rehang the door.

WALLPAPERING

WHAT YOU WILL NEED

Time. Wallpapering will average 10 to 20 minutes per sheet, longer if encountering trim.

Tools for Wallpapering. Wallpapering takes some very specialized but simple tools. As always, never skimp on quality. You will only regret it later. Most stores sell wallpaper application kits which include a full set of tools that will cover most of your needs. See the checklist at the end of the chapter for other tools you will need.

Materials for Wallpapering. Space is not available in this book to describe all the many types of wall coverings. Consult your supplier or a good wallpapering book for complete information. However, in choosing your wallpaper, always purchase the prepasted type with adhesive on the back. Avoid the older types where paste must be applied. You can spend days thumbing through a pattern book.

Estimating wallpaper materials. Multiple the perimeter of the room by the height of the walls to arrive at a total square footage. Divide this by 30. (The average roll covers 36 square feet, but there will be losses due to trim and pattern matching waste.) Some pattern matching and shrinkage require more rolls (check with your supplier). This new number is your number of rolls if you had no openings. Subtract ½ roll for each normal size door or window opening. This number covers your final needs. Purchase all rolls in one order to avoid variation in stock.

MOST COMMON MISTAKES

As with painting, the most important and often overlooked step is preparing the wall you are about to work on. Preparation, patience, and an eye for detail are all you need to avoid these common mistakes:

1. Not sanding, cleaning, and sizing the walls before applying the wallpaper.

2. Failure to soak the prepasted wallpaper long enough.

3. Failure to allow the wallcovering to cure the proper amount of time after soaking.

4. Letting the wallcovering paste dry on the woodwork.

5. Not positioning the strips of the wallpaper level and plumb.

6. Not getting air pockets out when smoothing the covering on the wall.

7. Not planning for pattern match-up and extra on top and bottom before cutting each strip.

8. Not estimating and ordering enough wallpaper for the job.

9. Not allowing the sizing to dry.

10. Not overlapping the wallpapers that have a tendency to shrink.

11. Using a seam roller on embossed wallpaper.

STEP ONE

PLANNING YOUR PROJECT

Margin of Error: Not applicable

Proper planning is essential to obtaining a professional-looking hanging job. Planning involves mostly understanding where the rolls will be applied and where they will meet at seamlines. Also, you have to consider adjustments so that patterns match, once you start to hang it.

The first thing you have to do is determine where you plan to start. This will determine the location of the point of mismatch — where odd-shaped pieces will need to be cut. You want to plan this so that these mismatch points are in the least visible locations. These mismatch points are more important when using a design with large patterns. With a neutral or a nondirectional pattern, you can begin at an inconspicuous corner or area of the room. Usually the best place to start with all wallpapers is an inconspicuous corner.

TIP: Before hanging wallpaper take the time to apply sizing to the wall (it's applied like paint but dries tacky). It assures adhesion while allowing for easy removal of the paper years later.

STEP TWO

PREPPING THE WALLS

Margin of Error: Not applicable

Follow the prepping in Step 1 above for painting. Also, there are a few additional steps that I recommend for a professional-looking job. It is important that the walls be very clean and free of any dust or debris.

If you are working on older walls, sealing the wall with a primer is not necessary. If the wall was painted with a flat oil-based paint, only cleaning and sizing is needed. However, shiny oil-based paints require a treatment with TSP or a deglosser for better adhesion.

If you are working with an untreated new wall or a latex paint-coated wall, apply an oil-based primer before papering. If in doubt, prime the wall. Also, spot prime any repaired areas that have fresh compound on them.

Wallpaper can be hung directly over old wallpaper. Be sure that it is in good condition and repair any rips, bubbles, or other problems. Be sure to check the seams and re-glue if needed. Apply a flat oil-based enamel undercoat to the wall and allow it to dry for 24 hours. Check to see if your new wallpaper requires a sizing. I recommend one. (With cloth-back vinyl hung over gypsum board that was never sealed, you need to apply a vinyl-to-vinyl primer before applying the new paper.)

Now apply a sizing. This step is sometimes overlooked, but it is worth the effort. Sizing is a liquid, applied like paint, that dries tacky. It not only assures good adhesion but also allows for easy removal of the paper years later.

Deteriorating Wallpaper

This can be one of the worst prepping problems. Usually you will not want to paint or paper over old wallpaper but will want to remove it instead. Often a home has several layers of old wallpaper that must be removed before painting or papering. If you do not plan to remove it, repair problem areas by re-gluing and working out any bubbles until it has a good smooth surface. If the areas are too bad, you will need to scrape away some of the paper and fill the area with compound and sand flush. Seal all old wallpaper with an oil-based primer, especially if it is a colored pattern.

allows you to peel the paper from the wall. Actually, this sounds a lot easier than it really is. This can be quite a frustrating and time-consuming task. You will need to get *all* the wallpaper off. If it does not peel off easily, be prepared to spend whatever time is needed to remove all the paper and glue.

To allow the steam to penetrate behind the wallpaper, nonporous wallpaper such as vinyl must first be scored with a puncturing roller or rough sandpaper before steaming. The teeth of a handsaw will also work.

When using the steamer, start at the top, and remove one strip of old wallpaper at a time. Working a broadknife be-

Figure 15. Use an electric wallpaper steamer. Be prepared for this process to go slowly.

The older wallpaper was not made to be easily removed as is the newer wallpaper. You will need a wallpaper steamer, as shown in Figure 15. This piece of equipment can be rented from a hardware, home center, or equipment rental yard. The steamer produces steam which dissolves the old glue and

hind the paper, work slowly downward allowing the steam to penetrate. After the wallpaper is removed, check the surface to see if there are any other wall conditions mentioned in Step 1 under Painting above. Be sure all glue and paper has been removed.

STEP THREE

MARKING A LEVEL LINE

Margin of Error: Exact

Starting at the inconspicuous corner you have chosen, measure to a point with your tape that is a distance from the corner of one inch less than the width of the wallpaper roll. Make a mark at this point. If your wallpaper rolls are 20″ wide, make a mark 19″ from the corner.

At this mark you will need to make an exactly plumb (vertical) line. There is a good chance that the corner is not plumb, so this process guarantees that you will be working from a plumb line. A common, and drastic, mistake in hanging wallpaper is to hang it out of plumb.

You can use a 4′ level or a wallpaper level (a straightedge with a level bubble), as shown in Figure 16, to mark this line on the wall. Also, a chalkline can be used. Be sure that the level bubble is reading true level, and then mark the line from the ceiling to the floor.

TIP: When cutting wallpaper with large repeating patterns be sure to alternate rolls — you'll save many feet when trying to match the pattern.

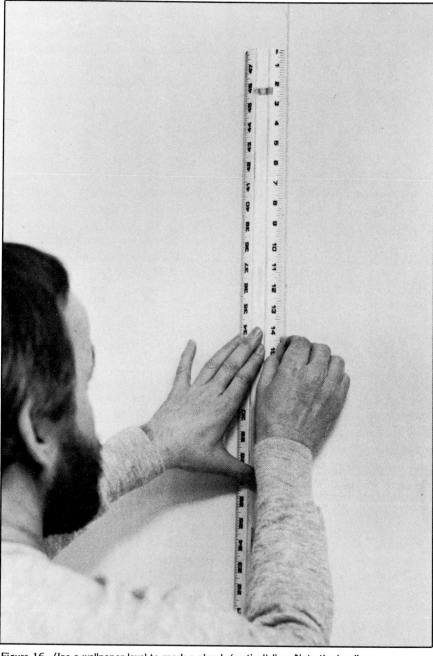

Figure 16. Use a wallpaper level to mark a plumb (vertical) line. Note the leveling bubble at the top of the level.

STEP FOUR

CUTTING THE WALLPAPER

Margin of Error: Exact

You are now ready to cut your first piece of wallpaper. You will need to cut the paper so that there is a 2″ overlap at the ceiling and floor. This excess will later be trimmed away. Also, you will want the pattern to break at the ceiling line. This pattern break line can be whatever you believe is most attractive. Hold each piece up against the wall before you cut it and mark where it will meet the baseboard and ceiling line. You can then use these lines when you hang it.

Cut the paper using a straightedge and a scissors or utility knife. Change the blade in the utility knife often to avoid ripping the paper.

STEP FIVE

SOAKING THE WALLPAPER

Margin of Error: Exact

Unlike the older types of wallpaper that needed paste spread on the back, most wallpapers today are prepasted with adhesives already applied. You simply soak the wallpaper in water and hang it. However, be careful that you closely follow the manufacturer's instructions. Not only is there a set period of time you need to let the paper soak in the tray, but also there is a set period during which, after it is removed from the tray, it must "cure" before being applied. This time varies from manufacturer to manufacturer, but is usually several minutes.

Most professionals apply paste even to prepasted wallpaper. They want that added insurance that it will properly adhere. With high-quality paper applied on a properly prepared wall, this is not needed. But consult with your supplier if in doubt.

The paper is placed in the tray of lukewarm water, rolled up as shown in Figure 17. The pattern side is in, and the tray is placed next to the wall directly below the area to be hung. Upon removing it from the tray, fold the wallpaper, pasted side to pasted side, so that it comes out flat, as shown in Figure 18. Be sure to fold the paper loosely and not crease it at the folds. This is called "booking." Allow it to cure to its maximum width before applying. Be sure that no dust or debris settles on the paper while it is curing.

Figure 17. Soaking the paper in the tray. Don't forget to let it cure.

STEP SIX

HANGING THE FIRST SHEET

Margin of Error: Exact

You are now ready to hang your first piece. Apply it so that one edge is exactly vertical and aligned with your plumb mark. Leave the bottom fold folded and, at first, work only with the upper part of the sheet. Be sure the mark for the ceiling is aligned so that there is a pattern break at the ceiling line. If you are working at an inside corner, which is often the case, wrap the one-inch overlap into the corner. See the section on inside corners below (Step 8).

Use a wallpaper brush to work out any bubbles, stroking the brush from the inside to the outside to push the air out. Start at the top and work your way down the paper. Keep working with the brush until all the bubbles are out and the paper is perfectly smooth on the wall. Be sure you stay aligned with your plumb mark as you work with the brush. Gently lift the bottom edge of the strip to free the sheet of any wrinkles.

After the upper part is smooth, release the bottom fold and position, using the palms of your hands. Then use the smoothing brush as you did above. Be sure there was no debris on the wall that you now see poking through. You will trim the paper after the next sheet is hung.

TIP: When removing non-porous wallpaper such as vinyl, be sure to score the paper to allow the steam of the wallpaper steamer to penetrate.

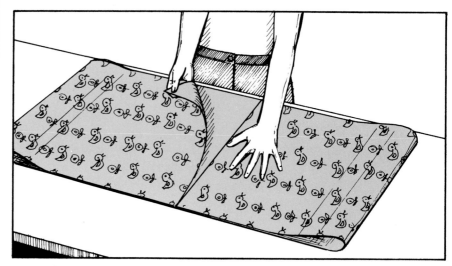

Figure 18. "Booking" the paper after it has soaked. Be careful not to crease the folds.

Figure 19. Applying the first sheet. Note the two-inch overlap at top and bottom.

Figure 20. Use the wallpaper brush to work out any wrinkles or bubbles. Work from the center out.

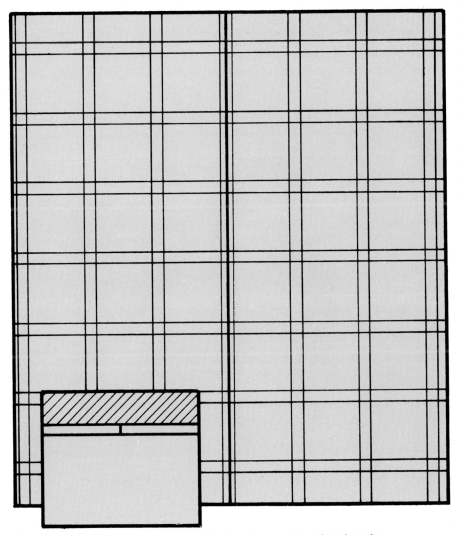

Figure 21. A butt seam is most common. The two pieces butt together where they meet. Be exact when doing this.

STEP SEVEN

HANGING THE SECOND AND SUBSEQUENT SHEETS

Margin of Error: Exact

Before cutting the second sheet, be sure that you have allowed for the pattern matching at the seamlines. To avoid waste, you can alternate between two different rolls with the larger patterns.

This second sheet butts snugly against the first. Do not overlap seams. (See Figure 21.) Apply this sheet as you did the first and maneuver it against the first with your hands. After this sheet is in place you can go back and trim the first. Use your straightedge or broadknife, as shown in Figure 23, to assure a good trim job, changing the razor blade for *each* strip of wallpaper applied.

After the sheets are in place, go over them with a large damp sponge to get out all the small bubbles and paste. Be sure to wipe up any excess paste at the seams and ends with the sponge before they dry. After 20 to 30 minutes, use a seam roller at the seams, as shown in Figure 23, to be sure they are well secured. Press the roller lightly to avoid a glossy area. This step is omitted with raised and flocked wallpaper.

STEP EIGHT

CORNERS & OPENINGS

Margin of Error: Exact

Corners, both inside and outside, are the more demanding part of hanging paper. In and of themselves, they are not that difficult. The problem is that the corners are seldom true plumb or vertical, and this is where the difficulty lies. You need to be able to hang your wallpaper plumb, even if the corners are not. This can be demanding and can take some time and care. Go slowly here, since this is where your new skills will be challenged the most.

Inside Corners

At both the top and bottom of the wall, measure the distances from the strip next to the corner to the actual corner itself. Add 1″ to the greater of the two measurements and cut a sheet lengthwise to this measurement. If, however, this measurement is within 6″ of your full sheet measurement, use a full sheet. If there is a sheet next to the corner, its edge can be used as a plumb line (let's hope that you have installed it plumb).

If there is no sheet at the corner, simply measure out from the corner the dimensions of a wallpaper roll less 1″ (for corner overlap) and draw a plumb line. This line will then be your guideline in hanging your first sheet. Since many times your first sheet is installed in an inconspicuous corner, this is the process you will use to install your first sheet.

Now simply hang the sheet as described earlier and wrap the excess into the corner. Since few corners are perfectly plumb, you will need to strike a plumbline on the adjacent wall, again at a distance from the corner of 1″ less than the dimension of the roll. Then apply another sheet and wrap the excess so it overlaps the first sheet. Now simply take your broadknife and your razor knife and cut the overlapping sheets in the corner and peel away the two excess pieces.

Outside Corners

If the outside corner is exactly plumb, and they seldom are, you can simply wrap the paper around the corner and begin from its edge on the other side of the corner. If it is not plumb, a little more attention is needed.

As with inside corners, measure at the top and bottom of the wall the distance from the last sheet to the corner. Add 1″ to the longest measurement and cut a sheet that size. If the measurement is within 6″ of a full sheet, use a full sheet.

Hang this sheet, cutting a diagonal slit at the corner at the top so it will bend around the corner. Hang it so that it is smooth and fold it smoothly around the corner. Now you need another plumbline on the intersecting wall. To do this, strike a plumbline on this wall with your wallpaper level. The plumbline should be the width of the roll from the corner. Now simply hang your intersecting piece to that plumbline. After both pieces are in place, make a new plumbline ¼″–½″ from the corner on the side of the corner. At this line, cut through both pieces of paper and peel away the excess. (See Figure 24.)

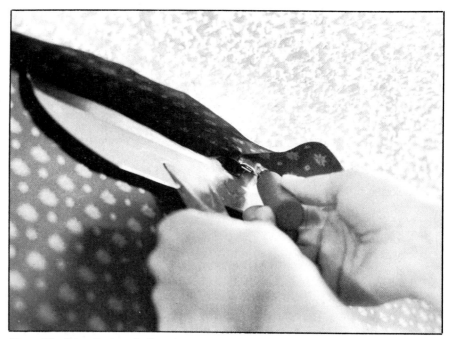

Figure 22. Using the broadknife and razor knife to cut the paper. Change blades often.

Windows and Doors

Openings for windows and doors offer a challenge to the novice. Also, you may encounter fireplaces, bookshelves, cabinets, and so on. To do this properly, don't try to cut the paper first and then apply it. Cut it after it is in place. If you are having trouble with complex areas, just step back, think about it, and try your best approach.

Simply hang your paper so that it is aligned with the adjacent piece and loosely press it against the window trim. Now cut away along the sides of the opening, but leave a 2″ excess, which you will trim later. Use a sharp razor and cut a 45-degree slit at the corners, both top and bottom, to the outside edge of the molding, ending exactly at the molding's edge.

Now press the paper against the molding with the wallpaper brush and then use your broadknife and razor knife to cut away the excess. Leave a hairline gap between the molding and the paper.

You will need to make a series of small diagonal cuts (as shown in Figure 26) around the sill area to fit all the little corners. Go slow and make small cuts to avoid over-cutting. Press the paper tightly against the molding and trim it where needed.

Finally, you will need to paper the area above and below the window with short strips. Be sure the vertical patterns below the window are aligned with those above and that the patterns match where they meet the paper hung to the sides of the windows. Be sure to wipe any excess glue off all the woodwork before it dries.

Light Switches and Outlets

After removing the plates from light switches and outlets and turning off the electricity simply cover over the holes as you hang the wallpaper. Then use your razor knife and make two diagonal cuts across the outlet or switch, about 3″ long, to expose the switch or outlet. Cut away the excess. You can cover their plates by tucking the wallpaper into the wall and replacing the cover.

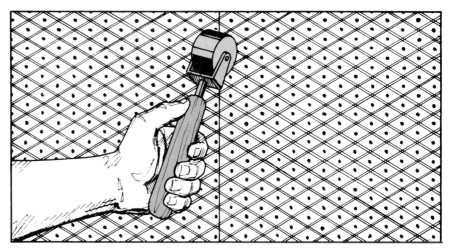

Figure 23. Use a seam roller at the seams 20–30 minutes after hanging the paper. Do not press too hard or you will gloss the paper.

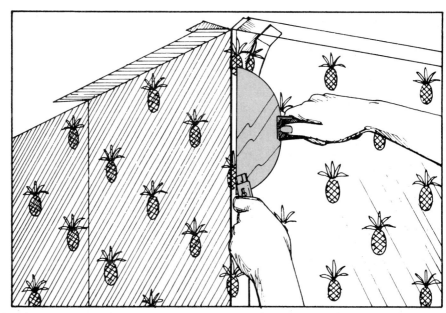

Figure 24. After you have measured a line ¼″–½″ from the outside corner, use your broadknife and razor knife to cut the paper at this line. Then remove excess.

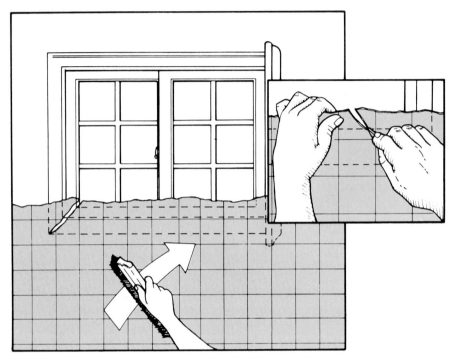

Figure 25. Use a razor to cut a 45-degree slit at both the top and bottom corners of the molding.

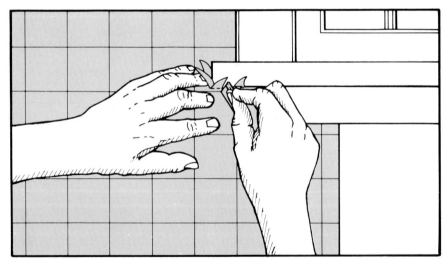

Figure 26. You will need to make small cuts around the sills. Gently cut to fit.

TOOLS AND MATERIALS CHECKLIST

Tools for Prepping Walls

Safety glasses or goggles	Can opener or widening tool
Respirator or face mask	Fan
Ear protectors	Hand sanding block
Rubber gloves	Orbital sander
Pry bar	Screwdriver
Paint scraper	Putty knife
Wallpaper steamer (rent if needed)	Sponge
	Cap or scarf
	Old clothes

Materials for Prepping Walls

Spackle (compound)	Self-adhesive drywall tape
Fine-grit sandpaper (100–120-grit silicon carbide)	Primer or adhesive pad
	Sizing (for wallpapering)
Detergent and ammonia or trisodiumphosphate (TSP)	

Tools for Painting

Drop cloths	Roller pan with screen
Ladders	
Buckets	Roller covers with appropriate naps
Paint edger	
Brushes, 4″, 3″, and 1½″	Roller handle
Angled sash brushes, 1½″ and 2″	Roller extender
	Paint guide

42

Materials for Painting

Masking tape, 2″ wide

Newspaper

Adhesive pad or primer

Paint

Paint thinner (with oil-based paints)

Aluminum foil

Rags

Tools for Wallpapering

Steel tape measure

Wallpaper level

Water tray

Seam roller

Wallpaper brush

Razor knife with lots of blades

Broadknife

Large sponge

Bucket

Pencil

Ladders

Materials for Wallpapering

Wallpaper

Wallpaper paste (if needed)

Paint remover or mineral spirits

Rags

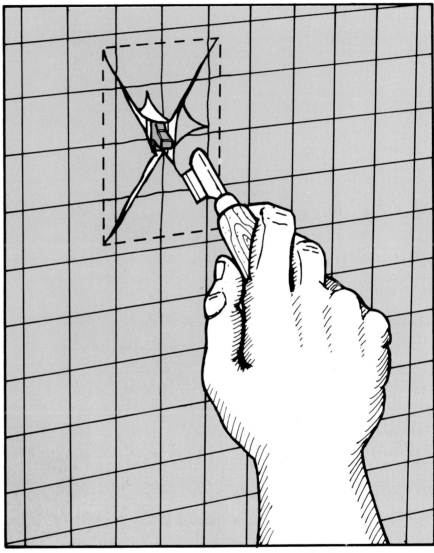

Figure 27. **Cover over the switches and outlets. Make diagonal cuts and trim the excess. Tuck the wallpaper into the wall and replace the cover plate.**

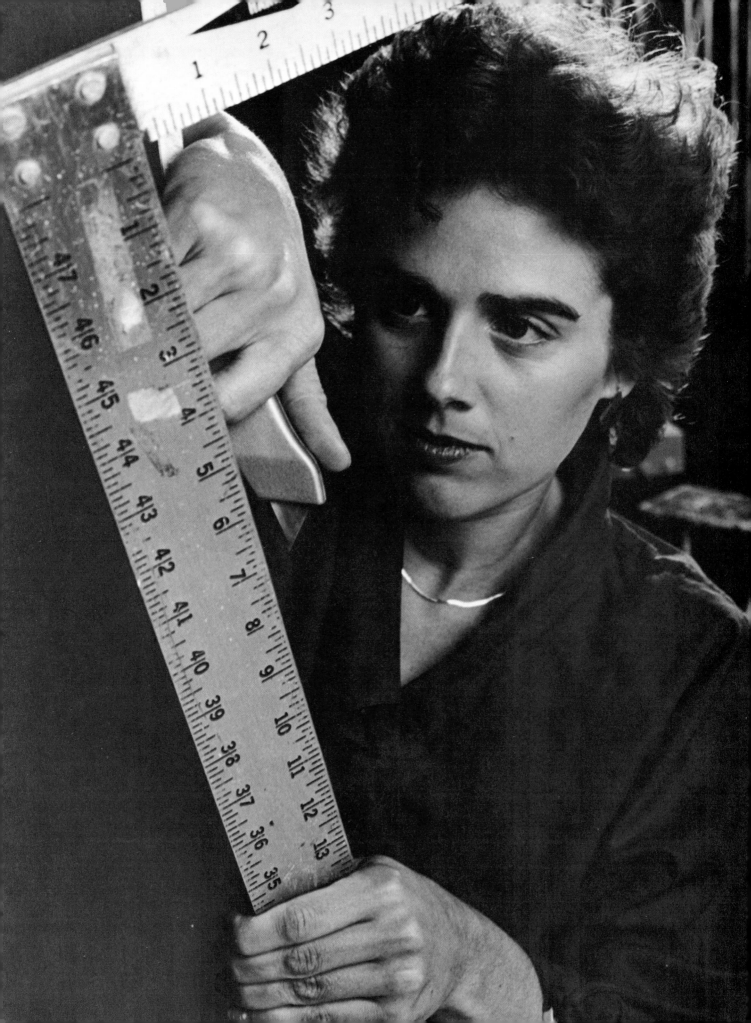

CHAPTER THREE

The Basics of Drywall
When Simple Painting is Not Enough

WHAT YOU WILL BE DOING

Before the advent of drywall, walls were usually a hardened, liquid plaster which was spread over wood slats (lath). Drywall is basically the plaster encased in large paper-covered sheets.

Drywall, often called gypsum, gyp board, or sheetrock, is made of a crumbly fire-resistant substance called gypsum. It is wrapped in a thick paper coating, is durable, and easily cut, trimmed, and repaired. In this chapter you will learn how drywall can be used to cover conventional bare stud walls or damaged lath and plaster walls.

Because of its unique construction, drywall can be cut, sawed, drilled, bent, nailed, glued, screwed, and painted or papered over.

In addition to being easy to work with, drywall is inexpensive. Though it can be difficult for a novice to finish to a smooth surface, if you practice your finishing in a closet or other area of low visibility you can master the techniques presented here painlessly. A poorly finished job can be quite visible, especially in a well-lit room. You may find a textured finish much easier to apply, since it does not require the perfection of a smooth finish. Once in place, the drywall can be painted or papered (unless it is textured), which makes it ideal for new interior design effects.

BEFORE YOU BEGIN

SAFETY

As you embark upon your home project, I stress that you develop safe work habits and stick to them.

1. Drywall is heavy and awkward to lift and maneuver. It is best to work in pairs, especially when working on ceilings and high areas.

2. Be careful when lifting so as not to cause unnecessary strain.

3. The proper respirator or face mask is recommended when sanding or sawing.

4. Be sure power tools are properly grounded.

5. Use the appropriate tool for the job.

6. Keep blades sharp. A dull blade requires excessive force, can slip and cause accidents.

7. Protect your eyes from gypsum dust by wearing safety glasses or goggles.

8. Observe proper use of stepladders. Never climb higher than the second step from the top — use a taller ladder instead. Be certain the spreader bars are locked in place and both pairs of legs are fully open. If leaning the ladder against a wall, a safe distance between the wall and the feet of the ladder is one quarter the height of the ladder. Do not use an aluminum ladder near electrical wires.

9. When setting a plank between ladders as a scaffold, be sure it extends a foot on each side and is clamped or nailed to its support.

Use the proper protection, take precautions, and plan ahead. Never bypass safety to save money or rush a project.

USEFUL TERMS

Corner bead. A protective metal cover for outside corners, to eliminate damage and crumbling of drywall and to effect a smoother finish.

Corner knife. A 90-degree folded blade for applying drywall compound to inside corners after taping.

Drywall nails. A barbed shank or annular ring shanked, concave-headed nail.

Drywall screws. Tapered headed no. 6 screws.

Greenrock. Moisture-resistant drywall for bathrooms and other damp areas. Usually one side of these panels is coated with green paper.

Mud. Drywall compound, vinyl spackling — the substance used to cover tape and nailheads and to smooth the wall to an even, unblemished surface.

Tape. Available in paper or fiber; used to cover the seams between drywall panels.

Taping knife. Wide, flat-bladed tools from 6″ to 10″ wide, for use in applying drywall compound to taped seams and nails.

WHAT YOU WILL NEED

Time. Time depends upon the type and extent of job being done.

Tools. Although you may have a number of tools useful to drywalling in your home toolbox, many specialized tools are available to make the job easier and the finished results more professional.

Ladder	$3/8''$ Drill	Mud knives (4″,	Goggles
Sawhorses	with a Phillips	6″, and 10″	Buckets and
Steel tape	head driver	widths)	sponges
measure	attachment (or	Corner mud knife	Flashlight
Drywall T-square	a cordless	Drywall square	Orbital sander
Carpenter's pencil	drywall screw	Utility knife and	Sanding block
Drywall hammer	gun)	blades	Tinsnips
Chalkline and	Scraper (plane)	Keyhole saw	
chalk	Mud trays	Dust masks	

If you plan to use adhesives to attach your drywall, you will also need a caulking gun. If you have a great deal of drywalling to get done, this can be made much easier with an air compressor fitted with a caulking attachment. This item can be rented if you do not have access to one. Reread the section on pneumatic tools in Chapter 1.

Tools and materials required for drywall application can be purchased at your home center or hardware store.

Materials. Standard drywall comes in various thicknesses — quarter inch, three-eighths inch, half inch, and five-eighths inch material. Thinner drywall offers the advantages of being lightweight and easy to manage. Thick drywall is stiffer and tends to go up flatter. The most commonly used drywall is $1/2''$ and $5/8''$ thick. Using a single layer of drywall thinner than this can result in a "spongy" wall. The standard panel is $4' \times 8'$, although $10'$ and $12'$ panels are available.

Moisture-resistant drywall is called greenrock and is specially treated for use in bathrooms and other damp areas. Its outer covering is of green paper.

The long edges of the panels are tapered to compensate for the thickness of mud and tape used to finish the seams, where two panels butt together. The basic materials you'll need are:

Drywall	Shim material
Vinyl spackling or joint compound	Butcher paper or cardboard for
Drywall nails, or	templates
Drywall screws	Metal corner beads
Drywall adhesive	Paper or fiber tape
Sandpaper (in various grades)	

PERMITS AND CODES

In some areas of the country, interior remodeling requires a building permit of some sort. In any event, the thickness and type of drywall to be used, as well as the nailing pattern employed, is sometimes governed by a local building code. I suggest you contact the office of your local building inspector before beginning work.

DESIGN

Drywall can be installed either vertically or horizontally. I suggest you plan your installation so that the least number of seams are created. Use this criterion to choose the size of drywall for your project and plan the application before proceeding. Remember that when two boards butt up against each other at their long edges, both must have a tapered factory edge where they meet. When using smaller pieces in odd-shaped areas, this will not always be possible. But do your best.

MOST COMMON MISTAKES

Given the number of steps involved in this project, the most common mistakes are listed separately with each relevant step. Note, however, that the most common mistake in working with drywall is not practicing the finishing steps before you do the actual work.

STEP ONE

PREPARING THE WALLS

Margin of Error: 1/8"

MOST COMMON MISTAKES

1. Neglecting to make provisions for insulation, ventilation, vapor barriers, plumbing, phone lines, wiring, and ductwork prior to the installation of drywall.

2. Neglecting to install nailguards where wires or pipes run within the studs, so nails or screws will not penetrate.

3. Placing seams at the side of a door or window.

Complete all electrical and plumbing work (such as installation of new outlets or wall and ceiling fixtures) before installing the drywall. This includes phone, cable TV lines, and alarm systems. Any leaks, poor ventilation, or other repairs should be taken care of before the drywall goes up. It won't make the walls look any better if a faulty pipe soaks your new walls within days. While you're at it, place metal nail guards over studs to protect wires and pipes. (Figure 1.) Also, be sure to complete any needed insulation, upgrading, or installation prior to drywalling.

Once you are sure all potential problems within the walls have been addressed, you can begin your layout work for drywall application. You'll want to mark the center of all wall studs on the ceiling and the floor for your vertical nailing pattern reference. If you are placing drywall over an existing wall, remove all the baseboards and note the locations of the nail holes in the wall

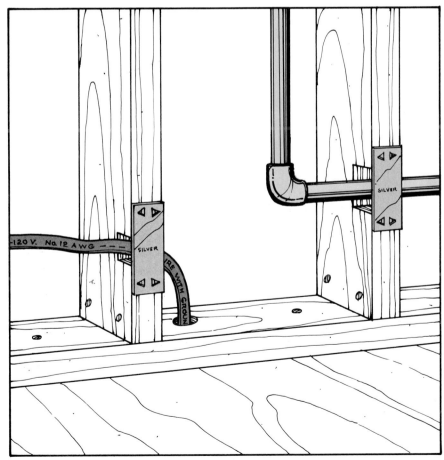

Figure 1. Nailguards protect wires and pipes from drywall nails.

surface. These nails will usually be in the center of a stud. Check this by drilling a hole ($1/8''$ drill bit) into the wall above a nail to find the stud. When you are confident you have found it, measure over 16″ (studs are usually 16″ or sometimes 24″ apart) and drill again until you find the next stud. Mark the stud locations on the ceiling and the floor and pop a chalkline down the center of the stud for your vertical nailing pattern reference. You may also wish to use one of the electronic or magnetic stud finders available on the market.

NOTE: Keep in mind, on a lath and plaster wall, you will need to drill through the plaster and lath before you locate the stud.

With open framework, observe your framework carefully to see if any studs (or rafters) are badly bowed and would cause the drywall to protrude or bow inward. This is especially critical around doors and windows where trim will later be applied. Correct these with shims or by chiseling, planing down, or even replacing the faulty studs if necessary before proceeding.

Figure 2. Using a scraping tool to smooth out the edge of a drywall panel.

STEP TWO

APPLYING THE DRYWALL

Margin of Error: $1/4''$

MOST COMMON MISTAKES

1. Not getting nail pattern inspected (check local code) before covering nails with compound and tape.

2. Not having insulation and utilities inspected (check local code) before covering with drywall.

3. Driving nails too deep so that they break the paper on the panels.

4. Not using drywall nails or screws.

Foot fulcrum

Figure 3. Use a fulcrum to support drywall lightly off the ground while nailing. Nail the nails directly across from each other in adjacent panels.

5. Not butting two panels of drywall at the beveled factory edge.

6. Not butting sheets at the center of a stud or rafter.

7. Applying the drywall sheets with the wrong side exposed.

8. Creating more seams than are necessary (i.e., using small scraps).

Final taping and mudding will go much more smoothly if the joints where sheets and odd shapes of drywall meet are smooth and able to fit closely together. Use a scraping plane or rasp on cut edges to smooth any roughnesses.

When you are positioning a drywall panel, align the top of each panel with the ceiling edge or the angle break to assure a clean edge. (Always install the ceiling panels first. The wall panels will help hold up the edges of the ceiling panels.)

All joints between boards should be positioned to meet over the center of a stud or rafter. The exception to this, of course, would be where the long edges meet on a horizontal application. Any gaps should fall close to the floor where a baseboard will cover them. To raise the panels you can make a foot fulcrum with two pieces of wood. (See Figure 3.)

The cumbersome application will go more easily if you start a couple of drywall nails at the corners and across the top of the drywall panel before you lift it into place. Once the panel is positioned, it will be easier to attach while another person holds it in place. Be sure to align each panel to meet over a stud.

Drywall nails vary. Some have cupped heads which make them easier to cover when mudding and taping. Those with barbed shanks increase holding power and reduce "nail popping." Nail along the edge of the panel about every 6″ or 7″ on ceilings and 8″ on center in the walls. In the middle of the panel, nail about every 12″. Check local code on this point for variance. It is advisable, if the studs are new wood, to double nail in the field, using 2 nails every 12″ instead of one. (See Figure 4.)

Hammer the nail firmly into the stud and until it is forced slightly below the surface of the panel — this is called dimpling. Also, be careful not to ding the edge of the panel when nailing or handling. Dings require extra mudding and finishing work. If you are using drywall screws, be sure you screw them to just below the surface of the panel.

TIP: Do not use aluminum ladders near electrical wires.

6″ on edges

12″ in center

(Double nail over green studs)

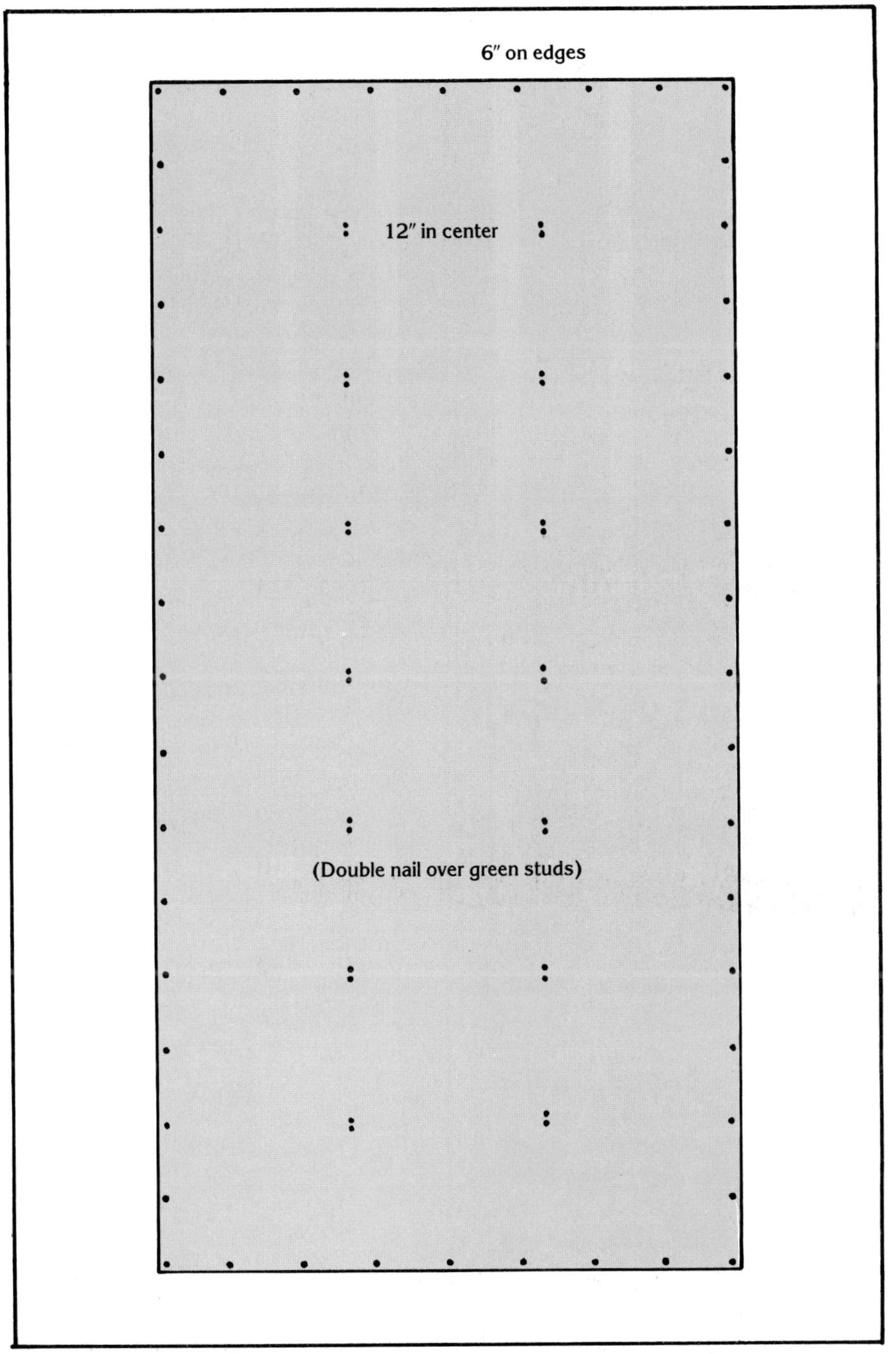

Figure 4. Nailing pattern for sheetrock. Check this with your local code.

Figure 5. Should you break the paper, drive a new nail directly below.

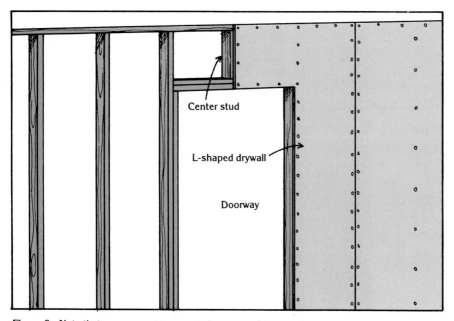

Center stud

L-shaped drywall

Doorway

Figure 6. Note that seams must accrue at the center of the opening and not at the edge of a door or window.

Whether using drywall nails or screws, do not break the paper when you are forcing the device below the surface. If the paper is broken, drive another nail or screw nearby to assure a good hold. It is advisable to have a special drywall hatchet or a cordless electric drywall screw gun for speed and ease of handling.

Place nails in adjoining sheets directly across from each other where they meet at a stud. This makes mudding easier. If you miss the stud, pull out the nail or screw and dimple the

hole to be able to mud and tape over it properly.

Another alternative to all these nail and/or screw holes is to apply the drywall with drywall adhesive. The adhesive should be applied with a caulk gun onto the studs in a continuous ⅜" zigzag bead. If you have access to an air compressor, there are caulking gun attachments that make this method almost effortless. Follow the manufacturer's instructions when using adhesive. The adhesive avoids nail holes that need to be finished with mud and reduces nail pops. Whenever using adhesives with panels, however, a minimum of 1 nail in each corner is needed to hold the panel in place.

When using adhesive, lay your stack of drywall panels over a stud so that the stud is in the center of the stack of panels, with the panel's backside facing up. This creates a slight bow in the panel which will force it into the stud and into the adhesive once the panel is applied.

Another reminder: as you apply the drywall try not to leave a gap between boards more than ⅛ to ¼ of an inch — less if possible. Larger gaps make taping more difficult. Before imbedding the tape over a seam, fill this void with joint compound. Never jam the sections of drywall together. They should be lightly butted but never forced.

Some areas require that you get your nailing pattern inspected (check local code) before covering the nails with tape and spackling.

TIP: When using adhesive, place your stack of drywall panels over a stud so that the stud is in the center of the stack of panels, with the back of the panel facing up. This will create a slight bow in the panels which will force it into the studs and into the adhesive once the panel is applied.

STEP THREE

CUTTING OPENINGS

Margin of Error: 1/4"

MOST COMMON MISTAKES

1. Dinging or damaging the edges of the panels.

2. Joining pieces so that the seam occurs at the edge, not the center, of the opening.

Applying drywall around openings like doors and windows calls for a little extra care and very accurate cutting. Never try to fit around a large opening with just one panel. You'll end up with an unstable panel of thin "arms" that are likely to break off from the main piece. It's best to work with two L-shaped pieces about the same size, with a joint that meets in the middle over the opening.

Joints must always meet at a stud but should never occur at the edge of a door or window. The door opens and closes at this point and the joint will eventually crack from the stress of the movement. (See Figure 6.)

Be particularly careful not to damage the board when cutting a notch or corner. Your cuts need to be clean and precise or the entire job will end up looking sloppy.

When covering around right-angle openings, use a drywall T-square or a chalkline to mark the board for cutting. Cut the shorter length first with a wallboard saw or keyhole saw. Then use a utility knife to score the longer cut. Use several light strokes with the knife to cut into the core. Position the cut over the edge of your worktable and snap the panel. Finish by cleanly undercutting the paper on the back side with the utility knife. Always cut with the good side up. (See Figure 7.)

Figure 7. Snap the drywall over an edge.

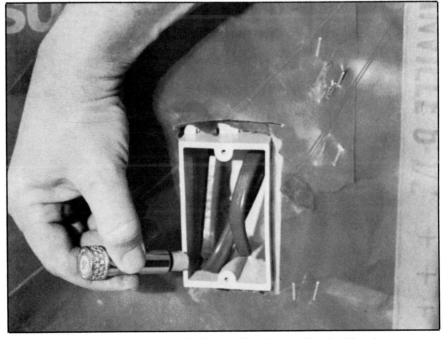

Figure 8. Outline the edges of the electrical boxes with colored chalk or lipstick and press drywall against it.

Figure 9. Use a drywall saw to cut out a hole for an electrical box after scoring with a utility knife.

STEP FOUR

ANGLES AND CEILINGS

Margin of Error: ¼"

MOST COMMON MISTAKES

1. Not applying the ceiling drywall before applying the drywall on the walls.

2. Creating more seams than are absolutely necessary (i.e., using small scraps).

Cutting a complex piece of drywall takes a bit of precision and may best be done with a paper or cardboard tem-

When cutting an opening to fit around a window, place the panel in position and mark the opening on the back of the panel. Use a drywall square or a clean straightedge to connect the points and make your cut accordingly. Cut the panel to fit to the edge of the stud at the rough opening. Do not let the drywall overlap onto the jamb or into the rough opening. For smaller openings like outlets, an efficient trick is to outline the opening with lipstick or colored chalk. Then fit the panel into place and apply hand pressure over the outlet area. The lipstick will transfer to the back of the panel for a cutting pattern.

Cut this patch out with your keyhole saw. Take care, when cutting from the back side of a panel, not to tear the paper beyond the patch hole area. Use the utility knife to finish cutting through the paper on the front side of the panel.

TIP: An alternative to paper tape is self-adhesive fiberglass or fabric tape.

Figure 10. Using "T" supports to support ceiling drywall until it is nailed in place.

plate. By taping something more flexible than drywall over the space to be covered and marking the dimensions on that; then using that pattern to transfer a precise pattern; your fit will be more exact. And your job will look more professional.

Ceilings and slants (like attic ceiling-walls) pose a serious problem in the form of gravity. More than one person will be needed to support each drywall panel as it is secured into place. You could use, instead, a 2″ × 4″ "T" if an assistant is not available. Actually, it would be best to use *both*, since, as you know by now, drywall is heavy, cumbersome, and not easily aligned overhead by one person, even if you're using supports. Make a supporting "T" by cutting a 2 × 4 to the height of your ceiling, *less* ¾″ (to accommodate the drywall). Nail a 3′ section of 1 × 4 attached to it as a support. (See Figure 10.)

Drywall screws used with a drywall screw gun are more efficient and convenient here (see Figure 11). The pattern for fastening with screws is a maximum of 12″ o.c. (on center) for ceilings; a maximum of 16″ o.c. in walls with studs placed 16″ o.c. When framing members are spaced 24″ o.c., the pattern for using screws would be a maximum of 12″ o.c. for both ceilings and walls. Local codes may vary on this point, however, so be certain to determine what is acceptable before beginning.

Again, I remind you that ceiling pieces should always be installed before wall boards. The wall boards will then serve as added support for the ceiling boards. Angled ceilings, however, may be installed after the walls without foreseen problems.

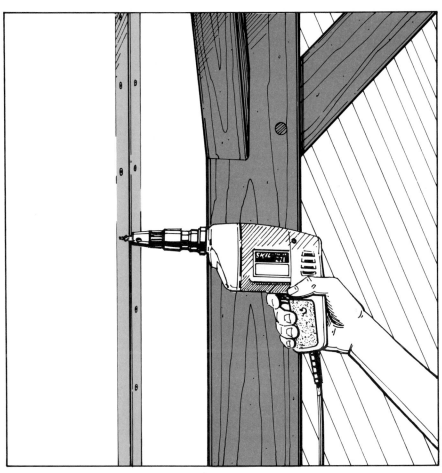

Figure 11. An electric screwdriver gun with screws is easier and quicker than nailing.

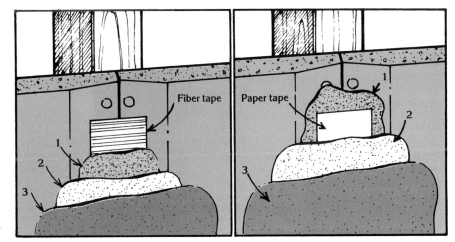

Figure 12. Self-adhesive fiber tape is applied directly to the drywall; the paper tape is applied to a thin layer of mud. Note how the edges of the panels are tapered to avoid a bulge at the seam.

TIP: When cutting around smaller openings like outlets, outline the opening with lipstick or colored chalk. Then fit the panel into place and apply hand pressure over the outlet area. The lipstick or chalk will transfer to the back of the panel and create a cutting pattern.

STEP FIVE

CURVES AND ODD SPACES

Margin of Error: ⅛″ to exact

MOST COMMON MISTAKES

1. Contaminating the compound with debris or dried chips of compound.

2. Not completely covering the tape with compound.

3. Creating more seams than are absolutely necessary (i.e., using small scraps).

Just as with angles, the easiest way to transfer the exact measurement from an odd-shaped space to the drywall is with a paper or cardboard template.

Tape or staple the paper to the stud and use a chalkline snapped down the center of each stud to mark the proper measurements on the paper. Transfer these measurements to the drywall. Cut small triangular slits in the paper and tape over these to the drywall with masking tape to secure the pattern and keep it from slipping. (See Figure 13.)

If you need to compensate for an angle being created, cut the template pieces slightly smaller (cut to the inside of the chalkline) than the actual space defined by the studs. As with other cuts, use the utility knife to make the long cuts and a keyhole saw for the crosscuts.

Fasten the drywall to the studs by the means you have chosen. With these pieces, tapered factory edges are not needed between adjoining pieces. Do smooth the cut edges for a more uniform joint, however.

TIP: To raise the panels, make a foot fulcrum with two pieces of wood.

Figure 13. Using a paper template to cut an odd shaped piece. Undercut pieces if installed at an angle.

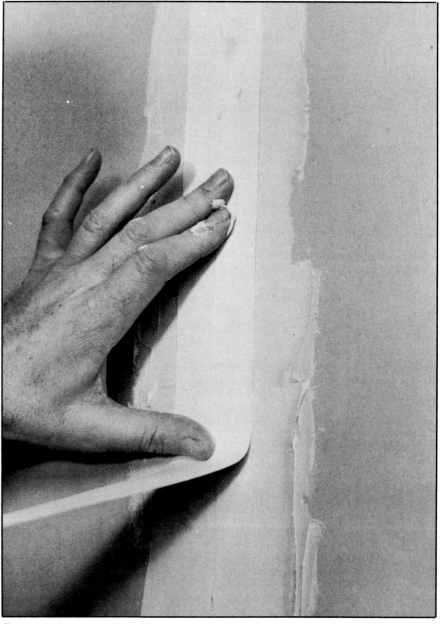

Figure 14. Paper tape is embedded into a layer of compound.

TAPE AND MUD

Now is the time to muster all of your patience and diligence, because the taping and mudding shows the flaws.

Many homeowners will carry the project to this point, then call in a professional to finish with finesse. If you are one of the more confident, take faith that a little practice in a less notice-able area (like, say, a closet) can go a long way. If, after that, you're still not sure, textured applications can be used. These are easier and often more suited to your creativity.

To achieve a smooth finish, all screw and nail heads must be covered with mud and seams taped over. Joint com-pound is known as mud. Conventional joint compound has a drying time of 8 to 24 hours, depending on the thick-ness of application. Allow longer for deeper cracks and crevices.

Working from a mud tray keeps dried pieces and bits of debris out of the can, and cleanliness is very impor-tant to a smooth finish. Keep the lid on airtight when you are not using it to keep it from drying out. Smooth the top of the mud flat and add ½" of water before sealing the can if it is to be stored for some time.

Compound can be purchased in 1- or 5-gallon buckets (or in powdered form, which you mix yourself). Unless you are doing a very small job, the 5-gallon bucket is a much better buy. As you are using the mud, scrape the in-side wall of the container often to keep residue from hardening and dropping pieces into the compound.

Drywall tape is available in paper tape, which is pre-creased and can be used on straight seams as well as cor-ner taping. Self-adhesive fiberglass tape can also be purchased. It has the ad-vantage of not needing a coating of mud underneath. This tape is recom-mended for the novice, except for use on the inside corners where it is neces-sary to use the paper tape.

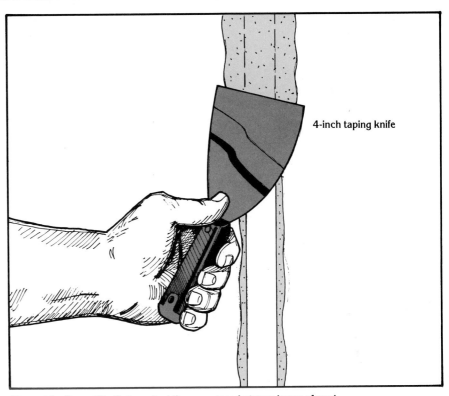

Figure 15. Use a 4" knife to embed the paper tape between layers of mud.

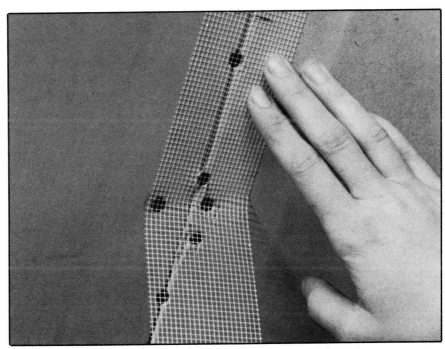

Figure 16. Self-adhesive fiber tape is applied directly to the drywall.

STEP SIX

APPLICATION OF TAPE AND MUD

Margin of Error: Exact

MOST COMMON MISTAKES

1. Not sanding between layers of drywall compound.

2. Not sanding the final coat of compound to a smooth finish.

Begin by covering all nail dimples, applying the mud flush with the panel.

If you have chosen to use paper tape at the joints, apply the first layer of mud with a 4" mud knife.

Apply enough mud to the seams for the drywall tape to adhere and to cover the entire seam.

Apply the tape and embed it into the mud. (Sometimes soaking the paper tape in water for a few moments aids this process.) Then, while the mud is still wet, apply a second layer to cover the tape completely. At the same time, draw your blade tightly over the surface to squeeze the mud out from underneath the tape so it is good and flat. Take care not to create any bubbles.

NOTE: A popular alternative to paper tape is self-adhesive fiberglass or fabric tape. With this type of tape, an undercoat of spackling is unnecessary. Simply apply the tape over the seam, then add a layer of mud over the tape.

Inside corners must be covered with paper tape because the fabric tape will not fold. Again, apply a layer of mud first, covering each side of the corner, then embed the folded tape. Finish smoothing the mud over and around the corner using a special corner knife. (See Figure 17.)

Outside corners require special metal corner beads to provide stability and protection to the drywall, since they are often brushed against and can be

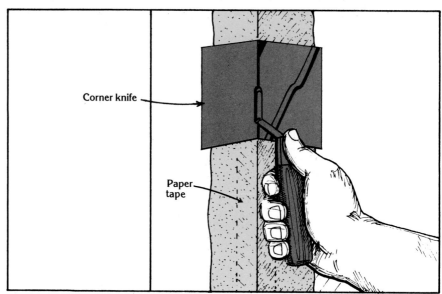

Figure 17. Using corner knife in inside corner.

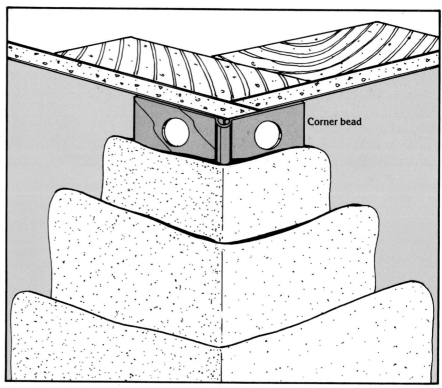

Figure 18. A metal corner bead protects outside corners from damage.

damaged easily. Cut the bead to fit the full height of the corner with tinsnips. Fasten it into the framing with screws or nails every 6". Then mud over it like any other seam, feathering the spackling out from the corner.

This first coat of mud should be completely dry before you go on to the next. If you want to speed things up, a heater with a fan will cut down the drying time considerably. Prepare the wall again before the second application. Use a mudding knife blade to scrape off any dried chips at the seams and nailhead areas. Then sand the first coat smooth with an orbital sander or sanding block using 80–100 grit sandpaper.

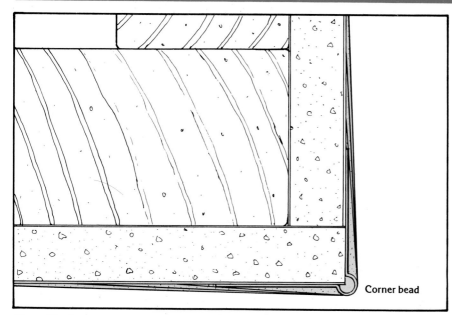

Figure 19. Corner bead covered by compound (top view).

ply compound to the inside and outside edges of the hole and fit the paper brim of the hat patch right over the bare gypsum. Now all you have to do is mud over the hat patch and allow it to dry.

When the patch is dry, use a knife blade to scrape off any dried chips. Lightly sand the patch; then apply another layer of mud. When this layer dries, scrape it, sand it lightly, then apply a final thinned-down coat of the spackling. Remember to sand once again prior to painting or wallpapering. Bare spackling on any wall repairs should always be covered with primer before paint or wallpaper application. This technique is illustrated in Step One of Chapter Two.

A safety note: When sanding, always use the paper face mask to avoid inhaling the dust.

You can opt for wiping it down with a large wet sponge in lieu of sanding, but take care not to soak the paper or wash away the spackling.

The second coat of mud needs to be thinned down with a little water and applied with a 6″ mud knife. Each coat you apply should be thinner than the last. Again, let this coat dry properly, then scrape it and sand or sponge it smooth. Be sure to feather the edges of the layers of compound at the joints so as not to build up raised areas there.

Apply the third coat with a 10″ mud knife for a smooth, even finish. Sand or sponge it smooth after this final coat as well.

NOTE: Only two coats of spackling are necessary for textured finishes. And, obviously, sanding and smoothing would have no merit.

Once the final coat has dried and been sanded, use a flashlight to check for blemishes. The light casts a shadow, which makes it easier to see the irregularities. A good smooth finish is essential before applying paint or wallpaper. Any inconsistency shows up.

Always do a final sanding or sponging just before preparing to paint or paper the newly applied drywall.

You will need to apply a primer-sealer undercoat to seal drywall and unpainted plaster or wallboard compound. Priming also prevents the base wallboard and outline of mudding applications from "showing through" any paint or wall coverings you may apply. Many primer-sealers are also "sizings," a preferred prerequisite to wallpapering. I recommend an oil-based primer for bare drywall. But be sure to check with your dealer for special considerations with your chosen wallcovering.

DRYWALL REPAIRS

Small dents and dings in drywall can usually be covered effectively with an application of wallboard compound and smoothed with sandpaper.

Larger holes need more complex surgery. We call this a "hat patch." Use a keyhole saw and utility knife to cut out the damaged portion. Clean out broken pieces around the edges of the hole. Remove a strip of the paper ½″ to 1″ wide around the perimeter of the clean hole. Then cut a new piece of drywall that is slightly larger than the hole. Carve away the gypsum on the back side of the patch until it fits the hole opening but leaves the paper on the outside of the patch intact. This is the "brim" of the "hat patch." Next, ap-

TOOLS AND MATERIALS CHECKLIST

Tools

Ladder	Mud knives (4″,
Sawhorses	6″, and 10″
Steel tape	widths)
measure	Corner mud knife
Drywall T-square	Mud trays
Carpenter's pencil	Drywall square
Drywall hammer	Utility knife and
⅜″ drill	blades
with a Phillip's	Keyhole saw
head driver	Dust masks
attachment (or	Goggles
a cordless	Buckets and
drywall screw	sponges
gun)	Flashlight
Chalkline and	Orbital sander
chalk	Sanding block
Scraper (plane)	Tinsnips

Materials

Drywall	Shim material
Vinyl spackling or	Butcher paper or
joint	cardboard for
compound	templates
Drywall nails	Metal corner
Drywall screws	beads
Drywall adhesive	Paper or fiber tape
Sandpaper in	
various grades	

CHAPTER FOUR

Paneling and Wall Systems

How to Make the Most of Your Living Space

WHAT YOU WILL BE DOING

Paneling is a dramatic and easy way to finish the walls of a room. Paneling comes in two basic forms — solid-wood boards in various widths (many of which are tongue-and-groove fit) and wood-faced 4′ × 8′ panels. In this chapter you will learn how to install wood-faced panels on several different surfaces, with special techniques to fit panels around openings and to custom-cut uneven intersections. One section describes the installation of tongue-and-groove solid-wood boards on a wall. In addition, you will discover some shortcuts and useful tips on trim for your new walls, as well as three types of shelving to complement them.

BEFORE YOU BEGIN

SAFETY

Although paneling is not a difficult do-it-yourself project, it is always a good idea to develop safe work habits and stick to them.

1. Use the appropriate tool for the job.

2. Keep blades sharp. A dull blade requires excessive force and can slip and cause accidents.

3. Wear the proper respirator when using adhesives with toxic fumes.

4. Wear rubber gloves when using solvents.

5. Be careful when lifting, to avoid unnecessary strain.

6. Don't smoke. Extinguish pilot lights and open flames when working with adhesives. Some are highly flammable.

7. Be sure tools are properly grounded.

8. Use all proper precautions when using power tools.

9. Use safety glasses or goggles whenever hammering or sawing.

TIP: When paneling is applied over existing white walls, a white streak can sometimes show through between the joints of two panels. You can avoid this by painting the existing walls with a 1 ½" dark strip at these points.

USEFUL TERMS

Furring. Usually 1" × 2" or 2" × 2" strips of wood attached to masonry or uneven walls to provide cavities in which to install insulation and a suitable surface upon which to apply paneling or wallboard.

Respirator. A device worn over the nose and mouth to filter out toxic fumes.

Scribing. A method of transferring the line of an uneven surface to a panel, making use of a compass.

Shim. Small wooden wedge used to even out furring strips, or to hold panels in place while attaching them to the wall.

Vapor barrier. Material to prevent buildup of moisture between insulation and paneling.

Wood-faced panels. 4' × 8' sections of plywood, one side laminated with hardwood veneer.

Sheet paneling

Figure 1. Installation of paneling over a drywall surface can be done with nails or adhesive.

WHAT YOU WILL NEED

Time. The installation of paneling and trim over bare studs will take 2 to 4 person hours per 100 square feet. When adding furring allow for 3 to 5 person hours per 100 square feet. When using adhesives allow for 2 to 4 person hours per 100 square feet.

Tools. Paneling an existing room or a new addition in the home can be a very satisfying project. The result is a look of invitation and warmth; and the process itself requires tools usually found in any home toolbox.

Hammer	Level
Tape measure	Circular saw
Drill and drill bits	Jig saw (for irregular cuts)
Nailset	Handsaw
Square	Assorted screwdrivers
Chalkline	Pencil

If you are paneling over masonry, you may want to rent a ramset or nail gun which will make the job of attaching the furring strips much easier. These guns fire a nail into concrete block of masonry using a .22-caliber cartridge. Though intimidating, they are safe when properly used. As an alternative, there are heavy-duty construction adhesives on the market which will effectively adhere furring strips to masonry. Check with your home center or hardware store.

If you plan to use an adhesive as a primary means of attachment, you will also need a caulking gun. An air compressor with a caulking gun attachment is a time- and effort-saving tool and can be rented if you do not have access to one. If you are unfamiliar with the use of pneumatic tools, read over the information on them in Chapter One on Tools before beginning work.

Other tools you will require include:

Compass	Finishing blades for your power saws
Finishing hammer	

When trimming, the following will be used as well:

Miter box and back saw	Coping saw

And if you add shelving:

Orbital sander	Chisel and mallet
Clamps	

Materials. You will also need to purchase various materials. Their needs are covered on the following pages.

Shims	Furring strips
Screws	Paneling insulation
Nails	Vapor barrier
Paneling adhesive	Trim pieces
Paneling boards of your choice	Caulk
Paneling nails	Shelving elements

PERMITS AND CODES

Paneling usually comes under the general catchall of "interior remodeling." In some areas, this may require a permit from the office of the local building inspector. Often any work in excess of a certain dollar amount (usually $100) requires a permit. I suggest you look into that possibility before beginning work.

DESIGN

Paneling is a good choice of wall covering for casual playrooms or dens and it can lend on air of elegance to a library or study. A well-chosen style can also be effective in more formal living spaces as well.

Use paneling to pull together spaces that may be separate but adjoining, such as familyroom/kitchens or in rooms with cathedral ceilings that expose portions of upper hallways or other rooms.

MOST COMMON MISTAKES

Even the most diligent worker sometimes makes a mistake. Keep in mind that the single most common mistake in any do-it-yourself project is failure to read and follow the manufacturer's instructions for the tool or material being used. Others are listed with each individual step.

STEP ONE

PLANNING YOUR PANELING

Margin of Error: Not applicable

MOST COMMON MISTAKE

1. Not taking the time to plan carefully before purchasing the materials for your project.

Properly chosen, paneling and shelving systems can enhance a room and make it a warm, inviting place to spend time. Become familiar with the varying colors and textures of today's paneling selections before making your decision. For example, a dark attic is more suited to a pastel panel, while a sunny family room would better accept a deeper tone.

The choice between sheet paneling and tongue and groove paneling is one of personal taste and expense. The solid wood tongue and groove is more expensive as well as more difficult to install. However, there are many people who find the richness of the natural wood to be well worth the extra expense.

To determine the amount of sheet paneling you will need, multiply the length of your wall by its width and then divide by 32 (the area of a 4 × 8 panel). For tongue and groove paneling, determine your area and consult with your dealer as widths of tongue and groove paneling vary. For molding, measure the linear feet. Avoid splicing short pieces by purchasing extra lengths of paneling from which to cut.

This chapter will discuss a variety of situations to help you choose the easiest, most cost effective method of applying your chosen paneling.

STEP TWO

APPLYING THE PANELING

Margin of Error: ¼" where covered by trim. Exact where exposed.

MOST COMMON MISTAKES

1. Neglecting to furr out an existing wall if needed, prior to installing the paneling.

2. Not adding insulation or a vapor barrier over an outside or basement wall.

3. Cutting panels face up with a saber or circular saw, thereby splintering the veneer panel.

4. Neglecting to check that each panel is plumb on the wall before applying the next.

5. Transferring measurements to the panel incorrectly or to the wrong side.

6. Not using a finishing hammer and finishing saw blades when working with paneling.

Figure 2. Using furring strips to install tongue-and-groove boards on a concrete wall.

Figure 3. Check to be sure panels are level and that adjacent panels meet over the centers of studs.

4" shim

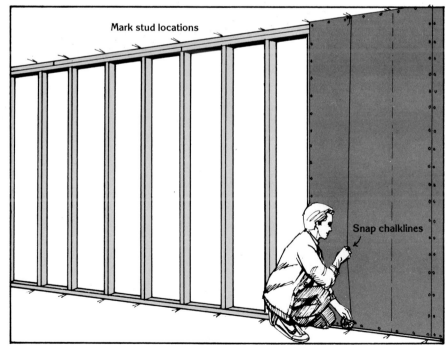

Mark stud locations

Snap chalklines

Figure 4. Popping chalklines down the center of the studs as nailing guides.

WOOD-FACED PANELING

Let's first discuss the easiest paneling situation — using wood-faced panels. Most paneling sheets come in 4' wide, 8' high sheets with a thin veneer surface. These are the most popular material on the market today and come in various styles, patterns, wood types, and quality.

PANELING OVER EXPOSED-STUD WALLS

This is the easiest paneling project because you are working with bare studs and have no structural or surfacing problems to contend with. You can use either a paneling adhesive or nails to attach panels to a stud wall. This is a matter of personal preference, although adhesive has the advantage of eliminating visible nailheads and reducing nail pops.

If you are using adhesive, use a caulking gun loaded with a paneling adhesive to apply a ⅜" zigzag ribbon of glue to the studs and top and bottom plates. Or, if you have access to an air compressor, the application of adhesive to the studs can be made even easier with a caulking gun attachment. Position the panel to the wall with edges aligned to the center line of the end studs. If no stud occurs at the edge, you will need to add one. To do this, simply toenail it into the top and bottom plate so that the center of the stud occurs where the two panels meet. Position the panel with a quarter-inch clearance at the top and bottom. Shim material can help you here to hold up the panel for clearance. Shims are small wooden wedges that can be purchased from your home center store or made from scrap wood at home. Or you can use a foot fulcrum to raise the panel into position.

Next, place a level against the edge of the panel to check that it is plumb, making certain your panel is in a correct position before nailing it into the studs. All paneling should be held in place with a minimum of one nail in each corner when using adhesive. If you are using nails, use one-inch color-coordinated paneling nails placed 6″ apart on all edges and 12″ apart on intermediate studs.

Use a finishing hammer to nail the panel along the edge enough to hold it in position, tack it at the top and bottom, and press your weight against it to make good contact with the adhesive. If you must rip a piece of paneling to fit an area less than 4′ wide, be sure to apply the factory edge against the factory edge of the adjoining piece. To avoid splintering, use a plywood blade and cut the panel from the back side.

PANELING OVER EXISTING WALLS

When paneling over an existing wall that is in good shape, you will need to mark off the positions of the studs for nailing reference. Studs are usually located every 16″ or 24″ on center. Tap along the wall with a hammer until you hear a solid sound, look for seams or drill a hole to verify that you have located the stud. Mark the position on the floor and ceiling and pop a chalkline to mark the center of the stud on the wall. Locate all studs for the entire area of wall space you will be paneling. Don't worry about drilling holes in the wall. These will be covered by the paneling.

The paneling nail must be long enough to go through the material firmly into the stud, so choose your nail lengths according to the material on your walls. Paneling nails come in different colors to match different wood types. Once inserted, they are practically invisible. I suggest nailing across the width of the panel to prevent bulges. The nails should be spaced 6″ apart around all edges and 12″ apart in the center. Many panel patterns are designed so that their V-grooves align

Figure 5. Gluing over existing wall is an alternative to nailing.

Figure 6. Cartridge-actuated nail gun (ramset) can be used to attach furring strips to concrete block wall.

PANELING OVER MASONRY OR DETERIORATED WALLS

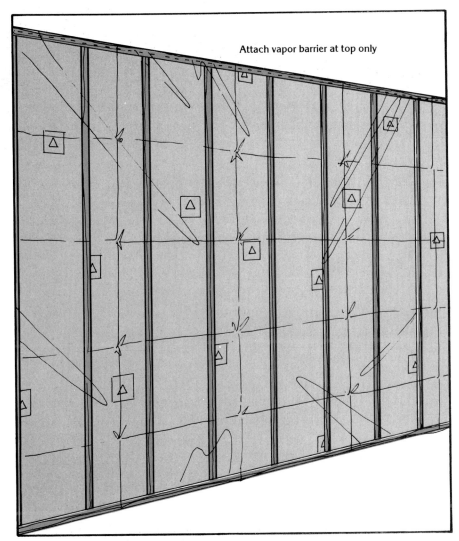

Attach vapor barrier at top only

Figure 7. Vapor barrier and rigid insulation installed over an uninsulated wall.

over studs, thereby allowing you to nail in the grooves.

When placing your panels in position, be certain they are plumb before nailing them permanently in place. To do this, simply hold a 4′ level against the edge of the paneling.

If you choose to use adhesive to attach your paneling over existing walls, measure over from a corner 48″ (the width of a panel) and snap a plumb chalkline vertically on the wall. This will tell you how far to spread the adhesive for each panel. Continue measuring and snapping plumb lines at 4′ intervals along the walls to be paneled.

Apply a ⅜″ bead of paneling adhesive around the perimeter of the area defined on the wall and an "X" bead connecting opposite corners (Figure 5). Here, too, an air compressor with caulking gun attachment would be a time and energy saver. Push the panel into the glued surface and use a level to make certain it is plumb before you tack it into position and glue it down permanently. The other panels will then align according to this first one. Again, keep in mind when using adhesive that all panels should be held in place with a minimum of one nail in each corner.

Because a masonry surface (or an old plaster wall with cracks, bulges, and loose plaster) is so hard to penetrate with paneling nails, and because it is such an uneven surface, "furring strips" must be added to such walls.

To attach the 2″ × 2″ furring strips, use either adhesive or a ramset, which can be rented from your local home center. Wear safety glasses and ear protectors when using a ramset, and be sure to use the right size nails and "bullets." (If the plaster wall is in really bad shape, you may wish to remove all the old plaster, rather than furr out. Use the claw side of a hammer to break the plaster away — right down to the studs, or at least the lath. This is a very messy, labor-intensive job and should be avoided unless absolutely necessary.)

Furring should be installed with a horizontal piece at the top and bottom and vertical strips 16″ on center, simulating a stud wall. Use a level on the furring strips and even out the irregularities in the masonry or plaster with shim material to get the furring surfaces level and even with each other. When this is completed you will have a wooden structure to hold the paneling solidly. If you are working on an uninsulated exterior wall, we also recommend cutting rigid foam-core insulation to friction-fit in the spaces between the furring strips. Measure the space between each furring strip separately, at both top and bottom. This will give you a custom friction-fit.

Next, add a vapor barrier of 6 ml. visquine. This is just a painter's plastic drop cloth to prevent the buildup of moisture between the insulation and the new paneling. You need only attach the vapor barrier to the top (Figure 7). Gravity and the paneling will keep it in place without puncturing too many holes in the plastic, which would destroy its ability to effectively keep moisture out. Now you can attach your paneling over the vapor barrier with nails. Adhesive cannot be used in this situation. Insulated walls that already have a vapor barrier do not require one directly behind the paneling.

STEP THREE

FITTING PANELS AROUND OPENINGS

Margin of Error: ¼" where covered by trim. Exact where exposed.

MOST COMMON MISTAKES

1. Overcutting window, door, and electrical openings.

2. Neglecting to have all electrical wiring and plumbing completed prior to application of paneling.

The easiest way to get an accurate door or window opening measurement is to have one person hold the sheet of paneling in place over the opening while another traces the line of the opening on the back of the panel. This works best for doors. If you are unable to get to the back of the panel, you will need to do it all with measurements as described next.

If you are not planning to butt the paneling up against the molding, carefully remove the molding with a pry bar, using a wooden wedge for leverage (Figure 8). Place the panel in position over the window, pushing it tightly butt up against the previously installed panel. Be sure that the ¼" gap between the floor and the panel is maintained with shims, and use a level to check that the panel is plumb. Place marks on the edge of the panel to indicate the top and bottom of the window or opening. Measure and record the distance from each mark to the side of the window. (See Figure 9.) Transfer these measurements to the back of the panel. Use a straightedge to connect the points.

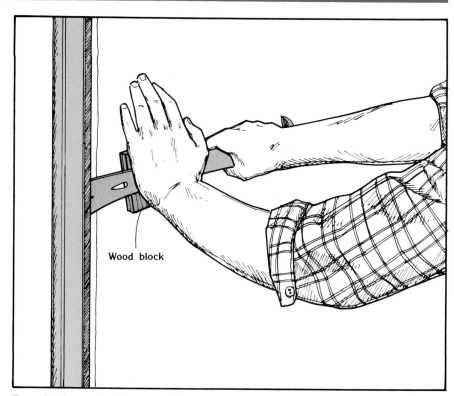

Wood block

Figure 8. Use a pry bar to remove door molding before installing paneling.

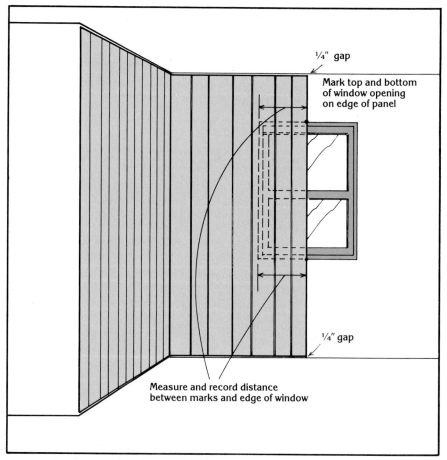

¼" gap

Mark top and bottom of window opening on edge of panel

¼" gap

Measure and record distance between marks and edge of window

Figure 9. Measure paneling to fit around doors and windows.

Building Out

When installing paneling over an existing wall, there can be a problem with the trim. The widths of original door and window jambs were calculated to fit the existing wall, and the addition of the new paneling makes the wall thicker by ¼″ or more.

There are several ways to approach this problem. You can replace all door and window jambs with wider boards, but this is costly and time consuming. (See Figure 11.) An easier solution would be to cut the panels to fit exactly up to the trim. This way, you would not have to remove the trim and replace it on top of the paneling to cover your mistakes. This is the easiest solution, if you are confident you can make good exact cuts. This is often difficult to do when ripping a long piece of paneling. If your cuts waver (Figure 12), it may be necessary to add small shoe molding between the paneling and trim to cover those mistakes.

Another method is to add ¼″ jamb extender strips to the jambs and then paint them to match. These strips

Figure 10. Outline lip of outlet box with lipstick or colored chalk. Whack paneling over box to imprint outline on back of paneling.

For smaller things like electrical boxes, mark the edge of the box with chalk or lipstick. Then position the panel over it (Figure 10). Give the panel a whack over the opening and the imprint should appear clearly on the back of the panel. Then, make your pencil lines and cut on the back of the panel to avoid splintering the veneer with your circular saw.

TIP: Use a painter's plastic drop cloth to prevent the buildup of moisture between the new insulation and the new paneling.

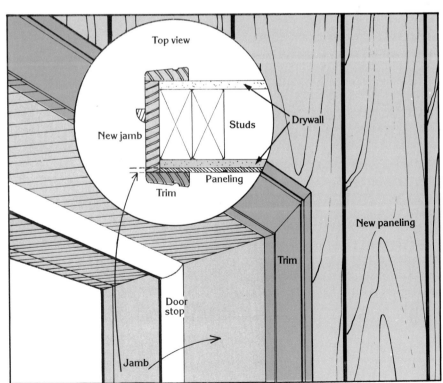

Figure 11. One method of trimming around new paneling is to remove the old jamb and replace it with a wider one.

leave a small gap between the old jamb and the new strip, which can be puttied and painted to match. These are usually available at home centers or mill-work shops.

A final option is to cut a groove on the back side of the trim so that it sets in the paneling and covers its edge.

This requires running each piece through a grooving process with a router or table saw (Figure 13). Inquire whether your supplier has a preformed piece of trim that will work. All three systems have their advantages and drawbacks. Consider the one that will work best for you.

Scribing

Now and then a panel must butt up against an irregular surface. With a fireplace, for instance, the wall goes from board to masonry, and you have a wavy corner to match up. For these situations, you will find "scribing" to be the easiest and most effective way of fitting the panel tightly in place.

Begin by measuring from the edge of the last full sheet to the very farthest point of the irregularity. Make a note of that distance, and then cut your panel to that width. Next, measure the distance from the edge of the last full sheet of paneling to the nearest point of the irregularity. Make a note of that distance. Subtract the second measurement from the first to get the "scribing distance." Then, position the panel you need to trim and fit so that it overlaps the last full sheet of paneling by the "scribing distance." (See Figure 14.) Use your level to position it plumb and tack it temporarily into place.

Set a simple dime-store compass to the "scribing distance." Hold the compass with the tip and the pencil horizontal; ride the tip along the irregular surface while the pencil runs along the panel you wish to trim (Figure 15). Trace the irregular line carefully from the top of the panel to the bottom. The result will be a line on the panel which should be the exact profile of the irregularity. This line can now be cut with a jig saw. Smooth the cut edge with a rasp or sanding block. Now glue or nail the panel into place. (A contour gauge can be used to transfer complex details accurately.)

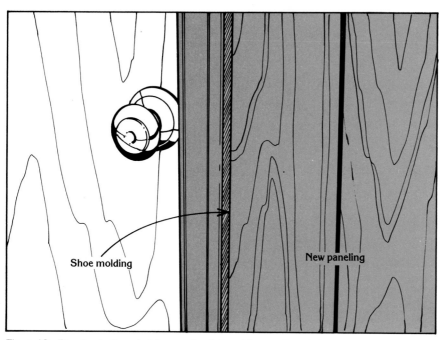

Figure 12. The simplest way to trim paneling is to cut it up to the existing trim and then install the shoe molding.

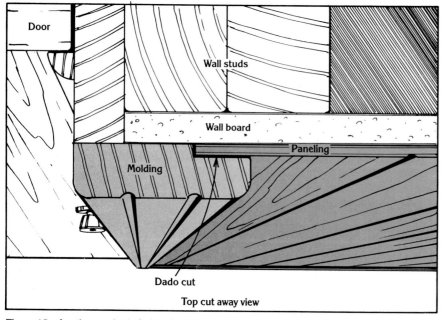

Figure 13. Another method of trimming around new paneling is to make a dado cut in the trim and replace it over the paneling.

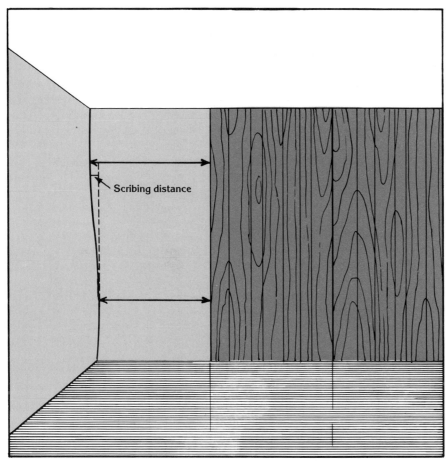

Figure 14. Overlap the paneling by the scribing distance. (Y − X = scribing distance.)

If you are starting at a corner that is irregular, measure out from the corner 48″ to the center of a stud. (See the section above on Paneling over Existing Walls to determine stud positions on finished walls.) Snap a plumb chalkline down the center of the stud to establish the position of the edge of the panel. Mark these positions on the ceiling and floor for a nailing reference. Place the panel snug into the corner as possible with a level on the opposite vertical edge to plumb the panel. Temporarily tack it in place at the top and bottom. Measure from the panel edge to the center line of the stud marked on the floor to determine your "scribing distance." This measurement should be the same at the ceiling and at the floor. Scribe and cut with a jigsaw, smooth, and install panel, as described above.

When applying paneling over existing white walls, a white streak can sometimes show through between joints of two panels. To avoid this, paint the existing nails with a 1½″ dark strip at these points.

Figure 15. Scribing panel using compass to fit irregular corner.

TIP: Miter cut the ends at a 45-degree angle so that the two pieces of molding overlap each other to make a cleaner-looking trim.

TRIM

STEP FOUR

APPLYING THE TRIM

Margin of Error: Exact

MOST COMMON MISTAKE

1. Leaving more than a ¼" gap at corners.

There are many styles of trim in materials such as wood, metal, and plastic. Trim is used to cover gaps at inside corners, floor and ceiling joints, or around door and window openings. Trim is the key to a successful job. With trim you cover your mistakes and thereby avoid the need for complete accuracy.

Floor and ceiling joints. The basic trim piece for a floor-to-wall or ceiling-to-wall connection is a quarter round or baseboard. It offers a clean, straight appearance and is easy to install. Simply nail it in place with finishing nails.

Outside corners. Place your paneling so that the edges meet as tightly as possible at an outside corner. If the intersection of the two pieces is neat enough it can be left uncovered. Special outside corner molding can also be applied.

Inside corners. If your walls are straight enough, and your paneling job neat enough, you can sometimes run one sheet tightly into the corner and butt the mate right up to it for a snug fit and a good-looking job. If this is not the case, however, a quarter round will work nicely here as well.

Outside baseboard corners. These pieces should first be cut to a 45-degree angle with your miter box and back saw. Nail them into place so they are snug. Then run the round part of your hammer handle or screwdriver shank tightly up the joint to seal any gap that may be left. (See Figure 17.)

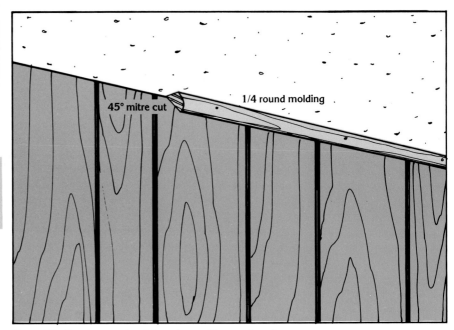

45° mitre cut   1/4 round molding

Figure 16. Quarter-round molding where ceiling meets wall.

Figure 17. Using shank of screwdriver to smooth outside edge of baseboard.

angle and cut away the wedged portion of the molding, following the outside line exactly. (See Figure 18.) This method transfers the perfect profile to the molding, which will then fit snugly over the mate at the wall.

Joints along the length of the baseboard. These can be ugly and tend to pull apart if merely butted up against each other. Another trick here is to miter cut the ends at a 45-degree angle so that the two pieces of molding will overlap each other to make a cleaner-looking trim. Apply some glue at the miter joint between the two pieces. This will keep the joint tight if the molding shrinks. You can allow the glue to ooze out of the joint and get tacky. Then lightly sand the joint, and the glue will mix with the sawdust and conceal the joint.

TIP: Trim is the secret to a successful paneling job. It covers your mistakes and thereby helps you avoid the need for greater accuracy.

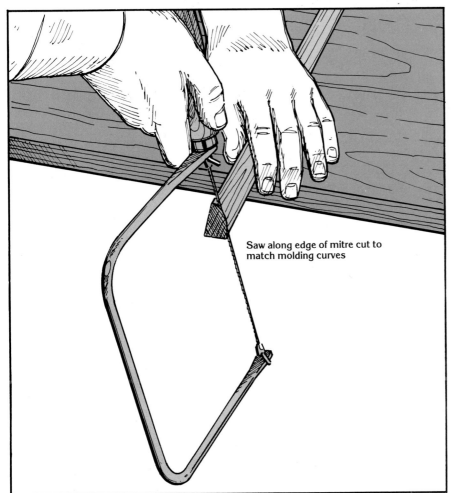

Saw along edge of mitre cut to match molding curves

Figure 18. Using a coping saw to cut quarter-round molding.

Inside baseboard corners. These can be tricky when you are using the types of baseboards that have curves and shapes to them. I do not recommend using a miter cut here because the nails have a tendency to pull the intersecting pieces away from each other, creating quite a gap, when attached. If you are painting, this crack can be filled with caulk and painted over. If you prefer the natural wood trim, a process called "coping" will give you a beautifully fitted corner every time.

Begin by butting the first piece of molding up to the wall and nailing it in place. The second piece should be placed in your miter box for a 45-degree cut with the inside wood grain showing on the front of the molding. Use a coping saw kept at a 90-degree

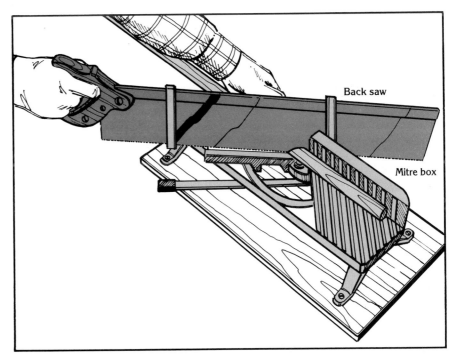

Back saw

Mitre box

Figure 19. Cutting a 45-degree angle with a miter box.

TONGUE-AND-GROOVE PANELING

The next type of paneling I will be discussing is Tongue-and-Groove Paneling. Paneling with solid wood T & G boards is more tedious than with hardboard panels, but their weight and stiffness mean they require less support. They also offer a real wood appearance. Special boards for paneling can be used, or tongue-and-groove hardwood flooring can be used.

STEP ONE

APPLICATION OF THE BOARDS

Margin of Error: Exact

MOST COMMON MISTAKES

1. Neglecting to furr out an existing wall if needed prior to installing the paneling.

2. Not adding insulation or a vapor barrier over an uninsulated outside or basement wall.

3. Cutting panels face up with a saber or circular saw, thereby splintering the veneer panel.

4. Neglecting to check that each piece is plumb on the wall before applying the next.

5. Transferring measurements to the panel incorrectly or to the wrong side.

6. Not using a finishing hammer and finishing saw blades when working with paneling.

When paneling vertically, because the boards are narrow pieces, you may need to put up horizontal furring strips (using adhesive or nails) so that the boards have something to hold onto.

Attach the furring strips horizontally across the studs every 24″ to create a solid backing. You can also install plywood over the existing walls. If you are paneling over existing wall material, you need to locate the studs and mark them on the floor and ceiling for nailing reference. See the section above on Paneling over Existing Walls.

If you choose to install this type of paneling on the diagonal or horizontal, furring is not necessary if the walls are in good shape. The boards will cross the studs at an angle and be adequately supported. Always start the boards in a corner with the groove edge facing the direction in which you are paneling. The boards can be glued or nailed to

the walls, or both. I recommend a paneling adhesive and toothed trowel, or a paneling adhesive applied from a caulking gun. Follow the adhesive instructions for application. If using the cartridge method for adhesive application, an air compressor with a caulking gun attachment will save you a great deal of time and effort.

Apply the boards in a stairstep pattern and be sure they are plumb. Use a small piece of paneling board as a pounding board to force two adjacent pieces together. The last piece, next to the intersecting wall, should be cut to size and its tongue slipped into the groove of the adjacent board. It should snap right into place. You may need to make a scribe cut, as described above in the section on scribing, under Wood-Faced Paneling; although corner trim often eliminates the need for scribing.

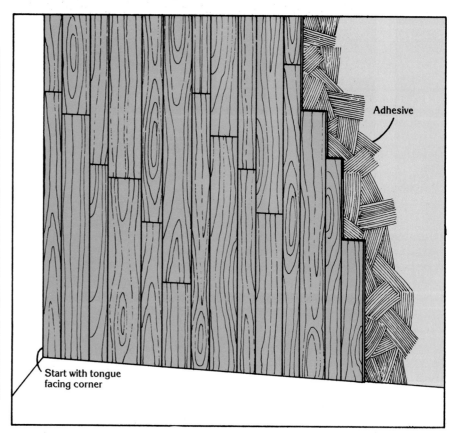

Figure 20. Installing the tongue-and-groove planks directly over drywall using adhesives.

FITTING BOARDS AROUND OPENINGS

First, remove all existing trim and apply full-size boards as close to door and window jambs as possible. Measure the distance from the edge of the last board to the edge of the opening. You will need to notch some boards, and cut others to specific length, above doors and windows and below windows. Then, very carefully, transfer these dimensions to your board, and, just as carefully, cut the boards out. If you are notching, cut only to within

¼" of your intersection of two cuts with the circular saw, and finish the cut with a handsaw if the board must butt up against existing trim, since the trim will not cover the cut. Otherwise, use a circular saw with the board face down so the circular blade doesn't cause the board to splinter. This step takes patience and care because you are working with such narrow pieces. Each board must be measured and trimmed separately. To apply trim, see Step 4 above under Wood-Faced Paneling.

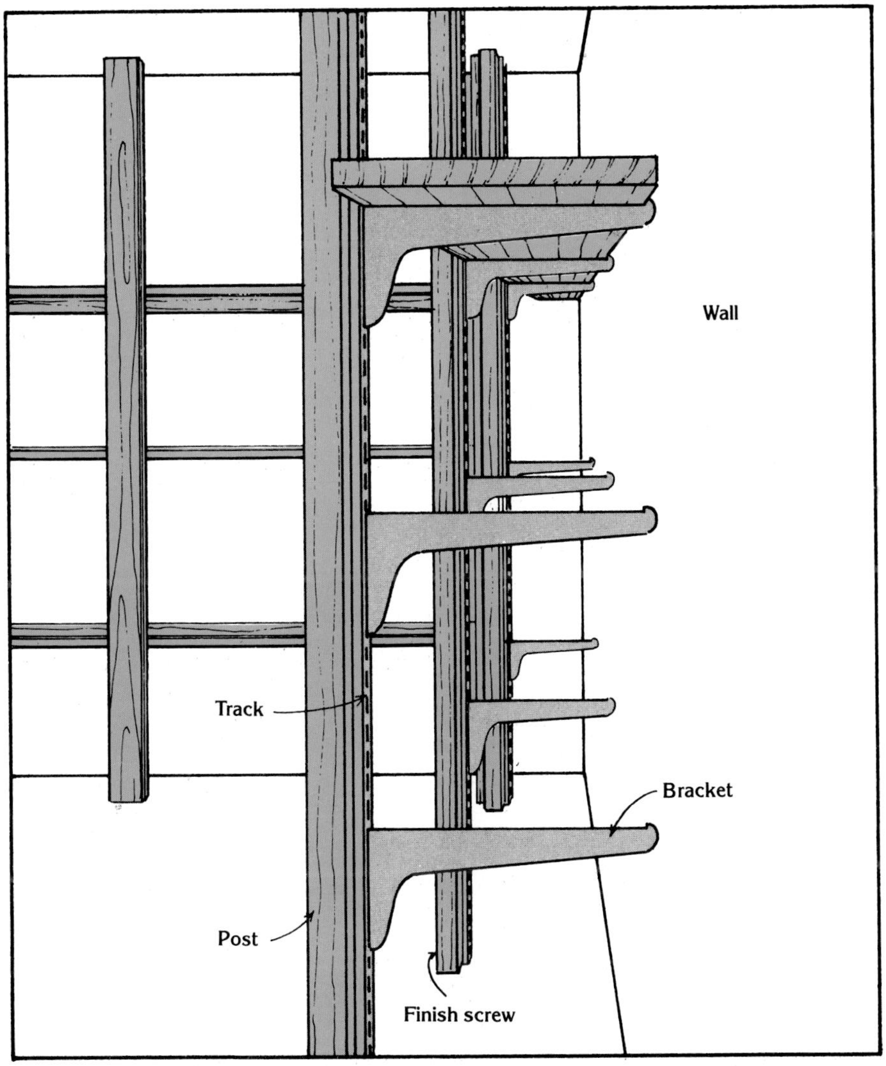

SHELVING SYSTEMS

The shelving systems below may be applied to both kinds of paneling discussed above. Properly planned shelves will enhance your newly paneled walls, as well as provide you with attractive storage space.

Planning

Always draw a plan of a shelving system prior to building. This minimizes any design and fitting problems you may have to work with. Use graph paper.

Take into account the visual effect you want from your wall system, what it will house, and the structural elements needed. Use your plan to aid you in making a materials list, so that you will have all necessary materials on hand when you begin building.

TIP: If you are paneling over masonry, you might want to use a ramset or nail gun to make the job of attaching the furring strips much easier.

Figure 21. Suspended shelving creates a pleasing effect.

73

SUSPENDED SHELVING

Probably the most common shelving system has been the one in which metal tracks are attached to a wall for hanging movable metal brackets. Wood or plastic shelves then rest on the brackets. This is a very simple system to construct. The main concern is that the tracks are attached to the studs behind the wall. The information in previous sections of this chapter help you locate the studs.

There is, however, an attractive alternative to mounting conventional shelving brackets directly to the wall when you don't want to detract from the visual effect of the paneling, or if you want more wood (or less metal) to show. Create front supports for the shelving system with posts running from floor to ceiling. Space them out from the wall the depth you want your shelves to be. (See Figure 21.) Attach them to the floor by drilling holes at the base and securing them with finishing screws. With these supports you can still use the inexpensive track-and-bracket construction. Attach the shelving brackets to the insides of the posts (facing the wall). This hides the tracks and minimizes the look of the metal.

CLOSET SHELVING

Aside from building your shelves from scratch, there are now many storage systems available, ready to assemble. I recommend you investigate these before beginning.

Attach $1'' \times 4''$ ledger boards to the closet wall at the height and length you wish your shelf to be. These ledgers should be level and attached directly to the wall studs for maximum support. The shelf board will rest on the lip of the ledger.

When adding a clothes hanging pole, you will need plastic pole supports which screw into the wall at either end of the closet. If the pole is very long, add a supporting pole bracket in the middle, attached to the ledger.

TIP: The application of adhesive to the studs can be made even easier by adding a caulking gun attachment to your air compressor.

RECESSED SHELVING

Many rooms have recessed cubbyhole walls, or even closets which you might like to open up, for exposed shelving.

It is a simple matter to measure and cut boards to fit vertically on either side of the alcove. Inexpensive hardware tracks can then be screwed plumb into the boards and adjustable clips installed in the tracks for multi-position shelving.

First measure and cut the shelving from plywood or $1''$ stock. Then, face the plywood with a 1×2 to cover up the rough edges. Next, add quarter round as trim pieces and paint the entire system to match the room's decor for an inexpensive and attractive wall unit. Adding sticky-back mirror squares at the back of a shelving system of this sort magnifies the space.

If you are using wood boards for your shelving, you will achieve a much finer finish with an orbital sander. The finishing process will go much faster and the result will be much smooth. It is worth renting one if you do not own one.

TOOLS AND MATERIALS CHECKLIST

Tools for All Projects

Hammer	Chalkline
Tape measure	Level
Electric drill (with	Circular saw
various drill	Jig saw
bits)	Handsaw
Nailset	Assorted
Carpenter's	screwdrivers
square	Pencil

Materials for All Projects

Shims	Adhesive
Screws	Beeswax
Nails	

Materials for Tongue-and-Groove Paneling

Tongue-and-	Color-coordinated
groove planks	nails
Adhesive	

Tools for Wood-Faced Paneling

Chalkline	Ramset
Caulking gun or	Compass
Air compressor	Finishing
(with caulking	hammer
gun	Finishing or
attachment)	plywood blades

Materials for Wood-Faced Paneling

Wood-faced	Furring strips
paneling	Rigid foam
Colored paneling	insulation
nails	Vapor barrier

Tools for Trim

Miter box with	Coping saw
back saw	Caulking gun

Materials for Trim

Quarter round	Finishing nails
Caulk	Carpenter's wood
Baseboard	glue
moldings	

Tools for Shelving

Orbital sander	Chisels and mallet
Clamps	

Materials for Shelving

Graph paper	1 × 2 board
1 × 4 board	Quarter round
Pole	Sticky-back
Plastic pole	mirror squares
supports	Posts
Supporting pole	Track and bracket
bracket	Shelf boards
Plywood	Finishing screws

CHAPTER FIVE

Ceilings

Installing and Replacing Suspended and Tile Ceilings

WHAT YOU WILL BE DOING

Because ceilings are perhaps more out of view than any other part of the interior of the home, their impact on the general feel or mood of a house is often underestimated. Along with the floor, they are the largest surfaces in the room. A visit to rooms that have different ceiling heights, materials, slopes, and angles will clearly demonstrate how much they affect the way a room feels. All too often they are overlooked in remodeling plans.

Ceilings are used not only as a design feature but also as a cover-up. Ceilings hide the framing of the floor or roof above, plumbing pipes, ductwork, electrical wire, insulation, and so on. Suspended ceilings (ceilings that are hung a set distance from the ceiling joists) work very well for this, because they create a cavity that allows for ease of access if repairs or further work is needed in this area.

In the past, the more common types of ceilings were lath and plaster (as were the walls) and wood planks. Metal ceilings were also popular because of their ease of installation and light weight. In the past few decades drywall (gypsum board) has re-placed lath and plaster as a wall and ceiling material. Indeed, drywall is nothing more than plaster already spread in a sheet. Drywall has become a very popular ceiling material. The tech-niques of working with drywall were presented in Chapter Three. Here we consider suspended acoustical ceilings and tile ceilings. In this chapter you will learn how to install both types of ceilings and how to make minor repairs to existing ceilings.

BEFORE YOU BEGIN

SAFETY

Always understand, develop, and adhere to proper safety practices. For installing ceilings, these include:

1. Use the appropriate tool for the job.

2. Use the proper dust mask or respirator when sanding and sawing.

3. Safety glasses or goggles should be worn whenever power tools are in use, or when hammering overhead (especially if you wear contact lenses).

4. Watch power cord placement so that it does not interfere with the tool's operation.

5. Keep blades sharp. A dull blade requires excessive force, can slip, and cause accidents.

6. Be certain the panels or tiles you purchase do not contain asbestos or any other material that could cause a health problem in your home. I recommend a nationally known manufacturer, respected for quality.

7. When using a stepladder, have both pairs of legs fully open and the spread bars locked in place, and never climb higher than the second step from the top. When bracing a ladder against the wall, a safe distance between the feet and the wall is one quarter the height of the ladder. Do not use an aluminum ladder when working near electrical wires. Consider using scaffolding.

USEFUL TERMS

Acoustic Ceiling. A ceiling which improves the quality of sound within a room. In our case, one with tiny noise-trapping holes to make it quieter.

Ceiling Joists. Overhead framing members of a room.

Ceiling Tiles. 12-inch squares cemented or stapled to an old ceiling.

Cross Tees. Gridwork which connects at right angles to runners.

Furring Strips. Strips of metal or wood attached directly with an old ceiling (perpendicular to ceiling joists) onto which ceiling tiles are clipped or stapled.

Runner. Main support grid for suspended ceilings, installed perpendicular to joists.

Suspended Ceiling. A ceiling lowered from the original ceiling or framework by a grid system, often used to hide exposed joists, rafters, ductwork, etc.

Tegular Panels. A two-level panel, the face being lower than the flange that rests on the grid.

Figure 1. Finished suspended ceiling.

WHAT YOU WILL NEED

Time. Installing either a tile or suspended ceiling in a 9′ × 12′ room will require 14 to 20 work hours, longer if unusual situations occur. This job is best undertaken by two people.

Tools. Suspended ceilings are hung from the ceiling joists with a metal grid. This creates the cavity between the joists and the ceiling where pipes, wires, and ductwork can be installed and worked on. A tile ceiling is either glued directly to an existing ceiling or onto "furring strips" that are glued or nailed to the existing ceiling. This type of ceiling works well either in covering over an older existing ceiling or where height is a consideration and a suspended ceiling would drop too low.

A suspended ceiling isn't hard to install and requires no exotic tools. The metal gridwork, especially the 12′ main runners, requires two people to install it, however.

Tile ceilings are even easier. They can often be glued over the existing ceiling if it is in good shape (but not over old tiles). Otherwise, wood furring strips are first nailed to the old ceiling or joists and the new tiles are stapled to these. A simpler system was recently developed. Instead of long furring strips, 4′ metal tracks are used. And instead of staples, clips snap onto the tracks to lock the tiles in place. Everything you need comes in one kit.

Many of the tools needed for either suspended or tile ceilings are the same. These include:

20′–25′ metal tape	Putty knife
Straightedge	Nails
Framing or combination square	Drywall pan
2–4′ Level	Handsaw
Sharp utility knife	Nail belt
Ladder	Face mask
Hammer	Safety goggles
Chalkline	Drill
Pencil	Miter box
String	Coping saw

Tools needed for a suspended ceiling only include:

Pliers	Wire
Aviation snips	

Tools needed for tile ceilings only include:

Fine-toothed hacksaw	Screwdriver

Materials

For suspended ceilings:

Eyehooks	Runners
Hanger wire	Cross tees
Wall molding	Tiles
Molding nails	Lighting fixtures

For tile ceilings

Furring strips	Shims
Adhesive	Tiles

PERMITS AND CODES

You probably won't need a permit to work on your ceilings, but check in with your local building permit department to find out about it. Often there is a minimum floor-to-ceiling height required (usually 7′6″). Also, you may need at least 5″ between any lighting fixture and the old ceiling.

DESIGN

Ceilings needn't just look nice; they can also do things: muffle noise, support lights, retard flames. An acoustical ceiling with tiny noise-trapping holes or fissures in the design is a wise choice for noisy rooms like kitchens and entertainment centers.

For rooms where fires are a possible concern, you can get ceilings made of mineral fiber, which is noncombustible. If you want to put lights in your new ceiling and relocate them without a lot of trouble, a suspended ceiling may be your best bet. You can buy fluorescent fixtures that easily fit into the grid system in place of a standard-size ceiling tile.

Suspended and tile ceilings have several advantages. The greatest of these is weight. The ceiling is the only area of the room where gravity is working against you. Installing and securing heavy ceiling materials (such as drywall) can be difficult. The acoustical ceiling uses space-age technology to create a ceiling that is both lightweight and durable. It is easy to install and secure because of its weight. Also, many types absorb sound and thereby add to the sound control of the room. It comes in many different styles, sizes, and colors and is easily obtainable from any home center or hardware store. You can get tiles or larger panels that look like marble, oak, and other natural materials, with the designs authentically hued, shaded, veined, and striated. If you prefer traditional white, pattern choices have broadened to include reproduction of bleached wood, sculptured plaster, and rough-troweled stucco.

MOST COMMON MISTAKES

Because of the complexity of this project the most common mistakes are listed once at the beginning of the chapter.

1. Not planning the ceiling layout on paper first.

2. Not checking local code for minimum ceiling height and clearance.

3. Failure to plan grids so they do not run into posts or columns.

4. Measuring the ceiling height line on the wall from a sloping floor, which creates a sloping ceiling.

5. Not laying out runners so border tiles will be more than half a tile.

6. Not installing the runners level.

7. Soiling the tiles during installation.

8. Neglecting to do the rough electrical work for the ceiling light fixtures before installing the ceiling.

9. Not allowing the required clearance between old ceiling joists or wiring and new ceiling light fixtures. Check your local code.

10. Neglecting to correct any ceiling leaks prior to installation of new ceiling.

11. Applying loose-filled or roll insulation directly on top of the ceiling panels rather than in ceiling joist cavities.

12. Installing ceiling below an existing ceiling that contains embedded radiant heat coils.

THE SUSPENDED CEILING

First let's deal with suspended ceilings. Again, these are used where enough room height is available to hang these from the ceiling joists or existing ceiling and still provide enough height between the floor and the new ceiling (usually a minimum of 7′6″ is required). The advantage of this type of ceiling over the tile ceiling is that it allows easy access to pipes, wires, and ductwork. This is very useful if you need to repair or add on to any of these systems. It is also useful in rooms where you want to reduce the ceiling height, either for aesthetics or for saving energy in rooms with high ceilings where hot air gathers at the top.

Suspended ceiling systems vary from manufacturer to manufacturer, but the systems are similar in their installation and whether or not they use 2′ × 4′ or 2′ × 2′ panels. Figure 2 shows the main pieces of a typical suspended ceiling.

Before beginning with the actual installation technique, let's look at an overview of how a typical ceiling goes together. Basically, there are only a few simple pieces that hook together to form the grid, and the panels are placed in the cells of the grid. The angle molding or wall molding is attached to the wall. This supports the runners that run the long way in the room. These runners are supported by wires that are attached to the ceiling joists by eye-hooks. Cross tees, running perpendicular to the runners, hold the runners together and create spaces or cells into which the panels are inserted. The panels are usually 2′ × 2′ squares or 2′ × 4′ rectangles.

Study Figure 3 closely before proceeding so you have a clear picture in your mind of how the entire system goes together. This is crucial and really the only difficult part of the entire ceiling installation.

Figure 2. The main pieces of a typical suspended ceiling.

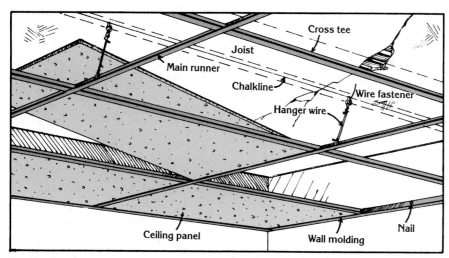

Figure 3. The anatomy of the grid.

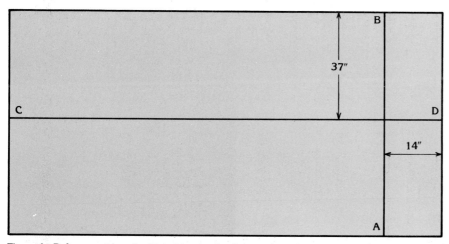

Figure 4. Reference strings in place at border the distance from the wall.

PLANNING YOUR CEILING

Margin of Error: Not applicable

Careful planning is essential for a successful ceiling installation. Avoiding or shortchanging this step will cause you to slap your forehead in frustration more than once. Plan well, and the rest of the job will go easily. Outlined here are the important issues in planning the ceiling installation.

Border Tiles

Border tiles are the tiles that run next to all the walls. Since rooms are rarely on exact 2′ or 4′ intervals, these tiles are often cut to fit. For appearance' sake, you want the border tiles on opposing sides of the room to be equal and all border tiles to be more than half a tile. You want to place both cross tees and runners in such a way that this is successfully accomplished.

First locate where your ceiling joists are running so you will know in what direction your runners are to run (perpendicular to ceiling joists). If the ceiling joists are exposed, there is no problem. If they are hidden within the old ceiling, you will need to use a hammer or a stud finder to locate them. Usually they run across the short dimension of the room. Then, with a chalkline, snap a line down the center of each joist on the old ceiling.

Now, using graph paper, begin to make a diagram of where all your runners and cross tees will go. First you must determine the size of all border panels. To do this, use the following formula.

Understanding the grid installation. Here are a few important things to note about the grid:

1. The runners, not the cross tees, run perpendicular to the ceiling joists.

2. The runners are hung from the joists with wire and eyehooks.

3. The cross tees run parallel with the joists and perpendicular to the runners.

4. The wires supporting the runners are often at an angle, since the holes in the runners into which the wires are threaded occur periodically and are not always directly below the wire.

5. Because the wires are often at an angle, each wire must be bent around a reference string to be sure their bends all occur at the same level.

6. The slots in the runners, into which the cross tees interlock, occur periodically along the runners. Because of this, these slots must all perfectly line up in the rows of runners so all cross tees will be on line and perpendicular to the runners. To achieve this, you will need to cut the first runner installed in each row to be sure the cross tee slots in each row of runners are aligned.

Determine the size of the border tiles so they are more than half a tile and equal. To do this, convert the room's short wall measurements into inches. If you are using 2′ × 4′ panels, divide this measurement by 48 (inches) if the panel length is to run parallel to the short wall. If you are using 2′ × 2′ panels, or if the panel length will run parallel to the long wall, divide by 24 inches. Take the remainder of this division and add 48 inches if the panel length will run parallel to the short wall and if you are using 2′ × 4′ panels. Add 24 inches if you are using 2′ × 2′ panels, or if the panel length will run parallel to the long wall. Half of this final figure equals the border dimensions at each side of the room.

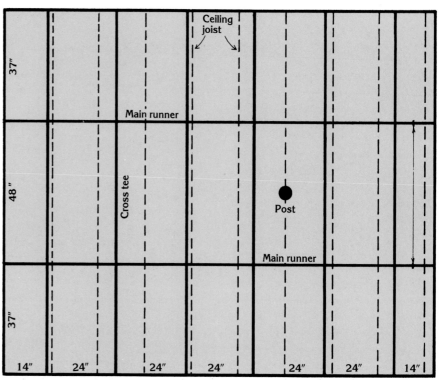

Figure 5. A typical sketch for grid layout.

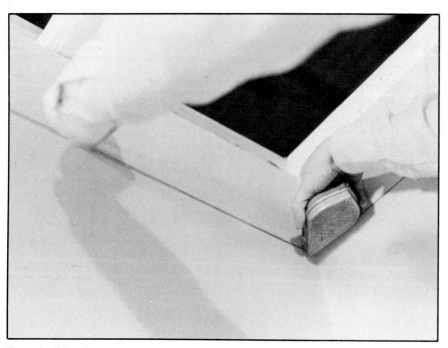

Figure 6. Using chalkline to snap level lines for wall molding.

Here's an example. For a room 10′2″ wide with the panels' length running parallel to the short wall and using 2′ × 4′ panels: Convert 10′2″ to 122″. Divide 122″ by 48″ = two full panel lengths and a remainder of 26″. Add 48″ to 26″ = 74″; then divide by 2 = 37″. Thus, the border panels at each side will be 37″. There will be one full-size tile and two 37″ border tiles (37 + 48 + 37 = 122). This dimension of 37″ also equals the distance of the first main runner from the sidewall.

Repeat these calculations using the length of the room to find the end border panel size.

Laying Out the Grid

Now that you have determined the size of the border tiles, you can draw the full grid on the graph paper (see Figure 5). Indicate the main runners on your graph paper by drawing the first and last runners at a border tile distance from the sidewalls and perpendicular to the ceiling joists. Add the in-between main runners at intervals of 4'. Using a different color pencil, mark the cross tees on the layout sheet. Start at the border tile distance from the end walls (14" in our example); then add the in-between cross tees every 2'. The cross tees will intersect with the main runners. If using 2 × 2 panels, additional cross tees will be used, locking into the perpendicular cross tees halfway between the main runners.

Columns or posts. If you have any columns or posts in the room that support the floor system of the floor above, these will have to be accounted for. This is a common occurrence in basements. The grid must be planned so that no runners or cross tees run into a column or post. If this is the case, you will need to make a slight adjustment so that the column falls in the open area of the grid. This may require unequal border tiles.

Light fixtures. Location of light fixtures will not require any changes in your grid, but they should be marked on the grid. Remember to do all your rough wiring before installing the grid.

Estimating the Materials

Wall moldings are available in 10' lengths. Measure the room's perimeter and divide by 10 to find the number of wall molding pieces you will need.

Main runners are available in 12-foot lengths. Tabs at each end of the main runners make it possible to join main runners for lengths longer than 12'. However, no more than two sections can be cut from each 12-foot length of main runner.

Cross tees come in 2- and 4-foot lengths with connecting tabs at each end. These connecting tabs are inserted into indentations that occur periodically in the runners, and cross tees.

Hanger wire of 12–16 gauges is needed to hang the runners every 4'. The wire at this point is 6" longer than the distance between the eyehook and the new ceiling.

Wire fasteners or eyehooks are necessary at each support point to attach the hanger wire to the ceiling joist.

Ceiling panels will be indicated by the layout. Allow enough to cut for border tiles. Also, purchase all needed lighting fixtures.

NOTE: The following system may vary from manufacturer to manufacturer, but most systems are similar. Also, the system is usually the same whether installing 2 × 4 or 2 × 2 panels.

STEP TWO

ESTABLISHING LEVEL LINES AND INSTALLING THE WALL MOLDING

Margin of Error: ¼"

The first thing you want to do is establish level lines on the wall at the height of the new ceiling. Remember that the code may require a minimum floor-to-ceiling height, usually 7'6". Also, you may need at least 5" between any lighting fixture and the old ceiling. Try to leave as large a cavity as possible, a minimum of 2", if no lighting fixtures are involved.

Marking the level lines can be rather simple if your floor is level. In this case, all you need to do is measure up in each corner the ceiling height (in our

Figure 7. Using level to mark level of wall molding.

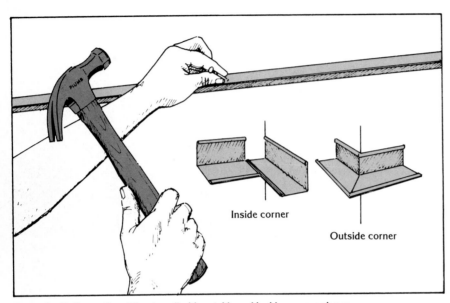

Figure 8. Nailing wall molding to wall with outside and inside corners shown.

Inside corner

Outside corner

POPPING CHALKLINES FOR THE RUNNERS

Margin of Error: ¹/₄″

Now you are ready to lay out chalklines, popped across the bottom of the ceiling joists (or existing ceiling), which will mark where the runners will be. You need to do some figuring before doing this. The object of this runner layout is to be certain that no border tile (the tiles that meet the wall) is ever less than half a tile (24″ with 4′ tiles). This process has been explained in the planning step. For example, imagine a room that is 10′2″ wide. We would first need to convert this measurement to be sure the border courses are at least half a tile, and also to assure that each border row on opposing walls will be equal. So we convert 10′2″ to 122″. This will allow us one full 4′ tile and two border rows of 37″ each (37 + 48 + 37 = 122). Using your tape measure, snap chalklines running perpendicular to the joists. These lines are 37″ from either wall, and this will leave a 48″ space in the middle (see Figure 5).

TIP: Locate wall studs by gently tapping on the wall with your hammer and listening for a solid sound (or you can use a stud locator which uses a magnet to find nails in the studs).

---

example, 8′), mark the walls at this point, and pop chalklines connecting these points (see Figure 6). You now have a level line running around the wall at ceiling height. You will nail your wall molding at this level.

The only problem here occurs if your floor is sloping. Then, if you measure up an equidistance at the corners, the ceiling will slope to match your floor. First, determine if your floor is level. You may be able to eye this, or use a level, or even a steel ball to see if it rolls to one area. If the floor is off level to any great degree (¹/₄″ or more), you will need to determine the difference at each corner and adjust your measurements. A long, 8′ level can be used here. Hold it level and determine the dip or rise of your floor. Perhaps you can measure down from the ceiling or joists above if they are level.

Another method is to simply use a level, an 8′ level would be most accu-

rate, and just draw a level line on all the walls starting from one point (Figure 7).

Next you will need to prepunch holes in the wall molding to correspond with the wall studs. You can locate these wall studs by tapping on the wall with your hammer and listening for a solid sound. Also, stud locators, which use magnets attracted to the wall covering nails, can be used.

Nail the wall molding to the wall around the entire perimeter of the room with the top edge of the molding lining up with the chalkline. If you are fastening this to a concrete block wall, use short masonry nails and direct the nail between the mortar joints and the edge of the block. If the wall is solid concrete or otherwise unable to accommodate wall molding, hang a section of runner directly next to the wall as a substitute. As shown in Figure 8, butt the molding at inside corners and miter cut at outside corners.

STEP FOUR

INSTALLING THE WIRE FASTENERS AND HANGER WIRE

Margin of Error: 1/4"

Now you are ready to attach the wire fasteners (eyehooks) and hanger wire that will support these runners. Screw the wire fasteners or eyehooks into the ceiling joists where the joists intersect the runner chalklines. Your eyehooks can be placed on 4' intervals so you do not need a fastener at every intersection. Then thread your wire through these eyehooks and securely wrap it around itself three times (see Figure 10). The wire should be long enough to

Figure 9. Use of scrap cardboard to hold masonry nail being driven between mortar joints.

extend below the level of the new ceiling at least 6". Add extra hangers and wire at light fixtures, one for each corner or as instructed by the manufacturer.

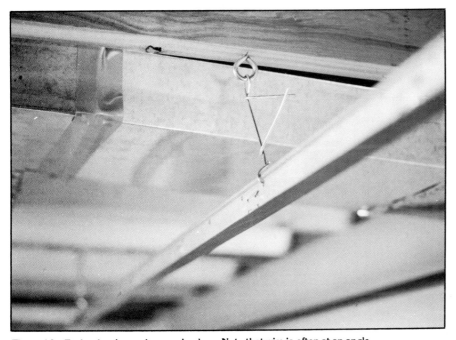

Figure 10. Eyehook, wire, and runner in place. Note that wire is often at an angle.

STEP FIVE

STRETCHING YOUR FIRST REFERENCE STRINGS

Margin of Error: Exact

Now you must stretch some reference strings that run exactly at the level of the bottom of the wall moldings. These strings will show you exactly where the runners and cross tees will be and will serve as guides to cut the runners and cross tees.

To stretch these strings, choose the corner of the room where you plan to start your installation. You will stretch only two strings: string AB, which will be the border tile distance from one wall (14" in our example); and string CD, which will be the border tile distance from the other wall (37" in our example; see Figure 5). Be sure the strings are at the level of the bottom of the wall molding so they will be out of the way while you install the grid. Check your strings with a framing square to be sure they are square. Adjust until they are, even if the border tiles will be irregular to accomplish this.

STEP SIX

MEASURING AND CUTTING THE RUNNERS AND STRETCHING NEW REFERENCE STRINGS

Margin of Error: ⅛"

The runners are now ready to be installed. The most important thing to remember here is that the runners have to be cut and installed in such a way that the cross tee slots in the runners occur exactly where each cross tee is planned to intersect the runners. The cross tees occur at line AB and then every 24" from line AB (see Figure 11). So you will need to cut the runners so a slot appears exactly along line AB. Slots will then automatically be aligned every 24" from there, since they are so spaced on the runners every 24". Measure and cut each runner so that the slots are aligned with line AB. Do not use the first runner for a pattern for the rest but measure each runner.

Now hold the cut runner at the level of the strings and next to string CD (see Figure 12). Locate the wire support hole (holes on tops of runners that hanging wires are attached to) that is farthest from the short wall you started at and closest to the first wire hanger from this wall. Circle this hole on the runner.

Carry this runner to the long side wall and rest it on the wall molding with the cut end butt against the short end wall. Mark the wall with a felt-tip pen or dark pencil through the circled hole (see Figure 13). Remove the main runner and drive a nail at this mark to attach yet another string to. Repeat this procedure on the opposite wall. Then stretch a string from nail to nail.

This string is used as a guide to bend your hanger wires at the proper place.

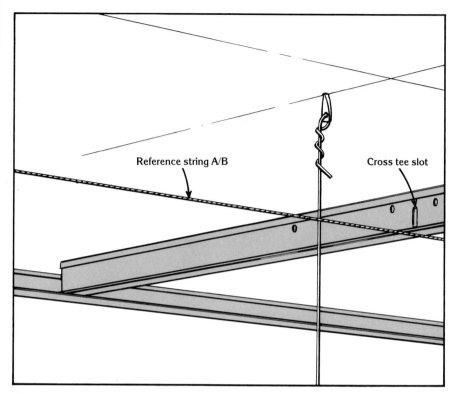

Figure 11. Reference string AB running aligned with cross tee slots.

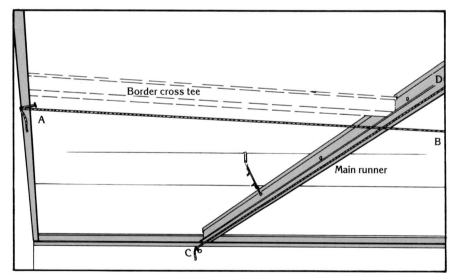

Figure 12. Cross tee location in grid. Note that wire hanger is at an angle.

Note that the string is running aligned with the wire support holes for the first set of wire hangers (though not necessarily the hanger wires themselves); *and* running level with these holes and therefore indicating where the wire must be bent at a 90-degree angle to insure that the runner is at its proper level.

Align each of the hanger wires to intersect with the string and make a 90-degree bend in the wire where it intersects the string (see Figure 14). Usually this will mean that the wires are at somewhat of an angle when in their final position, but that the runners will be hung perfectly level with the surrounding wall molding.

STEP SEVEN

HANGING THE GRID (CROSS TEES AND RUNNERS)

Margin of Error: ⅛″

You are now ready to hang the runners and clip in the cross tees. You can run additional strings to know where to bend each wire. You would run these strings aligned with each series of wire support holes that wires will be inserted into.

An easier way is to use a level placed on the runners and bend the wires as you go. To do this rest the cut end of the runner on the wall molding. Thread the first prebent wire hanger through the support hole. Remember this has been prebent so that the runner will hang at just the right level. The rest of the wire hangers are not. You can place a 4′ level on the runner and have someone hold it exactly level and then thread the unbent wire hangers through their support holes and bend them so that they keep the runner level. Wrap all wires around themselves three times after threading through the runners.

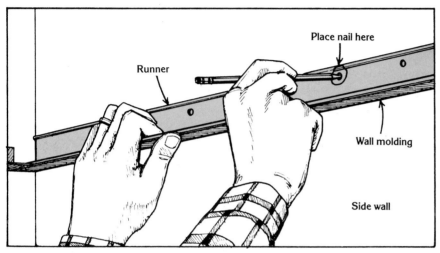

Figure 13. Marking location of first wire hanger hole on wall. Drive nail at this point.

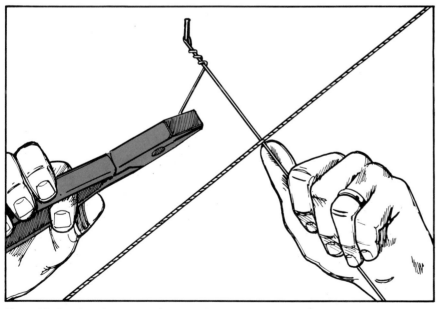

Figure 14. Bending wire around reference string.

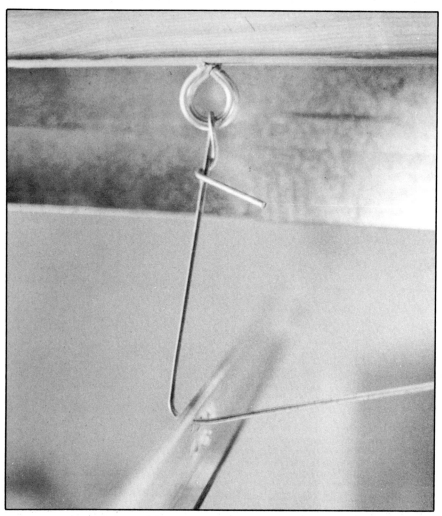

Figure 15. Bending wire at right angle.

As you work toward the opposite wall, connect the runner sections together as needed. Be very accurate with your measurements. You will need to cut the last piece to fit (you can use the excess piece to start the next row). As you connect and install the pieces, check to be sure that you have cut each runner so that the cross tee slots align exactly with the reference string AB. Also, you will have better support if you position an additional wire hanger close to the point where two runner sections are connected. Be sure you are always hanging the runners at the right level.

After all the runners are in place, install the cross tees. These 48″ pieces are installed every 24″ perpendicular to the runners (for 24″ × 48″ tiles). (For 24″ × 24″ panels, add a 24″ cross tee to the midpoint of the 48″ tee.) This should be a rather simple process if you have done everything up to here correctly. First install the full-size 4′ cross tees in the interior of the room. Once these are in place, lay in a few full ceiling panels to stabilize the system.

Now you must cut the cross tees in the border areas. Measure each border cross tee individually but use the string CD, not the runners, as a measuring guide. The runners still have a lot of play in them. To measure, align the edge of the first runner with the reference string CD, as shown. Then make your measurement from the side wall to the near edge of the runner. Measure and cut accurately. Repeat this process on the opposing wall.

Figure 16. Placing cross tee into slots on runners.

Figure 17. Cross tee slots need to be directly across from each other on adjacent runners.

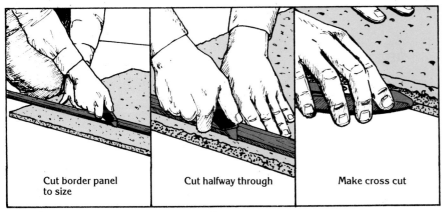

| Cut border panel to size | Cut halfway through | Make cross cut |

Figure 18. Three-step process to cutting border tiles.

STEP EIGHT

INSTALLING THE PANELS

Margin of Error: Not applicable

Installing the full panels is as easy as just slipping them into the grid from below and dropping them into place. Be sure you wear clean gloves or have clean hands so you don't soil the white tiles.

The border panels will need to be cut to size. Usually the larger 24″ × 48″ flat panels require only a straight cut with a sharp knife or saw to fit between the grids and the wall molding.

The tegular 24″ × 24″ panels (tegular means two levels — or that the face of the tile is lower than the grid level). In this case you will have to cut in a flange on the freshly cut edge so it will fit the grid. To do this, measure the size of the opening plus the flange. Place this panel in position in the grid. The cut side without the bevel and flange must rest on the wall molding. Draw a pencil line where the wall molding meets the border panel. Be sure the opposite end of the panel is centered in the grid.

Remove the panel and lay it face up on a flat surface. Cut along the pencil line in such a manner that your utility knife (use a sharp one) only penetrates half the thickness of the panel. Finally, using your utility knife, laying it flat on the table, cut into the side of the panels, halfway through its thickness, to meet up with your original cut, thereby creating the flange. Now install this in your grid. (See Figure 18.)

STEP NINE

OPTIONAL SITUATIONS

Margin of Error: Not applicable

Boxing around Basement Windows

As shown in Figure 19, build a three-sided valance around each window. You can use ¼" plywood for the top and 1 × 6 pine for the three sides. Be sure you build the valance wide enough to allow the window to open and long enough to provide for an open drapery. In most cases, allowing 9" on either side, a total of 18", is sufficient for open drapes.

Attach the top of the valance to the bottom of the ceiling joist and install the wall molding for the lay-in panels at the desired level. Curtain rods can be attached to the inside of the valance.

Boxing around Iron Support Beams and Ductwork

Many basement areas have horizontal iron support beams that support the first floor. To box around these, proceed as follows:

Construct wooden lattices to attach to both sides of the support beam. Use 1" × ½" wood strips (1 × 3 cut in half) and 1 × 3 center supports spaced every 16" to construct the lattice. Nail the lattice to the wooden floor joists running on top of the iron beam.

Enclose the support beam by nailing a finishing material, drywall, paneling, etc., to the lattice. Attach the same material to the bottom of the lattices to cover the bottom of the beam. Attach outside corner molding. Now, onto this finished box, simply snap a chalkline at the height of the new ceiling and nail the wall molding along this line. This process can also be used for ductwork.

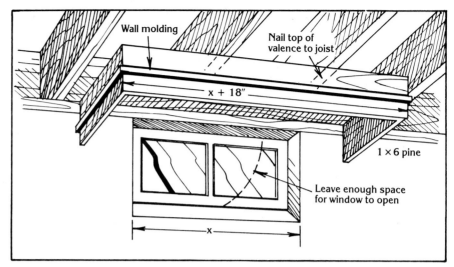

Figure 19. Boxing around a basement window.

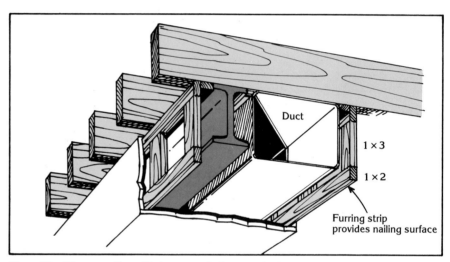

Figure 20. Often you will need to box around a beam or duct.

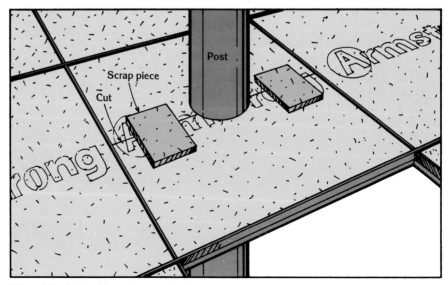

Figure 21. Cutting tiles to fit around column.

Figure 22. **Inserting light fixture and panel into grid.**

Figure 23. **Installing face plate of light fixture into fixture.**

Fitting around Columns and Posts

Cut the panel at the midpoint of the column. Then cut semicircles to the size required for rejoining panels to fit snugly around the post, as shown in Figure 21. Make all cuts with a very sharp utility or fiberboard knife.

When the two pieces of panel are rejoined in the ceiling, glue scrap pieces of material to the back of the panels.

Installing Electrical Lighting Fixtures

Electrical lighting fixtures are easy to install in suspended ceilings. Usually it is best to install all your rough wiring before you begin the project. However, since there is often a cavity between the panels and the joists, and since the panels can be removed, it can be done afterward, though this takes considerably more effort. You can use either incandescent or fluorescent fixtures. The fluorescent fixtures often come with a translucent panel that fits directly into a panel cell. Incandescent fixtures are either flush mounted or recessed. Also, you need to be more careful with these types of fixtures, because they get a lot hotter than fluorescent. The incandescent fixtures come with adjustable arms that are attached to the ceiling joists to carry the weight. A hole is cut in the panel for the fixture. Also, a finishing collar fits around the fixture to hide the rough-cut hole. (The details of wiring are discussed more fully in Chapter 9.)

Care of the Ceiling

Caring for a suspended ceiling is an easy matter. Should a panel become water damaged, marred, or very dirty, it can simply be replaced. Also, the panels are washable and can be painted.

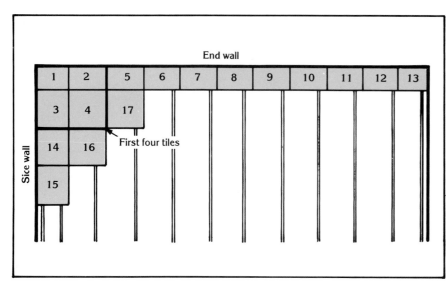

End wall

| 1 | 2 | 5 | 6 | 7 | 8 | 9 | 10 | 11 | 12 | 13 |

| 3 | 4 | 17 |

First four tiles

| 14 | 16 |

| 15 |

Sice wall

Figure 24. Installation pattern for ceiling tiles. Install in pyramid pattern.

The second type of ceiling I discuss in this chapter is the kind composed of standard ceiling tiles. These tiles are usually 12″ square and come in assorted patterns. They attach directly to the old ceiling, or to wood or metal furring strips. They leave no cavity as do suspended ceilings. Unless you use the clip method described below in Steps 1–7, you attach them permanently, and they cannot be removed as easily as the suspended panels. They are, however, quick and easy to install and work well where you do not want to lower the ceiling height. They are excellent for covering up existing ceilings, especially old cracked plaster. If your ceiling is water damaged, be sure you correct the leak problem before you begin.

Often the tiles can be installed directly over the existing ceiling, if it is in good condition. Existing ceiling tiles, however, must be removed first. The tiles can be installed in a bathroom if there is a vent window or fan.

The type of installation I show here is a new improved method using metal "furring strips" and clips. These strips, or tracks, are attached to the ceiling joists and support the tiles. The clips make it possible to remove ceiling tiles without damaging them in order to correct minor mistakes, insert light fixtures, or reach wiring and pipes between the joists. You merely slide the clip back along the track to release the tile. This system reduces nailing by two thirds. Since the metal tracks don't have to be spaced precisely 12″ apart as do wood furring strips, this system gives you a greater margin of error. And it doesn't require that you saw the tracks: they simply overlap at the end wall.

It is the latest and simplest system to use. It comes in a kit with all needed materials and instructions on the box as to how to estimate the quantity of tiles needed. Steps 8–11 below cover installation using conventional wood furring strips.

STEP ONE

PREPARATION

Margin of Error: Not applicable

Be sure to leave your tiles in open boxes in the room for at least 24 hours, so they can become acclimated to the temperature and humidity. Also, fix any leaks or moisture problems before beginning. Inspect the ceiling for dips, swells, and other irregularities and chart these out on paper.

STEP TWO

LAYING OUT THE CEILING

Margin of Error: ¼″

The layout for ceiling tiles is somewhat simpler than that for the suspended ceiling. The main thing you are planning for are the border tiles. These are the rows of tiles that run along the walls of a room. You want to plan these tiles so that they are never less than 6″ (½ tile). Rarely do room dimensions work out in exact 12″ intervals.

For example, let's assume the width between two of the walls is 9′8″. If we made no adjustments, there would be 9 full-size tiles and two border rows of 4″. To correct for these small border rows, convert 9′8″ (116″) into 8′20″ (116″). In this way you can have 8 full-size courses and two border rows of 10″ each. Work out a similar layout in the other direction (in our example, 12′4″ converts to 11 full-size tiles and two 8″ border tiles. In this way, all four border rows of a rectangular or square room are more than 6″, and the two opposing border rows are equal.

STEP THREE

LOCATING THE CEILING JOISTS

Margin of Error: 1/2"

The metal furring strips need to be nailed to something solid in order to hold the ceiling and prevent it from sagging. The ceiling joists, the wooden framing members that hold up the existing ceiling, will work fine when the furring strips are nailed perpendicular across them. Use a nail everywhere a furring strip crosses a joist. If the ceiling joists are exposed, this is a simple procedure. If there is an existing ceiling, a little more work is required.

First you must locate the joists and mark them on the existing ceiling so that you will be able to nail the furring strips to them. If there is an attic above, you may want to crawl up and determine the direction the ceiling joists run. Usually they run across the short dimension of the room. Using a hammer, and tapping on the ceiling, you should be able to determine where the sound is more solid. Drill a hole or drive in a nail to be sure you have located a joist. You can also use stud finders. Some new ones on the market actually measure the density behind the finish materials to locate studs and joists. Locate either end of each joist where they rest on the wall and then use your chalkline to pop a line down the center of each joist. Once you have located the first joist, all the others should be located 12", 16", or 24" from each other. It is still best to test with a nail or by drilling, since, in many older homes, and some newer ones, these distances are not always dependably the same.

STEP FOUR

INSTALLING THE FIRST ROW OF METAL FURRING STRIPS

Margin of Error: 1/2"

After marking the location of the joists on your existing ceiling, you are now ready to install metal furring strips (tracks). These strips usually come in 4' sections. There are a few things to remember about installing these strips. They must be well secured to the ceiling joists, level, and parallel. In many old houses, the ceilings often have waves and buckles in them. This can cause problems, since the tile ceiling will be equally wavy if this is not corrected. Study the ceiling before applying the strips. Use a level, or straight board, placed against the ceiling, to see if you can determine any buckles or other irregularities. Note any particularly bad problems. As you install the strips, use wooden shims, placed between the ceiling and the furring strip, to fill out any dips in the ceiling (see Figure 26). Smaller dips, 1/4" or so, usually will not need shims, since the strips can span these on their own. Just be sure that the strips are level within 1/4", even if the existing ceiling is not.

Begin with your first row by the wall. Do not nail this right next to the wall, but rather 1" away from the wall. Nail at each joist with the nails provided in the kits. It is a good idea to give the strip a tug to be sure it is well secured. Use 2 nails for every 4' of track nailed into the joists. You do not want it to start sagging after the tiles are up. Continue placing the 4' strips 1" from the wall. It

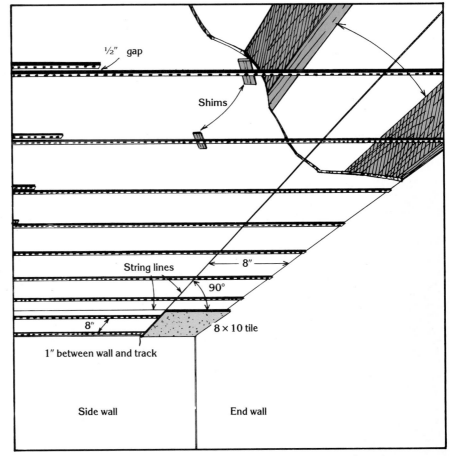

Figure 25. Reference strings and tracks in place. Note shims are level to tracks and reference strings are at a border tile distance from end wall.

is not essential that the ends of the strips butt right up against each other. There can be as much as a ¼" gap between each 4' strip. Also, the joints do not need to meet over a joist. Just be sure that the tracks are on line, since you may need to attach a clip over the junction of two tracks.

When you reach the other end of the wall you may need to cut a section of the 4' strips to fit the last section. This can be done with a fine-tooth hacksaw.

STEP FIVE

INSTALLING THE REMAINING ROWS

Margin of Error: ½"

After this first row is in place, proceed with the second row. Remember, this row will be used to hold the odd-sized border row. When you install this second row of furring strips, do so so that they are placed a distance from the wall that is the size of the border tile less 2". In our example, where we have 10" border tiles, this second row would be placed 8" (10 − 2 = 8") from the wall!.

Measure along as you go; be sure you keep a constant 8" from the wall. Nail this row up in the same manner as you did the row next to the wall. Be sure to stagger your joints. This means that the joints between two 4' sections of strips should not occur at the same place in two adjacent rows, but rather should be staggered. This assures that there will not be a series of joints in a row across the furring strip row that could cause a noticeable dip.

After the second row is installed, begin the remaining rows. These are all placed 12" apart. Again, the next to the last row should be at a distance from the wall equal to the size of a border tile less 2" (8", in our example). The last row should be 1" from the wall.

STEP SIX

SQUARING THE CEILING WITH STRINGS

Margin of Error: Exact

If your walls are meeting at true right angles so that the room is a perfect square or rectangle, you can omit this step. Unfortunately, in many homes, especially older ones, this is not the case. In these instances you must set up strings that are at true right angles and lay the tiles according to these strings. The strings will serve as guides for installing and cutting the border tiles. If you omit this step, the tile ceiling will look strange and out of line with the walls.

You will need to set up two strings that run at the level of the new ceiling and out from each wall the width of the border tiles at that wall. (See Figure 26.)

The strings are attached to nails temporarily driven into the walls. The two strings will intersect at a corner. The strings are placed in such a way so as to outline the edge of the two intersecting border rows. Let's say that one row is a 10" row and the intersecting row is 8".

Set up one line so that it is at the level of the ceiling and running 10" from the wall. Do the same with the intersecting string so that it is running 8" from the wall. Once these are in place, take a framing square and, holding it steady, see if the two strings are square. Remember, if they are just a little off square over the 2' arm of the square, the walls could be a few inches off over the distance of the wall. Be sure, therefore, that each line is running *exactly* along each arm of the square. If they are not, adjust one of the strings (preferably the one that outlines the border row that will be least noticeable from below) until the lines are exactly at right angles. You now have a square reference with which to start installing the tiles.

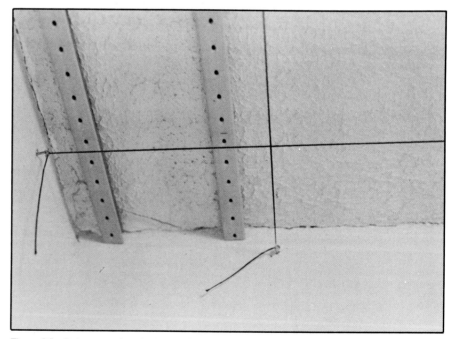

Figure 26. Strings are placed a border tile distance from each wall and at right angles.

STEP SEVEN

INSTALLING THE TILES

Margin of Error: ⅛″

You will begin installing your tiles in the corner of the room where the two strings intersect.

You will need to cut border tiles to fit. Cut the tile *face up* with a sharp utility knife. Cut the tile so that the edges next to the wall are the cut edges with no tongues or flanges. The edges pointing toward the interior of the room will be the factory edge (see Figure 30).

After cutting your first few tiles, snap a clip into the first two tracks and push the clips flush against the wall, as shown in Figure 31. Place the first tile in the corner and push the cut edge of the tile into the clips. Secure the other edge of the tile by snapping on clips into the tracks and pushing them onto the flange. Be sure your hands are clean, or wear clean gloves, so that you don't soil the tiles.

Install the next three tiles that surround this first corner tile. Make sure your tiles fit snugly into the corner and line up with the border reference string lines. This is very important, so take your time. Adjust until they are perfectly aligned.

Once these first four tiles are in place, continue with the installation progression. When you reach the opposite side wall, cut the border tiles ½″ short of the wall to leave a gap for any expansion due to moisture. Install the remaining diagonally across the room.

To install the last tile in a row, snap a clip on the end of each track and push it flush up against the wall. Cut the last tile to fit so that it is ½″ short of the wall. Position the tile in place, then slide the clip into the edge of the tile with a screwdriver, as shown in Figure 32.

Finally, nail on any molding. Paint or stain the molding before installing it. Be sure to nail the molding every 24″ into the wall studs, not the ceiling.

Figure 27. Sliding clips along track and into tile.

Figure 28. Final row of border tiles going in. Note clips are in place and border tiles are ½″ shy of wall.

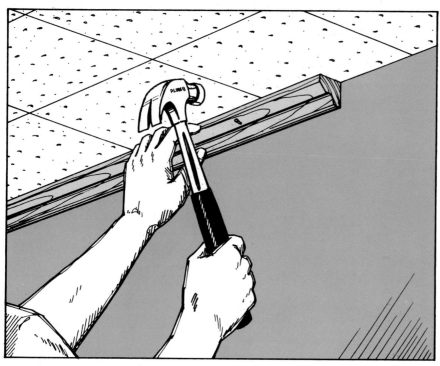

Figure 29. Be sure to nail molding to the wall, not the ceiling.

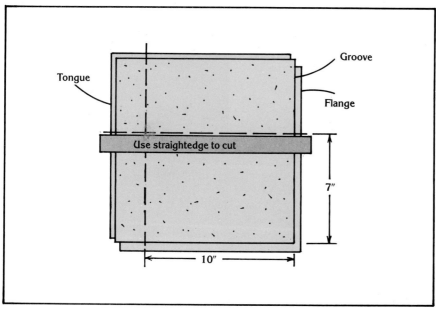

Figure 30. Cutting border tiles.

STEP EIGHT

INSTALLING WITH WOOD FURRING STRIPS (WHEN APPLICABLE)

Margin of Error: ¼″

As mentioned above, tile ceilings can also be installed using wood furring strips. Some manufacturers require this type of system. Preparing for installation and calculating the border tiles are the same as for the clip method (Steps 1 and 2 above).

The furring strips are nailed perpendicular to the joists. If the joists are exposed, there is no problem. If you are installing these over an existing ceiling, you will need to locate and mark the joists as described under the clip method in the preceding steps.

If you are installing 12″ × 24″ tiles, furring strips must be installed on 12″ centers. When stapling 24″ tiles to furring strips, make sure that the tiles run lengthwise along the furring strips, not perpendicular across them.

Use two 8-penny nails at each joist to keep the strips from warping. If you are nailing over a lath and plaster ceiling, longer nails may be needed. You need to penetrate into the joists at least 1″. Use a 4′–8′ level to be sure the strips are level. Use wooden shims where needed.

The first furring strip is flush up against the wall, as shown in Figure 35. The second strip is positioned so that its *center* is the same distance from the wall as the width of the border tile that butts against that wall *plus* ½″ to allow for the stapling flange of the tile.

For example, if the width of the border tile that butts against the wall is 10″, add ½″ to the 10″ width and position the second strip so the center is 10½″ from the side wall.

After installing the second strip, work across the ceiling, nailing furring strips spaced 12″ on center (from the center of one strip to the center of the next). Be exact. Nail the final strip flush against the wall.

When two furring strips are joined, the butt joint should always be over the center of a joist. Never allow these joints to fall in between joists where they cannot be nailed. Also, stagger the joints so that joints in adjacent rows do not fall on the same joist.

STEP NINE

SQUARING THE CEILING WITH STRINGS

Margin of Error: Exact

Same as explained above for clip method.

STEP TEN

INSTALLING THE FIRST ROW OF TILES

Margin of Error: ⅛″

After your lines are in place, you can start to cut the border tiles. Cut them face up with a sharp utility knife. Include the face and flange of your tile in your measurement. Because the walls are often uneven, each border tile should be cut and measured individually. Cutting these tiles ¼″ shy of the actual measurement will make these tiles fit easier. The gap between the wall and tile will be covered later by molding.

Cut the tiles so that the cut edge is against the wall and the factory edge points toward the interior of the room. Cut them so that the outside edges of the flanges line up exactly with your reference strings. Fasten each tile with four ½″ or ⁹⁄₁₆″ staples, two in each flange (use six staples for 12″ × 24″ tiles).

Work across the ceiling, installing two or three border tiles at a time, and fill in between with full-size tiles. When you reach the last row of tiles, measure and cut each tile individually. If the stapling flange isn't large enough for stapling, face nail the tile in place near the wall where the nailhead will be hidden by the molding.

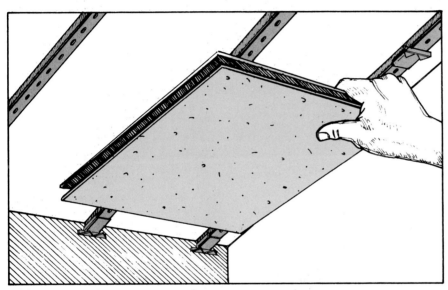

Figure 31. Installing border tile. Note that the cut edges are against the wall.

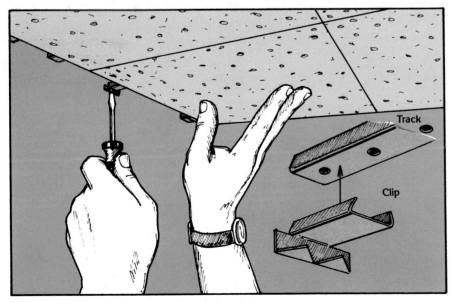

Figure 32. Slipping clip into the last tile with screwdriver.

Figure 33. Using utility knife and straightedge to cut tiles. Be sure blade is sharp.

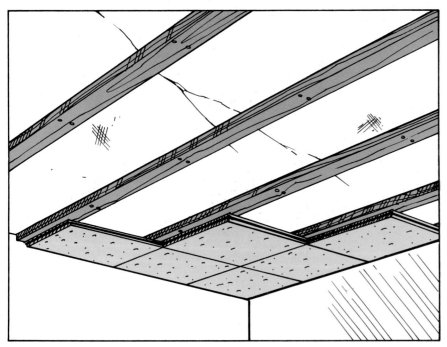

Figure 34. Wooden furring strips can be nailed directly to the old ceiling and the tiles stapled to these.

STEP ELEVEN

INSTALLING THE MOLDING

Margin of Error: Exact

Same as in the clip method described above.

TOOLS AND MATERIALS CHECKLIST

Tools For Suspended Ceilings

Pliers	Drill
Dust mask or	Chalkline
respirator	Utility knife
Safety glasses or	Miter box
goggles	Framing square
Tape measure	Nail belt
2′ to 4′ level	Coping saw
Straight edge	Aviation snips
Hammer	

Materials For Suspended Ceilings

Eyehooks	Cross tees and
Hanger wire	panels
Suspended	Lighting fixtures
ceiling system	Luminous panels
with wall	Molding
molding	Molding nails
Runners	

Tools For Ceiling Tiles

Fine-toothed hack saw	Hammer
Screwdriver	Drill
Dust mask or respirator	Chalkline
	Utility knife
Safety glasses or goggles	Miter box
	Coping saw
2' to 4' level	Nail belt
Straight edge	Aviation snips
	Tape measure

Materials For Ceiling Tiles

Metal furring strip kits	Ceiling tiles
	Molding
Shims	Molding nails

Materials For Boxing Basement Windows

¼" plywood	Nails
1" × 6" pine	

Materials For Boxing Support Beams

1" × 1½" wood strips	Nails
	Drywall or paneling
1" × 3" wood strips	Corner molding

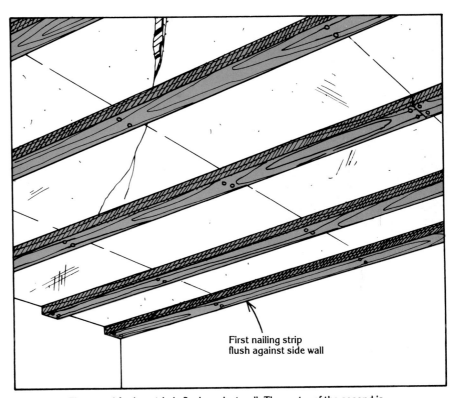

First nailing strip flush against side wall

Figure 35. First wood furring strip is flush against wall. The center of the second is the width of the border tile plus ½".

CHAPTER SIX

Vinyl Flooring
Installing and Maintaining

WHAT YOU WILL BE DOING

In this chapter I discuss the variety of vinyl flooring materials on the market today and the techniques used to install them. There are now more patterns, colors, styles, and installation choices than ever before, and vinyl floors are an easy, affordable way to customize your floors.

I will detail and illustrate floor preparation, template use, cutting, and installing sheet vinyl flooring; as well as application of perimeter bond materials and full-spread adhesive floors. In addition, there are complete instructions for installing a self-adhesive tile floor. Finally, I discuss the application of vinyl flooring over concrete.

BEFORE YOU BEGIN

SAFETY

1. Provide adequate ventilation with window fans when using adhesives, as some are toxic.

2. Extinguish pilot lights and any open flames when applying adhesives which can be flammable.

3. The proper respirator should be worn when using substances with toxic fumes.

4. Wear rubber gloves when working with solvents.

5. Keep blades sharp. A dull blade requires excessive force, can slip, and cause accidents.

6. Goggles or safety glasses should be worn whenever hammering, prying, or cutting materials.

7. Many older existing floor materials may contain asbestos fibers. Avoid sanding or dry scraping them, because inhaling asbestos fibers or dust may cause asbestosis or other bodily harm.

8. Use the proper protection, take precautions, and plan ahead. Never bypass safety to save money or rush a project.

USEFUL TERMS

Full-spread adhesive. Requires trowel and application of adhesive under the entire vinyl floor.

Ledging. A condition where one side of seam overlaps another.

Parameter bond. Attached only at walls and seams where flooring shrinks after installation to tighten over the floor.

Template. A paper pattern used to assure accurate error-free installation.

Underlayment. A layer of plywood applied under the vinyl to level and flash, or even out a deteriorated floor.

WHAT YOU WILL NEED

Time. Most vinyl floor installations can be completed in one or two days by a single worker. If restructuring is needed, extra time will be necessary. For a 9 × 12 room, using perimeter bond sheet vinyl or self-adhesive tiles, plan on 7–9 work hours. Full-spread adhesives will require 9–11 work hours.

Tools. Vinyl floor installations require very few tools that are not in every homeowner's toolbox.

Pry bar	Notched blade or utility knife
Utility knife	Notched trowel
Handsaw	Rolling pin or seam roller
Hammer	Staple gun
Scissors	Chalkline
Pencil or ball point pen	Carpenter's square
1″ wide ruler	

A hair blow dryer might come in handy, to heat up tiles for making complicated cuts.

Materials.

Craft or butcher paper	Adhesive
Do-it-yourself installation kit	Seam sealer kit
Masking tape	Staples
Sheet vinyl or tiles	Vinyl wall base

If it is necessary to restructure your subfloor before laying the vinyl, you may also need:

Leveling compound	¼″ plywood
¾″ T & G plywood	6 penny ring shank nails

PERMITS AND CODES

Replacing floors comes under the coverage of remodeling and may be regulated by local building codes. A permit may be necessary. Many areas require a permit if more than $100 of work will be done. Always check your local building code before beginning work.

DESIGN

Often you will be replacing a floor because it is damaged or worn — you will not be completely redecorating a room at the same time. In this situation the decor aspects which you are retaining will give you clues as to which way to go with color and pattern for your floor.

The color you choose will be determined by the predominant color of the room. Neutral tones and single color dominant rooms will make your decision easy. For an obviously multi-colored space you will need to determine which color you prefer to emphasize.

For pattern selection, keep in mind that patterns can be combined but are most effectively done by using one large pattern, one medium pattern and one small pattern distributed among walls, fabrics and flooring. These of course should be color-coordinated.

If your floor offers a wide expanse of uninterrupted space, a larger pattern may be used. If, however, it is broken up spacially, has alcoves or is interrupted by counters or appliances, a more pleasing effect will be accomplished with a smaller pattern.

You can utilize the pattern to create a visual span from one space to another by repeating like shapes in three by three sections both vertically and horizontally.

MOST COMMON MISTAKES

The single most common mistake in any vinyl flooring project is applying the flooring over an improperly cleaned or prepared floor — such as a basement floor that has a moisture problem. The other frequently made mistakes are listed before each step.

SHEET VINYL FLOORING (PERIMETER BOND)

STEP ONE

PREPARING THE FLOOR

Margin of Error: Floor should be level within 1/8", with gaps no larger than 1/4"

MOST COMMON MISTAKES

1. Not leveling the floor and/or applying an underlayment if needed.

2. Not making the needed repairs before beginning the job.

When laying a new floor, you will need to remove all furniture and appliances from the room. Do not attempt to merely move furniture from one side to the other because you will need space in which to maneuver. Also, the floor will need some time to set once it is installed. So move out anything that isn't attached.

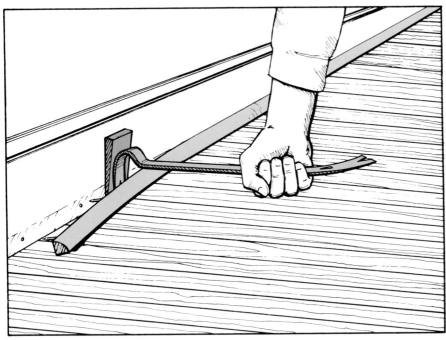

Figure 1. Removing shoe molding with a pry bar and a wedge.

Remove the shoe moldings, trim pieces, door thresholds, and floor grates carefully, using a pry bar and a scrap of wood for a leverage wedge so as not to mar the baseboard (Figure 1). This will enable you to fit the flooring right up to the baseboard. Any minor imperfections along the cut edge of the new flooring will be hidden underneath the molding when you replace it. (If you are using full-spread adhesive, take a moment here to review other special floor preparations you may need to consider for that type of bonding. See the section on Full-Spread Adhesive Sheet Flooring.)

A scrap of cardboard will support your handsaw so you can undercut the bottoms of the doorway moldings to allow for the flooring to slip underneath. Keep the saw blade flat against the cardboard when doing this (Figure 2). If your floor is level, dry, and structurally

Figure 2. Using a tile to undercut door jambs.

sound, with an even finish, you will need no other prep work than to sweep and vacuum thoroughly, then mop the floor with a mild cleaner. If the flooring will have a seam, the 6″ strip of floor directly under the seam should be very clean and free from any wax or finish so the adhesive will have something to hold on to. Use a heavy-duty detergent or wax remover to clean this strip.

If the floor is badly sloped or dipped, fill those areas in with leveling compound. Install an underlayment of ¼″ plywood. Plan the seam so they do not match those of the flooring underneath. Over an open joist system, first apply a layer of ¾″ tongue-and-groove plywood as a subfloor. Check local code for specific recommendations.

Nail the underlayment with 6 penny ring shank nails every 4″ to 6″ around the edge and every 4″ in the middle. Check local code on this requirement as well. Leave ¼″ gap at the baseboard and ¹⁄₁₆″ between sheets to allow for expansion and contraction of the wood.

STEP TWO

MAKING THE TEMPLATE

Margin of Error: Exact

MOST COMMON MISTAKE

1. Neglecting to make or properly use a template when working with sheet vinyl.

A template or pattern is essential for accurately cutting your vinyl floor. Craft paper, butcher's paper, or the paper that comes in the do-it-yourself installation kits works wonderfully. The template will enable you to transfer accurate measurements to the vinyl flooring without making unnecessary or awkward cuts during installation.

A trick to keep the pattern from shifting while you work is to cut little triangles in various areas of the paper. You can then tape it to the floor with masking tape pressed over the cutouts.

Tape overlapping paper edges together, keeping the pattern smooth and flat as you progress. For working with a floor large enough (over 12′) to require two pieces of flooring, there are special seam-fitting, pattern-matching, and seam-sealing steps. Usually flooring comes in 12′ widths. It is best to lay out the flooring so that the seam will fall in a low-traffic area if at all possible.

Many floors have irregular, odd-shaped, or just plain hard-to-fit objects like molding, pipes, a commode, or fancy baseboard joints. Use smaller pieces of paper when trying to pattern an irregular section of the floor, adding them on to the main template with tape.

If at all possible, when flooring a bathroom, remove the toilet. This makes it easier to conceal the cut under the fixture, making the job look more professional. First shut off the water supply valve, then remove the drain tank and supply line. Unbolt the

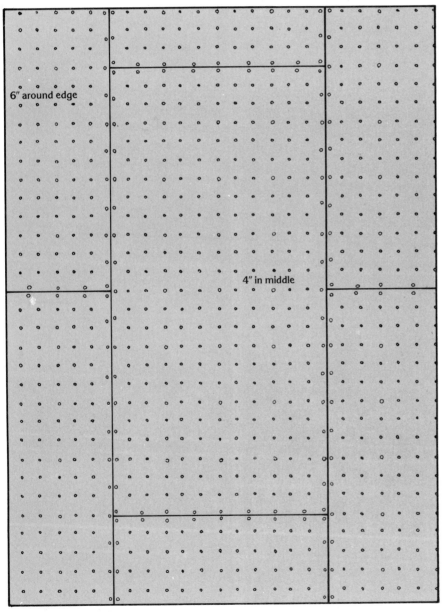

6″ around edge

4″ in middle

Figure 3. Nailing pattern for underlayment.

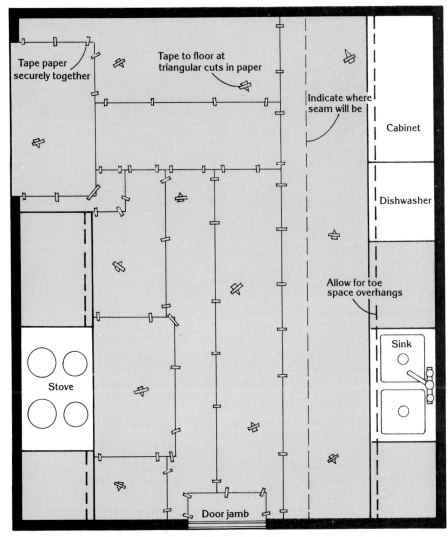

Figure 4. Typical paper template, after marking and installing.

Labels in figure: Tape paper securely together; Tape to floor at triangular cuts in paper; Indicate where seam will be; Cabinet; Dishwasher; Allow for toe space overhangs; Sink; Stove; Door jamb

Figure 5. Cut out small triangles in the paper and use masking tape to hold paper in place.

toilet and lift it from the drain pipe. (After you install the new floor, you will need to remove the old wax seal under the toilet, install a new wax seal, and re-seat the toilet.)

Marking around pipes and fixtures takes a bit more care. Mark the center of the objects by butting your paper template up to the object and marking the center edge. With scissors, cut a slit in your template from the center edge to the wall. Now crease the paper template along both sides and cut out the opening. Always check and make any necessary corrections to be certain the opening is an exact fit.

If you are unable to remove a doorway molding, slip the template under and cut it to fit the jamb.

If the wall molding cannot be removed for whatever reason, you will need to match the edge line made by the molding very precisely. Do this by pressing pieces of paper into the crease where the molding meets the floor. Cut these out with scissors at the crease and tape them to the overall pattern.

If you are using an installation kit (some manufacturers provide these for their sheet vinyl products), the accompanying roller disk will aid you in marking your pattern. When using this roller, leave about ½″ gap between your template paper and the wall. The roller disk is designed to transfer the wall line to the pattern paper, leaving an exact 1″ space between the pencil line and the wall (Figure 6). This means this line on the template is actually one full inch shy of the wall everywhere you use that roller disk. With this method, when you transfer your template to the vinyl, you must be sure to use a 1″ wide straight-edge placed along your outline mark. It will put that inch back onto the flooring when you mark it. If you don't have a kit, you can use a 1″ wide ruler or a paint stirrer with a ball point pen cartridge taped to its edge. Whether you

TIP: When you purchase self-adhesive vinyl tile, buy about 5 percent more tile than the total area you plan to cover.

use an installation kit with a disk roller, a makeshift marker, or just press the paper up to the wall, creasing it for your outline, it is best to work a short distance at a time. Do not try to mark a wall in one continuous line.

Make a note on the pattern identifying the position of any object you had to fit around, so that you can check its fit and its relative location one last time before you complete the installation. When you have finished your template, you should have a paper floor with all of the "landmarks" clearly indicated. Now you should be ready to get an accurate transfer of your paper pattern onto the vinyl material.

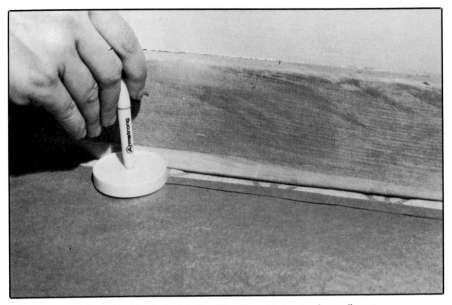

Figure 6. A roller, provided in the installation kit, will enable you to draw a line exactly 1″ from the wall edge.

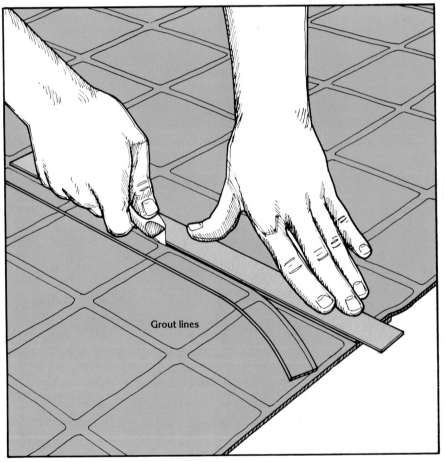

Grout lines

Figure 7. Overlap the two pieces and double cut the seam along the grout line.

STEP THREE

CUTTING THE VINYL

Margin of Error: Exact

MOST COMMON MISTAKES

1. Laying out the template on the wrong side, thereby cutting the floor backwards.

2. Not lining up the template seamline with a pattern (grout) line on the flooring material.

Unroll the new flooring face up on a clean, smooth surface. (Otherwise, small stones or dirt can become imbedded in the back, eventually wearing through or tearing the new floor.) The basement, garage, attic, or driveway is probably the best place for this. However, if working outside, don't expose the vinyl to direct sunlight.

Overlap the vinyl pieces where the seams will fall. Check the two sections for pattern match all along the overlap and at each corner of the pattern. If you are working with a strongly pronounced design that calls for a perfect match, keep both pieces running in the direction they came off the roll.

Tape the two vinyl sections firmly together after they are matched so they won't move when you cut them. You will double cut straight through overlapped edges of the two pieces so they fit together perfectly (Figure 7). Getting a good-looking seam is not difficult if you make your cut in a simulated grout line or other pattern feature that can serve as camouflage. Be sure to keep a sharp blade in the utility knife. (You may want to practice before trying the cut on the flooring.)

After you have made your cut, double check the pattern match before continuing. Then tape the seam together.

Compensate on both sides for any out-of-line walls by shifting the template in a direction that will split the difference of the error. Lay out your paper pattern or template over the flooring material so that the seam now falls in a low-traffic or low-visibility part of the room. Be sure that you are not positioning the template upside down and that you are cutting the flooring as you want it. If possible, avoid positioning a line in the vinyl pattern too close to the out-of-line wall.

Once you have the template situated where you want it, tape it to the vinyl through the triangular slits, just like you taped it to the old floor.

NOTE: Remember to transfer the 1″ back onto the floor where a roller or 1″ marking guide was used. Use great care where an exact transfer connects to the inch-wide marking guide points.

The ball point pen lines are easily removed with a soft cloth and mild detergent.

Use a notched blade knife or a utility knife to trim the vinyl. Many kits include a notched blade knife. In any case, always make sure the blade is as sharp as possible. Cut very carefully and true along your line for a precise fit.

Once the floor has been cut out, roll the floor up with the pattern showing on the outside and the narrow protruding areas on the outside end of the roll.

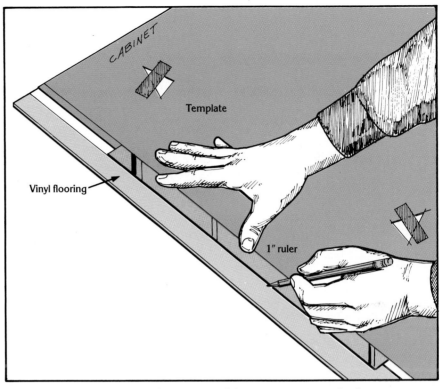

Figure 8. Using a 1″ ruler to transfer the needed 1″ from paper template to flooring.

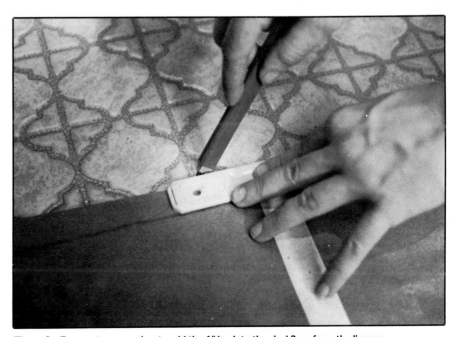

Figure 9. Be sure to remember to add the 1″ back to the vinyl floor from the line on the paper.

TIP: Use the 3-4-5 triangle technique to check that your lines are perfectly square.

STEP FOUR

INSTALLING THE FLOORING

Margin of Error: Within ¼" at edges, exact at seams

MOST COMMON MISTAKES

1. When estimating the amount of sheet vinyl or perimeter bond material, forgetting to account for pattern matching at a seam.

2. Unrolling perimeter bond sheet vinyl too early, or waiting too long to lay it, thereby causing it to shrink before it is permanently laid in place.

3. Neglecting to use flooring materials with the compatible adhesive and appropriate trowel at seams.

Figure 10. Use a sharp utility knife to cut the vinyl flooring.

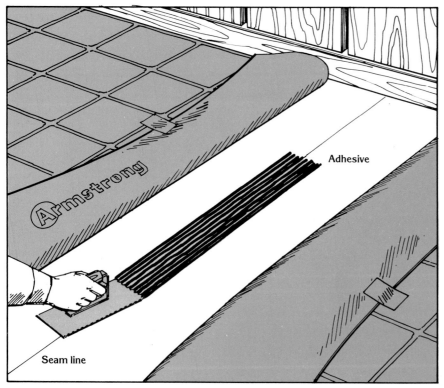

Figure 11. Tape back vinyl and trowel adhesive over penciled seamline.

Perimeter Bond Sheet Vinyl Flooring

Carry your roll of cut vinyl flooring into the room in which it will be installed. Carefully unroll and position it over the clean, dry floor, matching up the landmarks you indicated on your template.

Carefully assess your cutting job. If any additional trimming needs to be done, this is the time to do it — *before* any adhesives have been applied.

The first part of the new floor to be secured is the seam. This is done by applying the adhesive along the floor between the two sections of flooring. First, gently fold back one section and temporarily tape it back out of the way. Draw a pencil line along the edge of the other section to mark the seamline. Gently fold back the second section and tape it out of the way.

Apply a band of adhesive to the underlying floor surface along the seamline, using the recommended notched-tooth metal trowel (Figure 11). Remember that the old floor needs to be clean and free of wax.

Figure 12. Perimeter bond flooring requires only stapling at the edges. Staples will be covered by the shoe molding.

Figure 13. Roll back vinyl and apply adhesive with a toothed trowel. This application is used for full spread adhesives only.

Check the manufacturer's recommendations at this point. Some require only a 3″ band (1½″ on either side of the pencil line); others may require as much as 6″ of adhesive — 3″ on either side of the seam.

Apply the adhesive all along the pencil line to about 1½′ away from any cabinets. You want to stop the adhesive here, so that, once the seam is pressed together and rolled, you will be able to fold back the flooring under the cabinets to apply adhesive there. You have to glue the areas under cabinets. You cannot get a staple gun under the cabinet overhang.

Lay one piece into the adhesive, and then the other. Make sure the edges of the vinyl are tight against each other. If you don't, you'll get a condition called "ledging" where one side rides up higher than the other. Dirt can build up here and draw attention to the seam.

Now go over the seam with a rolling pin or seam roller, to press the vinyl into the adhesive and eliminate ledging.

To prevent moisture from getting under the floor along this seam, use a special seam sealer kit. Read and follow the instructions carefully. When applying solvent, hold the bottle at the proper angle and don't wipe up any of the excess. It will dissolve, and you won't see it after a short time. Give the seam a few hours to set up before walking on it.

Use the adhesive, as instructed, on the perimeter areas that are visible without a molding or in areas where you are unable to use your staple gun. Roll the edge back, apply the adhesive in the proper amount with the notched trowel or manufacturer's suggested applicator, and press it into place with the roller.

For the edges that will be covered by the quarter round trim, I find that staples applied with a staple gun work best. They are fast and provide great holding power. In addition, there will be fewer problems with temperature and humidity than there would be with adhesives. Staple close to the wall so the molding will cover the staples (see Figure 12).

This type of vinyl floor, being perimeter bonded, will now contract slightly, tightening like a drumhead over the

109

next 24 to 48 hours. Because of this, wait until the floor has contracted to its final tension before moving the furniture and appliances back onto it.

Finishing up is a simple matter of replacing the trim and thresholds you removed at the start of the project.

NOTE: These days, vinyl floors are made to be "no-wax." Once the floor has contracted into its final position, all you have to do is damp mop. As always, follow the manufacturer's suggestions for cleaning and care.

Full-Spread Adhesive Sheet Flooring

Full-spread adhesive is fast becoming the least popular type of vinyl flooring. It cannot be removed as easily as other floorings, should you decide to install another floor at a later date. Check around to see if your chosen pattern is available in a perimeter bond application, before you opt for the full-spread. If your pattern is available only in a full-spread application, try to limit its installation to small rooms. It is much too cumbersome to try to align on larger floors already spread with adhesive.

1. Check your floor carefully to ascertain that it is dry, level, and structurally sound. See Step One on Preparing the Floor for modifications.

2. Full-spread adhesives need floors that are smooth and free of grease, dirt, and any irregularities. Clean the floor well.

3. Follow the template procedure described in Step Two.

4. One of the most important things about working with adhesives is that you use the correct type of applicator or trowel and adhesive. This information will be included in the manufacturer's instructions. The adhesive should be applied to as much of the floor as will allow you to properly place the sheet vinyl and give you some working and adjusting room.

5. If you are applying a seamed floor, lay the smaller section first. Follow the instructions for seams as described in the section above on Perimeter Bond Flooring.

6. If you have done a careful job of outlining the odd and irregular shapes of the floor, and of transferring the template to the right side of the flooring, getting the sheet floor to fit should present no problems. If possible, remove the toilet and run the flooring underneath.

7. Once the flooring is in place, I recommend you go over it with a rolling pin or a 100-lb. roller. This assures the floor's getting a good bond with the adhesive. Roll from the center of the floor out toward the edges, to get rid of all the air bubbles and waves.

SELF-ADHESIVE VINYL TILES

Self-adhesive vinyl tiles are perhaps the easiest type of floor to put down. Because of the sticky backing, there is no need to mess with gooey adhesives and seam sealers. You need only acclimate the tiles to the room's temperature by storing them there overnight in open boxes. This is especially important when installing floors over concrete. Also, when you purchase tile, you want to have about 5 percent more tile than the total area you plan to cover, to account for border tiles.

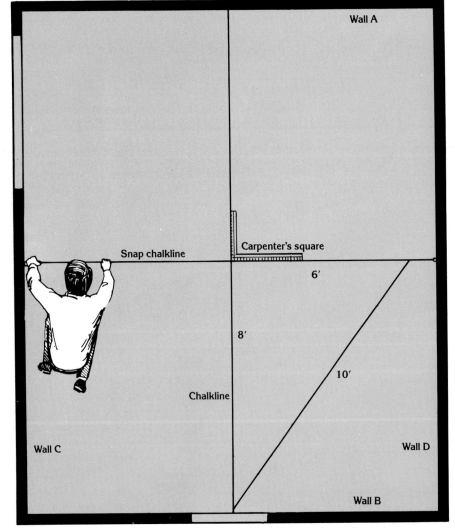

Figure 14. Measure for the midpoints of the lines using a 3-4-5 triangle to be sure layout lines are square.

STEP ONE

PREPARING THE FLOOR

Margin of Error: Floor should be level within ⅛″ and with gaps no larger than ¼″

MOST COMMON MISTAKES

1. Not making needed repairs before beginning the job.

2. Not leveling the floor and/or applying an underlayment, if needed.

3. Not purchasing 5 to 10 percent more tiles to account for border waste.

Self-adhesive tiles require a bit more floor preparation than sheet vinyl. They need a flat as well as a smooth surface upon which to adhere.

When laying a tile floor, you will have a more balanced floor if you work from the center of the room outward. You will need to establish layout lines and find the center of the floor. You must also be sure the seams in the tiles do not line up directly over seams in the under floor.

First, measure to find the midpoints of two opposing walls (Wall A and Wall B in Figure 14). Stretch a chalkline between the midpoints of these walls and snap it (Line A/B). Measure for the midpoints of the other two opposing walls (Wall C and Wall D).

Before snapping the second line (Line C/D), place a carpenter's square in the center where the two lines would intersect. If necessary, adjust the second line (Line C/D) so the two intersect at a 90-degree angle. These lines must be perfectly square. You can check this easily with the 3-4-5 triangle technique.
3-4-5 Triangle. Start at the intersection of the layout lines and measure 6′ along Line A/B. The measure 8′ along Line C/D. The measurement between points A/B and C/D will be exactly 10′ if

the lines are perfectly square. (You can use any multiple of 3-4-5, but it is best to use the longest possible, to assure the greatest accuracy.)

If the lines are not perfectly square, adjust Line C/D until they are. Do not adjust Line A/B! Lay loose tile from the center point along Line A/B to the wall. If the space between the last tile and the wall is less than half a tile, offset Line C/D one-half tile (6″ with 12″ tiles) closer to the one wall and snap a new Line C/D. Repeat this process by laying tiles along Line C/D and adjusting Line A/B. This will assure equal borders on opposing walls. And all borders will be more than half a tile.

TIP: Always install tiles by working toward the center of the room.

STEP TWO

LAYING THE TILES

Margin of Error: Exact

MOST COMMON MISTAKES

1. Not laying out and squaring your working lines when placing square tiles.

2. Placing a pattern line too close to an irregular wall, thereby accentuating the out-of-line wall.

3. Neglecting to lay the floor tiles in the direction indicated by the arrow on the back of the tile.

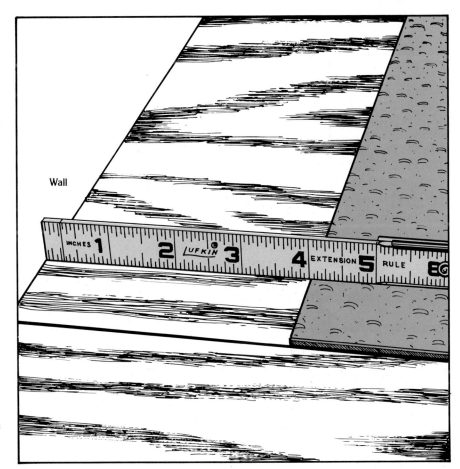

Wall

Figure 15. If the last tile by the wall is less than the space of half a tile (as shown), move the center line over half a tile space.

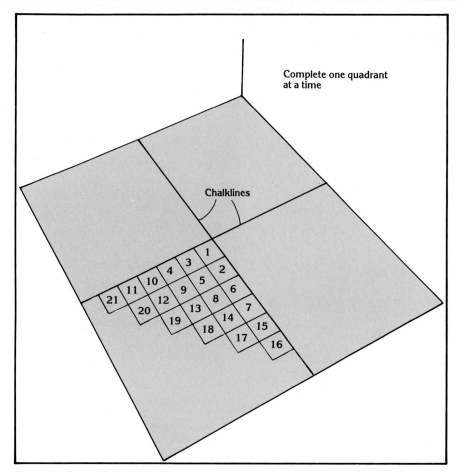

Figure 16. Pattern for laying tiles.

After making sure your floor is clean of debris and dirt, begin laying the tiles. These vinyl floor tiles should be installed in a certain direction, indicated on the back of the tile by an arrow.

Beginning at the intersection of the working lines, the first tile goes down along the first working line (Line A/B), with the second along Line C/D, as shown in Figure 16. Continue to lay the tiles within the quadrants, working out toward the borders. Be sure they are snug so that they will end up properly at the wall and leave a good finished look.

Tiles are easily cut with a utility knife or a pair of scissors, and will cut even easier if you first warm the tile with a blow dryer. This is especially helpful when making a cut to fit around an intricate shape. In the case of a complex cut, a template of butcher paper or craft paper is needed as well. Cut the paper to fit around the obstruction, then trace the pattern onto the tile.

A consistently accurate method of cutting a border tile for a perfect fit, even though the wall may be slightly out of line, is this: Lay the tile you want to cut squarely on top of the tile that is already in place on the row adjacent to the border row. Take another loose tile and butt it up against the wall so it overlaps the tile you want to cut. It then becomes a straightedge for cutting the border tile. Score the tile to be cut with a utility knife. The border tile should then break cleanly along that line and fit into place perfectly.

When fitting border tiles along irregular or curving walls, a template is a necessity. As you place your paper tile in position, crease the paper (as you push it into the corner or curve) as tightly as you can possibly get it. Mark the crease with a pencil as accurately as you can manage. Transfer the pattern to the tile (making sure the tile is facing in the proper direction) and make your cut very carefully along the line with a utility knife.

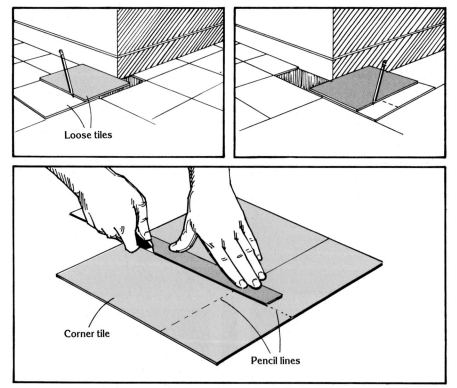

Figure 17. The sequence for cutting a tile at an outside corner.

TIP: Try to avoid full-spread adhesive vinyl flooring because it is difficult to remove.

STEP THREE

REPLACING THE TRIM

Margin of Error: Exact

MOST COMMON MISTAKE

1. Installing the trim before the tiles are all in place.

Once your newly laid, self-adhesive tile flooring is in place, you can replace the trim pieces and door thresholds. Where it was necessary to install an underlayment, you may need to use a reducer strip. Install this, according to the manufacturer's instructions, where the newly laid floor meets another that is not exactly at the same level. Another option for trim is a self-adhesive vinyl wall base, available in 2½″ × 48″ and 4″ × 48″ sections.

DRY TILES

Dry-back flooring tiles that need an adhesive can be laid the same as sticky-backed tiles. Follow the manufacturer's instructions for specific preparation, adhesive and trowel use, and drying time. This type of flooring, like the full-spread adhesive sheet vinyl, can be difficult to remove later.

TIP: To keep the pattern from shifting while you work, cut little triangles in various areas of the paper. Then, tape it to the floor with masking tape pressed over the cutouts.

APPLYING VINYL OVER CONCRETE

When faced with a situation in which you must apply sheet vinyl or tiles over concrete, note the following special considerations.

The concrete *must be dry*. New concrete should be cured to a hard, dry, non-powdery finish. New concrete should also have a minimum of a 4-ml. moisture barrier between the ground and the concrete slab.

To be on the safe side, test *all* concrete subfloors for moisture. I recommend you test at a time that is most likely to produce moisture — a rainy month, for instance. This test can be done in three different ways. Perhaps the easiest is to completely tape down 2′ × 2′ polyfilm squares in a variety of places on the floor. Leave these for 24 to 48 hours; then check for condensation under the plastic.

A second test involves chipping small sections of concrete from the floor in several areas. Apply to each chipped area a 3 percent Penophalen in alcohol solution. This can be purchased at most drugstores. A red color reaction indicates moisture is present in your floor. Chipping the concrete protects against the possibility that a concrete sealer had been applied without your knowledge.

The third test involves the use of calcium chloride crystals, also available from a druggist. Make a 3″-diameter putty ring on the slab, place ¼ teaspoon of the calcium chloride within the circle, then cover this with a water glass to seal off the crystals from the air. If the crystals are dissolved within 12 hours, the slab is too wet.

To effectively carry an applied floor, a concrete subfloor should have a density of 90 pounds per cubic foot or more. A lighter slab tends to hold moisture longer, as well as retain a scaly or chalky surface. Either moisture or retention of concrete dust can lead to problems.

TOOLS AND MATERIALS CHECKLIST

Tools for Perimeter Bond Sheet Vinyl

Scissors	Notched blade or
Pencil or ball	utility knife
point pen	Rolling pin or
1″ wide ruler	seam roller
Notched trowel	Staple gun

Materials for Perimeter Bond Sheet Vinyl

Craft or butcher	Sheet vinyl
paper	Adhesive
Do-it-yourself	Seam sealer kit
installation kit	Staples
Masking tape	

Tools for Full-Spread Adhesive

Scissors	Notched blade or
Pencil or ball	utility knife
point pen	Rolling pin or
1″ wide ruler	(rented) 100 lb.
Notched trowel	roller

Materials for Full-Spread Adhesive

Craft or butcher	Sheet vinyl
paper	Adhesive
Masking tape	Seam sealer kit

Tools for Self-Adhesive Vinyl Tiles

Chalkline	Scissors
Carpenter's	Hair dryer
square	Pencil
Utility knife	

Materials for Self-Adhesive Vinyl Tile

Tiles	Butcher or craft
Vinyl wall base	paper

Tools for Floor Preparation

Pry bar	Handsaw
Utility knife	Hammer

Materials for Floor Preparation

Leveling	¼″ plywood
compound	6 penny ring
¾″ T & G	shank nails
plywood	

CHAPTER SEVEN

Hardwood Floors
Refinishing, Repairing, and Installing

WHAT YOU WILL BE DOING

A hardwood floor is perhaps the most beautiful and durable flooring you can use. In recent years these floors have experienced something of a comeback. Earlier in this country's construction history, they were the most commonplace of all floorings. With the advent of vinyl and linoleum flooring, and later with the widespread use of carpeting, they began to decline in popularity.

Part of their comeback, other than just the appreciation of the product itself, has been the introduction of new types of hardwood flooring systems. Not only are these new types as beautiful and as durable as the earlier tongue-and-groove plank flooring, but also their ease of installation makes their application a rather simple do-it-yourself project, even for a novice. This may surprise many people, since it appears to be rather difficult and best left to professionals or to the more experienced do-it-yourselfers. This is not really the case. Both parquet and plank flooring can easily be installed by novices in a weekend.

In this chapter I discuss three areas of hardwood flooring: refinishing and repairing existing hardwood floors, installing parquet floors, and installing plank (strip) flooring. For the most part, I discuss installing the prefinished floors. These floors are already stained and have the protective top coat applied. You can, however, install unfinished hardwood floors. After they are installed they need to be finished by sanding, staining (optional), and application of a protective finish. The techniques for doing this on a newly installed unfinished plank floor are similar to those discussed under the refinishing section of this chapter. There are some differences, however; mainly in the fact that the thicker unfinished strip floorings require a special nailing gun for proper application.

BEFORE YOU BEGIN

SAFETY

As you exercise your do-it-yourself skills, develop safe work habits and stick to them.

1. Safety glasses or goggles should be worn when power tools are in use, especially if you wear contact lenses.

2. Always unplug your power tools when making adjustments or changing blades, drill bits, or sandpaper.

3. Be sure your tools are properly grounded.

4. Watch power cord placement so that it doesn't interfere with the tool's operation.

5. Wear ear protectors when using power tools, because some operate at noise levels that damage hearing.

6. Be careful of loose hair and clothing so that it does not get caught in power tools.

7. The proper respirator or face mask should be worn when sanding, sawing, or using substances with toxic fumes.

8. Use adequate ventilation with window fans. Keep away from heat sparks and flames when applying adhesives or mastic. Some are highly flammable.

9. Wear rubber gloves when using solvents.

10. Use the appropriate tool for the job.

11. Keep blades sharp. A dull blade requires excessive force and can slip and cause accidents.

12. Seal all heating and air conditioning ducts and electrical outlets. Wood dust can ignite.

13. Take care in storing oily rags which can spontaneously combust.

14. Use the proper protection, take precautions, and plan ahead. Never bypass safety to save money or rush a project.

USEFUL TERMS

Floor register. An opening in the floor, usually covered by a grate, which brings heated or cooled air into a room.
Glazier's points. Small metal triangles used to hold glass panes in their frames.
Penetrating sealant. A finish that soaks into the wood as well as providing a hard finishing surface.
Polyurethane. A synthetic rubber polymer sealant for wood.
Reducer strips. Prefabricated door thresholds for use where two rooms with different floor levels come together.
Shoe molding. Decorative and functional trim pieces used where walls and floors meet.

Surface finish. A finish that provides a hard surface coat without penetrating the wood.
Underlayment. A supporting floor which provides a smooth, level surface upon which to lay a finished floor.

WHAT YOU WILL NEED

Because the requirements for working on existing floors and those for installing new floors are so different, I have listed separately what you will need at the beginning of each project.

PERMITS AND CODES

Some areas require permits whenever you spend over a certain amount on any repairs or remodeling. Sometimes this figure is as low as $100. Check with your local municipalities to see if you need a permit. Usually only a small fee is required, and often this ordinance is not enforced. Other than this, no permits or inspections apply in these projects.

MOST COMMON MISTAKES

Because of the complexity of the work, the most common mistakes are listed with each step of each project.

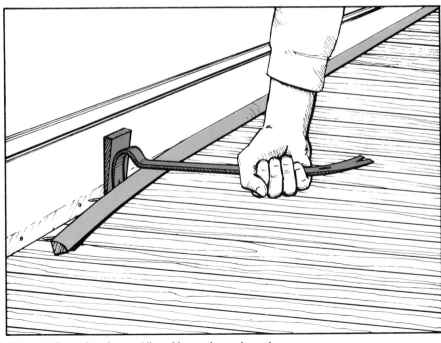

Figure 1. Removing shoe molding with a pry bar and a wedge.

REFINISHING AND REPAIRING EXISTING HARDWOOD FLOORS

WHAT YOU WILL NEED

Time. Repairs are difficult to assess for time. The extent of repair work will determine this. Refinishing a 9′ × 12′ room will require 8–18 work hours. Remember, however, that added time will be needed between steps to allow coats of finish to dry properly.

Tools. Except for a few specialty tools, most of the tools you will need to refinish hardwood floors are the common ones in a household toolbox. These include:

Hammer	Rags
Nailset	Tack cloths (sticky rags that pick up fine dust)
Paint scraper	Masks for dust and toxic fumes
Lamb's wool mop	Fan for ventilation
Paint tray	

If repairing, also:

Tape	Chisel
Power saw	Drill

Specialty tools:

Shop-type vacuum cleaner	Edge sander
Drum sander	

The drum sander is a large sander used on the main body of the floor. The edge sander is especially designed to sand the floor where it meets the wall, areas the drum sander will not reach. The shop vacuum is needed to remove as much dust as possible before you apply the stains and protective finish. All these tools should be available to rent at your home center, hardware store, or rental equipment yard.

Materials

Sandpaper	Protective finish
Wood dough	Flooring (if needed for repair)
Stain	

Very often an older hardwood floor will seem to be in such bad condition that the only remedy is to cover it over with carpeting, tile, or a new hardwood flooring. Usually the floor is salvageable, at a lot less expense than you had imagined. The advantage of hardwood floors is their durability and often their ability to be rejuvenated after years of use. The floors are usually structurally sound and, with sanding and refinishing, can be brought back to their previous beauty. If the floor is, however, beyond repair, you will need to either cover it or replace it.

PREPARING AND REPAIRING THE FLOOR

Margin of Error: Not applicable

MOST COMMON MISTAKES

1. Not setting nailheads below floor level.

2. Not removing shoe molding.

Before beginning your sanding work, some prep work will probably be in order. Take a close survey of the floor. Note if any pieces are so badly damaged that they need to be replaced. Note where there are any nailheads above the level of the flooring. These will have to be countersunk with a nailset and hammer, or they will tear the sandpaper. Remove the shoe molding where the floor meets the wall. Try to remove this gently so that it can be reused and nailed back into place, once the refinishing is completed. Also, note where there are any bad ridges or cupped boards, because these areas will take extra sanding. Finally, before sanding, sweep and vacuum the floor well, and seal off the room from the rest of the house so that dust will not spread. You may even want to consider using plastic and tape around the edges of all doors leading into other areas of the house.

Repairing squeaky or cupped boards. Squeaky boards are annoying, but often can be easily fixed. Try fixing them with the simplest technique: inserting a shim from below the floor, between the floor joist and the area where the floor is squeaking. Sometimes, even tapping the squeaking area with a hammer and 2 × 4 wrapped in a towel will work. Also, try squirting some lubricant such as graphite, talcum powder, floor oil, mineral oil, or wood dough between the boards. You can even try forcing metal glazier's points between the boards every 6″ to separate the boards.

If these simpler techniques are not working, try drilling a pilot hole through the board, nailing from above with a finishing nail, and then countersinking the nail and filling the hole with wood dough. This technique also works for repairing cupped or warped boards. If the floor joists are exposed from below, you can drill a pilot hole up through the floor joist and/or subflooring and ¼″ into the squeaky board. A drill bit stop will be useful here to prevent drilling through the floor surface. Wrapping masking tape around the bit will work as a drill guide. Then you can grab the board from below with a ³⁄₁₆″ round-head wood screw with a large washer. This technique of screwing the flooring from below also works when repairing cupped or warped boards. One other possible solution is to add metal joist bridging or wood blocking between the joists near the squeak. This will often stiffen the floor and eliminate the squeak.

Badly warped or cupped floors. Some floors may be badly warped or cupped, due to moisture. In this case it is not practical to repair each board individually. Instead, I recommend you sand the entire floor down to an even level. Use your drum sander and a rough grade of sandpaper and make diagonal passes across the cupped areas until they are all smooth and level. Later you will have to sand with the grain in order to work out all the unsightly sanding marks left by the diagonal sanding.

Damaged boards. Badly marred or damaged boards often need to be replaced. You will need to cut and chisel these out of the floor and replace them with new boards. To do this, adjust the blade on your circular saw to the thickness of the damaged floor to avoid cutting the subfloor. Use a plunge cut and saw down the center of the board, taking care not to cut into the good boards at either end.

Using a hammer and chisel and a pry bar, remove the damaged board, again taking care not to mar any adjacent boards. Cut a new piece the exact length and remove its tongue so that it will fit into the opening. Also chisel off the tongue of the board protruding into the space. (See Figure 5.) Install the new board, applying two ¼″ beads of subfloor adhesive to its bottom, and insert it into the opening. Finally, pre-drill pilot holes through the new board into the subfloor and nail the board with finishing nails. Countersink these nails and cover with wood dough.

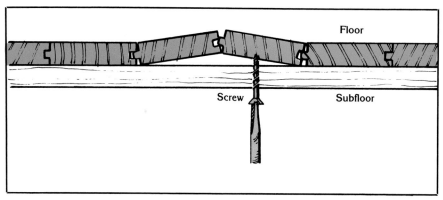

Figure 2. Using a screw to pull down warped floorboard.

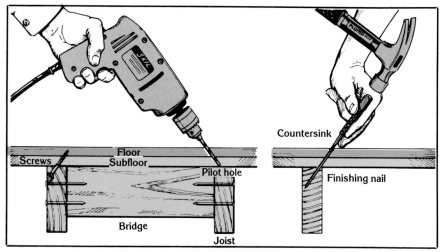

Figure 3. Various ways of securing warped or squeaky floorboards.

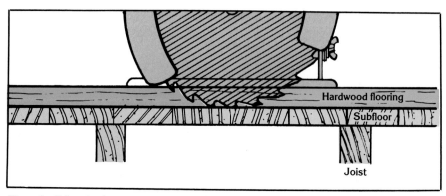

Figure 4. Using circular saw to cut a groove in damaged board.

TIP: Spread a sheet of plywood over the newly laid tile to be used as a "kneeling board" as you work. This will allow you to avoid stepping directly on the tiles.

STEP TWO

PREPARING THE ROOM FOR SANDING

Margin of Error: Not applicable

MOST COMMON MISTAKE

1. Neglecting to adequately prepare the floor.

After you have prepared and repaired the floor, you will need to take a few additional steps before sanding. Remove all furniture and preferably the drapes. If you do not want to actually remove the drapes, you can fold them, hang them with a coat hanger from the drapery rod, and then slip a large plastic bag over them and tightly seal the bag. Remove floor registers and seal them with plastic, as well as any heating or air-conditioning ducts. Search out any protruding nailheads and countersink them with a nailset. Also, remember that sanding produces a very flammable dust, so turn off all pilot lights and electrical appliances. I also recommend that you seal off all electrical outlets. Seal the room tightly from the rest of the house to avoid dust problems. However, open a window and use a window fan to provide adequate ventilation while sanding.

Before beginning to sand, remove all the shoe molding (the baseboards are usually left in place). To remove the shoe molding, use a utility knife to carefully cut through any thick paint layers between the baseboards and the molding. Carefully pry the molding loose with a pry bar and a wooden wedge so as not to mar the baseboards. Number each piece so you will know where it goes when you are ready to replace it.

Use a putty knife and wood dough to fill all the small holes and cracks. Be sure the wood dough matches the color of the unfinished flooring. Allow the wood dough to properly dry before sanding. After all this is done, sweep the floor well and vacuum with a good heavy-duty shop vac.

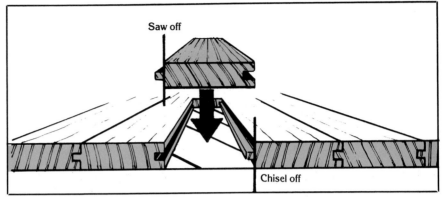

Figure 5. Cutting off the tongues so new board will fit in.

Figure 6. Applying adhesive to back of new piece of flooring.

Figure 7. Using a putty knife and wood dough to fill cracks.

STEP THREE

SANDING THE FLOOR

Margin of Error: Everything level within 1/8"; no old stain remaining

MOST COMMON MISTAKES

1. Allowing sander to gouge floor.

2. Not removing all of the old stain.

3. Leaving high spots or ridges.

4. Not using an edge sander.

5. Not sanding with fine paper.

Most oak floorings are 3/4" thick and can be sanded a number of times. Some may be thinner floors — 1/2", 3/8", or 5/16" — and these must be refinished with caution to avoid sanding through to the subfloor. Remove a floor register and measure the thickness of your flooring. If it is thinner than 3/4", consult a professional floor refinisher.

If yours is a 3/4" flooring, you are now ready to begin sanding. This is the only difficult part of the entire process. You need to be very careful here or you can gouge the floor past repair. I have seen this happen to a friend who had not bothered to learn the proper use of the drum sander. Fortunately, the gouge was in an area covered by a sofa, but you do not want to start arranging your furniture according to your gouges.

When you rent the drum sander, be sure you get a manufacturer's instructional manual and some hints and a demonstration from the store where you rented it. Be sure it's in good shape and functioning well. And check to be sure you have all the dust bags, special wrenches, and attachments. The machine is powerful and, if not used properly, can quickly gouge your floor beyond repair. If you feel you are not strong enough to handle the drum

sander (it requires no great strength and can be handled by most women), ask someone else to help you. You may want to practice on a piece of plywood, or with fine sandpaper, until you get the hang of it. Always use a dust mask. Ear protection is recommended as well.

Purchase several grits of "open face" sandpaper. Coarse grits will be needed for the rough sanding and for removing the old finish. Finer grits will be needed toward the end of the sanding process to provide a smooth finish. If you need

to remove paint or to sand cupped boards, start with a 20-grit paper. To remove shellac or varnish, a 36-grit will do. For the second sanding, a medium, 80-grit paper is used; and the final finish sanding requires a fine, 100-grit paper. The actual number of sanding passes, from 2 to 4, will depend on the condition of your floor and the build-up of old finish and wax.

Be sure to buy enough paper. The average room will require 10 sheets of each grade for the drum sander and 10

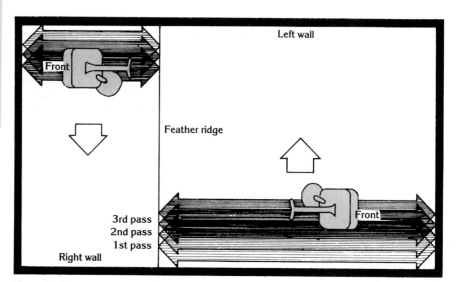

Figure 8. Recommended pattern of sanding.

Figure 9. Using professional drum sander to refinish floor.

sheets of each grade for the disc sander. Get a surplus and return what you don't use.

Your first process in sanding involves using the rough-grit sandpaper. You will not only be removing any previous finish, stain, or discoloration, but also leveling the floor to a smooth surface. There may be warped boards or ridges where the boards come together. If the floor is very bad in these areas, you may need to sand diagonally across the floor with a rough-grade sandpaper until the floor is smooth. Then sand with the grain of the floor to get out the sanding marks left by the diagonal sanding. Except for sanding these badly cupped areas, always sand with the grain of the floor.

Use a coarse grade in the beginning, unless the floor is in very good condition. Be sure the paper is properly installed and be prepared to change it regularly. The heat will melt the old finish, and this clogs the sandpaper.

As you begin sanding, remember never to turn the sander on while the sandpaper and drum are touching the floor. Tilt it back by the handle until it is out of contact, start the sander, and, when it reaches full speed, slowly lower it until the sandpaper touches the floor. Begin to move the moment the drum touches the floor. Let the sander pull you forward at a slow, steady speed. You can sand both forward and backward, but always keep the sander in motion. *Never allow it to stop while turning.* Sand in straight lines along the grain pattern of the flooring. As you approach the end of your run, lift the sander while it is still moving forward.

We recommend sanding two-thirds of the floor in one direction and one-third in the other, as shown in Figure 8. Whenever you need to reposition the sander, be sure the drum is off the floor. Overlap your back-and-forth passes to be sure you are sanding all areas thoroughly, and to assure an even finish with no sanding marks. Go forward and then return over the same area as you go backward. Move sideways in 3″–4″ increments to overlap each pass.

After you have done the main body of the floor with the rough paper, use an edge sander where the floor meets the wall and in other areas missed by the drum sander. Again you will be using coarse-grit papers. Follow the manufacturer's instructions with this machine, because it can also gouge the wood, but not as easily as the drum sander.

After the first sanding, check to see if any nails are now protruding, and, if so, countersink them. Fill all dents, gouges, and cracks with wood dough and allow it to dry. Then repeat the process with both the drum and edge sanders with medium-grit paper.

Repeat this process for the final coat; but before beginning this coat, use a high-quality hand paint scraper to get to any areas the power tools could not reach, such as under radiators and in corners. Do a good job, because this determines the quality of the final finish. Also, if there are any nail holes, dings, or other holes in the floor, fill them with wood dough of a similar color as the flooring and sand flush with the floor surface.

Figure 10. Using edge sander where floor meets wall.

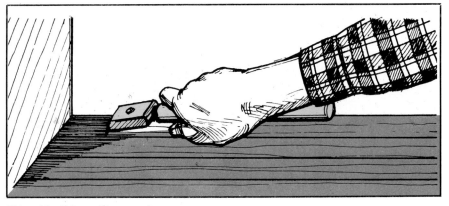

Figure 11. Using paint scraper in corner.

TIP: Remember to open a window and use a fan to provide adequate ventilation while sanding.

Figure 12. Using professional buffer with steel wool pad to sand between coats.

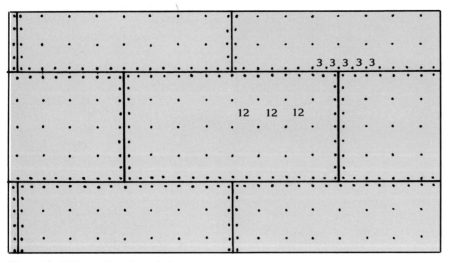

3 3 3 3 3

12   12   12

Figure 13. Nailing pattern for underlayment.

STEP FOUR

APPLYING THE STAIN

Margin of Error: Not applicable

MOST COMMON MISTAKES

1. Not removing all the dust.

2. Staining unevenly.

It is best to finish the floor and apply a protective sealant as soon as possible after sanding the floor, preferably the same day. This protects the floor from moisture and other problems that could cause the wood grain to rise and create a rough surface. Before you begin finishing the floor, you need to be sure that it is perfectly clean and free of dust or debris. Also, carefully check for any flaws or imperfections.

Fill cracks or holes with wood dough, allow it to adequately dry, and then sand smooth. Sand off any swirl or sanding marks. If there are stains that cannot be removed by sanding, try bleaching them out. Wearing gloves and goggles, use an undiluted household bleach applied directly to the center of the stain. In a few minutes the bleach should lighten the stain. Apply enough bleach to blend the stain with the color of the wood. Then wash the bleached area with warm water and let it dry. Vacuum the floors well and go over them with a tack cloth. These cloths are sticky and, when rubbed across the floor, pick up all the fine dust. Rub your entire floor well with cheese cloth. Also, clean up any areas where dust has settled, so that it does not get on the surface.

Staining the floor is optional. You may want to just put on the protective finish and let the natural color of the wood show through. If you decide to stain it, visit some other rooms with various color stains to see how you like it, once it is down. Often the sample stain at the store will give a very different effect when a large area like a floor is that color. Also, you may want to test a small area of your floor before applying it everywhere. If the floor is still blotchy after sanding, you may need to stain it in order to arrive at an even coloration.

Before staining, you may want to apply a special wood sealer to the flooring. This is especially important if you are applying the stain to a softwood floor. This is not the heavy-duty protective finish to be applied last, but rather a light-weight sealer that simply seals the open pores of the wood. This makes an even application of stain much easier. Some wood sealers are colored and stain and seal the floor in one application.

Applying stain may be trickier than you think. It takes some concentration and skill to get a good even finish with no blotchy areas where the stain is unevenly applied. The sealer will help here, as the pores will be sealed and the stain will not penetrate as deep or as quickly.

Pour all the stain you need into one container and mix it thoroughly to assure an even application. You can apply the stain using rags, brushes, or a roller. Go carefully and be sure it is penetrating to give an even color. Apply a generous coat and, after 5 to 10 minutes, vigorously wipe with a rag to remove excess stain. The amount of time you allow it to set on the floor will determine the degree of darkness provided. We recommend buffing the floor with a professional buffer and a #2 steel wool disc and thoroughly vacuuming before the final finish coat is applied. As always, follow the manufacturer's instructions closely.

Keep rags handy to wipe up any excess. The pigments of the stain are in suspension, not in solution, so the stain must be stirred regularly during application. Be sure never to store oily rags together. There is always the threat of spontaneous combustion.

STEP FIVE

APPLYING THE PROTECTIVE FINISH

Margin of Error: Not applicable

MOST COMMON MISTAKES

1. Not sanding after every coat.
2. Not stirring the finish properly.

There are several different types of protective finishes. The most common are penetrating sealers or surface finishes, including polyurethane, varnish, and shellac. Penetrating sealers (mentioned under staining) penetrate the pores of the wood, so the finish wears as the wood wears and can be retouched with wax in heavy-traffic areas. They come tinted or clear. These penetrating sealers are often used as an undercoat with surface finishes; but be sure the two finishes are compatible before you begin.

Surface finishes provide a tough, clear coating over stained or sealed wood. Polyurethane has pretty much replaced varnish, shellac, and lacquer. Often a heavy-traffic wax is applied over the polyurethane.

Finishes come in a clear gloss finish (high gloss) and a satin finish (low gloss). The high gloss shows dust easier.

TIP: Test a small area of the floor before applying stain. Often the sample stain at the store will give a very different effect when used on your large and particular floor.

Figure 14. Using a tile to undercut door jambs.

Applying Polyurethane

Be sure to buy the slower-drying air-drying polyurethanes. Novices will have trouble with the faster-drying moisture-cured types that professionals use. Be sure whatever type you use is compatible with any undercoat you may have.

When working with polyurethane, be sure that it is well stirred before you apply it. The hardeners settle in the bottom and, if it is not well stirred, the floor will not dry evenly. Use a paint stick or install a bent coat hanger in a drill that has a variable speed. Stir at a low speed so as not to create bubbles in the polyurethane. Ventilate the room well and wear a mask made for use with toxic fumes. In ventilating, however, be sure you're not creating a dust problem that will cause dust particles to settle on the wet floor.

It is best to apply the finish with a lamb's wool applicator and a paint tray. A brush is used at the walls and in hard-to-reach areas. Apply the polyurethane evenly, moving the applicator in the direction of the grain.

Usually three or four coats are applied. You will need to sand with a fine-grade sandpaper between each coat after they have dried. The drying time will differ according to the humidity and temperature. Be sure you don't begin sanding until the previous coat is *entirely* dry, with no tacky feel. Sand with a professional buffer equipped with a #2 steel wool disc. This is much easier than using a hand sander. Hard-to-reach areas should be sanded by hand. Vacuum after each sanding, and then go over the floor with a damp mop to remove all the dust. The second coat can be applied across the grain. The final coat does not need buffing.

After your final coat, wait until it has dried, and move in. For a few days the protective finish may "outgas" fumes, which may be rather unpleasant; but aside from that, the fumes should be gone after a week or so. Some professionals choose to apply a heavy-traffic wax over the floor for one final coat of protection.

INSTALLING PARQUET FLOORS

Some people look at parquet floors, with all the small, beautiful inlaid pieces, and think, "What patience and skill the installer must have had!" Actually, patience and great skill is no longer needed to install this beautiful flooring. Quite the opposite is true. It is one of the simpler do-it-yourself projects. This is because all those little pieces have been prefabricated together into larger tiles. Because of this, and the fact that it comes prefinished, it is no more difficult to install than vinyl floor tiles.

WHAT YOU WILL NEED

Time. Plan on approximately 10 to 15 work hours to complete a 9′ × 12′ room, longer if underlayment is needed. This can be a one person task.

Tools.

Carpenter's pencil	Eye protection
Hammer	Pry bar and wood wedge
Utility knife	Extension cords (heavy duty)
Heavy duty shop vacuum	Chalk line and chalk
Fan(s)	Jigsaw
Tape measure	Notched trowel
Carpenter's square	150 lb. roller
Ear protectors	Handsaw
Respirator/face mask	

Materials. If adding an underlayment before laying your floor, you will need

Leveling compound	Particle board or luan mahogany
6-penny ring shank nails	plywood

If you are only laying the parquet,

Mastic or adhesive	Reducer strip
Parquet tiles	Adhesive cleaning solvent
Plywood	Rags

STEP ONE

PREPARING THE EXISTING FLOOR

Margin of Error: Within 3/16″ of level

MOST COMMON MISTAKES

1. Installing over a badly damaged, damp, or sloping floor.

2. Not correcting problems before applying floor.

Oftentimes the wood parquet floor can be installed directly over an existing floor. Sometimes, however, you are not so lucky. Be sure you closely inspect your floor to ascertain how much preparation will be needed. It's tempting to just forge ahead, but resist the temptation, because, if a badly damaged or uneven floor is not properly prepared, you will not be satisfied with the final product. Also, if you are using adhesives to apply your new floor, you will often have to remove old resilient sheet or tile floors, if the floor is not in good shape, and prepare a clean surface for the adhesive to adhere to. Applying a new plywood or hardboard subfloor directly on top of it may be easier. If, however, the resilient floor is in good shape and well bonded, simply removing old wax by rough sanding or scrubbing with a household scouring compound will suffice. Many cannot be applied over rubber tiles. Check manufacturer's instructions.

If the problem is just a few small dings and gouges, these can be quickly prepared with some wood putty. The real problem occurs if the floor is not level or has a lot of bumps, dips, or ridges; or if the floor is spongy and the substructure inadequate. A visual inspection may suffice. You may want to use a level or a steel ball that will roll to the low spots if the floor is not level. Also, check the corners to see if they are dipping. Sometimes, if the floor is off level, you can correct it by installing support from below. This may not be easy to do and may not level the floor adequately. The floor needs to be level within 1/4″ over 10′.

If the floor is very uneven or very much off level, I recommend that you apply a thin layer of underlayment over it. An underlayment is simply a thin (3/8″–1/2″) piece of plywood, hardboard, or particle board spread over the floor to create a new smooth and level surface.

If the floor is simply rough with ridges and small dips or gouges, installing the underlayment will suffice. If, however, the floor is off level, you will need to fill in the low areas before the underlayment is applied, to create a level floor. Use a leveling compound in all the low and dished areas, and then allow it to dry before installing the underlayment. Be sure that the underlayment is well secured to the old floor or you will have squeaks. To do this, use a 6-penny (6d) ring shank nail. Ring shank nails have a greater holding power than regular nails and are used specifically for this purpose. Nail every 4 to 6″ around the edges and every 4″ in the middle (see Figure 13). Also, leave a 1/2″ gap between the plywood and the wall all the way around, to allow for any possible expansion of the plywood. Many professionals leave a 1/16″–1/8″ gap between the plywood sheets as well. This

expansion could cause buckling or warping over an extended period of time.

Also, check to be sure there are no loose boards if you are not using a new underlayment. Repair these before beginning. When applying directly over an old floor, countersink any protruding nails and sand off any paint, wax, or varnish that might affect the adhering ability of the adhesive. Clean the floor thoroughly and remove the shoe molding (the baseboards are usually left in place). Use a utility knife to cut the paint where the shoe molding meets the baseboard. Use a pry bar, hammer, and a wedge to remove the shoe molding, being sure not to mar the baseboard as you go. Number each piece of shoe molding so you know where to install it later. Also, check to be sure all water and moisture problems are solved. You may want to install a 4–6 mil. polyethylene sheet to cover the ground directly below the house if you are installing the flooring over the crawlspace. This will help reduce cupping due to moisture.

After the underlayment is installed (assuming one was needed), your last step in preparation is to "undercut" your door jambs. This avoids a lot of notching. Undercutting is a process of cutting away some of the door jamb (the trim around the door) so that the new parquet flooring can be installed underneath it rather than notched around it.

To do this, simply take a scrap piece of parquet to act as a guide for the correct thickness and place it on top of the floor in front of the jamb. Then, holding your handsaw flat as shown in Figure 14, cut away the bottom of the jamb the thickness of the parquet. After you have done this you are ready to start installing the flooring.

TIP: If you can't get a roller, a kitchen rolling pin and all your weight will adhere vinyl to the floor sufficiently.

STEP TWO

LOCATING YOUR LAYOUT LINES

Margin of Error: 1/4″

MOST COMMON MISTAKES

1. Not using layout lines.

2. Not making the 6″ adjustment when needed.

As with vinyl floor tiles, you need to mark your floor with "layout lines" that will guide you in installing the parquet floor tiles. Two lines are used that cross approximately in the center of the floor and divide your room into four equal quadrants. The tiles are then laid out from the center where the lines cross toward the corners. Do this process correctly, because it will affect the final outcome of the project considerably.

First, find the center of the room and establish your layout lines. In Figure 16, walls A and B are 20′6″. Wall D is the wall of highest visibility, having a wide opening from the dining room, so you will want a full tile at this opening. Using increments of a full tile (usually 12″), measure along walls A and B from wall D approximately 1/2 the room, 10′. Snap a chalkline AB at these points. This is your first line. Now find the midpoints of walls C and D and snap your second line.

You may now need to make some adjustments to these lines. You want border tiles along walls A and B that are equal in width and more than 1/2 a tile. To do this, measure line AB (176″), divide it by 2, then divide that result (88″) by the size of the tile (12″). If more than 1/2 a tile remains along walls A and B, do not offset your chalklines. If, however, the remainder is less than half a tile, as in our example, 4″ (88 divided by 12 = 7′4″) you would end up with two 4″ border tiles and 14 full-size tiles.

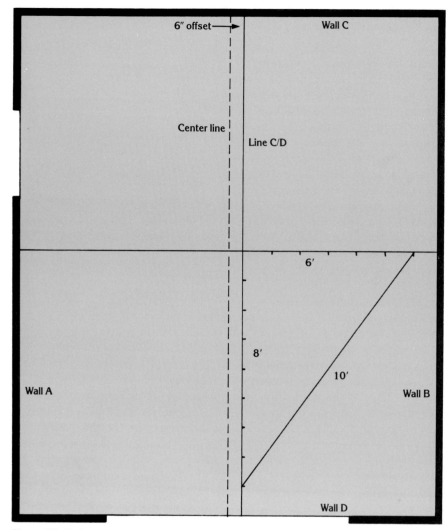

Figure 15. Typical layout pattern for parquet floor.

Labels within figure: 6″ offset, Wall C, Center line, Line C/D, 6′, 8′, 10′, Wall A, Wall B, Wall D

STEP THREE

APPLYING THE ADHESIVES

Margin of Error: Not applicable

MOST COMMON MISTAKES

1. Using wrong adhesives.

2. Applying when adhesive or room is too cold.

3. Using wrong trowel.

After the subfloor has been properly prepared, clean and vacuum well and be sure there are no protrusions from nails, splinters, and so on. Be sure to provide good ventilation, such as a window fan, because adhesive fumes can be toxic. Also, extinguish all pilot lights or open flames since some adhesives are highly combustible.

Be sure you have chosen the proper adhesive for the flooring, and follow the manufacturer's instructions closely. Most adhesives should be stored in a room heated at 70 degrees for 24 hours before applying. I also recommend that you store the wood tiles loosely in the room for at least 24 hours so they can acclimate to its temperature and humidity. If you have not been able to store the adhesives in a heated room before applying, you can place the unopened can in hot water to heat it up.

Use a toothed trowel and spread the adhesive in the area you will be working in. Spread up to, *but do not cover*, your working layout lines. Follow the pattern of laying tiles as shown in Figure 18. Be sure you spread no more area than can be covered in two to three hours. Hold the trowel at a 45-degree angle to get even ridges. Too much adhesive will squeeze between the tiles. Too little will not provide proper adhering. ⅛″

Remember, we want border tiles that are 6″ or more. To do this, offset the center chalkline by ½ tile (6″). This will now be our second layout line CD, which will leave a border tile of 9″ in our example along walls A and B. (You can also check this out by simply dry laying your tiles to see how they will work out.)

Before proceeding, however, you must check to be sure these two layout lines are perfectly perpendicular to each other. If all the walls were perfectly parallel, the lines would be at right angles. This is rarely the case, and usually the walls are off parallel a little.

Use a 3–4–5 triangle to check this (Figure 15). A 3–4–5 triangle has one side that is 3 (feet, inches, miles, etc.), another that is 4, and the third, 5, so that the angle across from the 5 side is a right angle. (You can multiply these by the same number and it will work; i.e., 6–8–10, 15–20–25.

Start at the intersection of the two lines and measure 6′ along line AB and then 8′ along line CD. Mark these points and measure the distance between them. If this distance is 10′, the lines are exactly parallel. If the distance is other than 10′, adjust only line CD until you have arrived at an accurate 3–4–5 (6–8–10) triangle. Do not move line AB or you will have odd-cut tiles at the visible doorway.

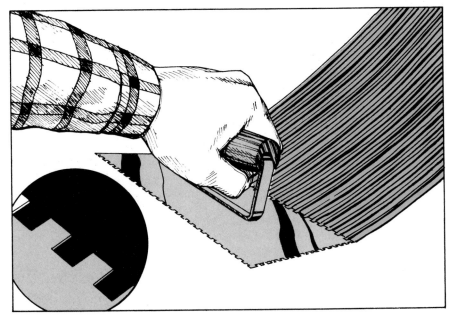

Figure 16. Using a toothed trowel to apply the mastic. Each manufacturer will recommend a certain size.

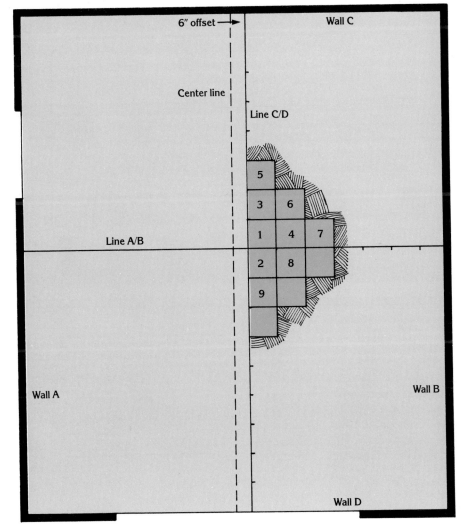

Figure 17. Installation pattern of parquet floor tiles.

ridges are about right. Let the adhesive thicken and become tacky according to the manufacturer's instruction (usually 1 hour) before laying the tiles. Once it has properly set up you can begin flooring.

STEP FOUR

LAYING THE TILES

Margin of Error: $1/8''$

MOST COMMON MISTAKES

1. Not leaving a $1/2''$ gap between tiles and the wall.

2. Not allowing adhesive to properly set up.

After your adhesive has set up you can start laying the tiles. This is where the fun begins. Everything you are doing will be your finished work, so go slow and do a good job. Lay the tiles in the pattern shown in Figure 17 or in one described by the manufacturer. Usually this is done in a pyramid fashion. Place the tiles exactly up to your layout lines. Here is where your previous accuracy will pay off.

The tiles are tongue and grooved and should fit easily together. Occasionally you may need to use a mallet or hammer and a block of wood to force them together. Avoid sliding the tiles or stepping on them for 24 hours after they are laid. You may want to spread a sheet of plywood as a kneeling board over the newly laid tile as you continue to work. In this way you avoid stepping directly on the tiles. Be sure there is no adhesive between the board and the tiles.

Take special care in laying your first 10 to 12 tiles, because these will determine the appearance of the entire floor. Be sure you have them right. Also,

127

check to be sure there is no debris lifting the tiles. Engage the tongue and grooves of the tiles as you lay them next to each other, but don't slide them into place.

Every few tiles stop and tap the tiles with a mallet or hammer and a block of wood to be sure they are properly seated. If any adhesive gets on the tiles, clean it immediately with a rag soaked in solvent. Never apply the solvent directly to the tiles or it could mar their finish.

You will need to cut the border tiles to fit. This is best done with a fine-toothed handsaw, though a power jig saw can also be used. Don't forget to leave a ½″ gap between these border tiles and the walls (see Figure 19). Many manufacturers recommend placing a cork expansion strip in this gap.

Figure 18. Laying the parquet tiles in a pyramid fashion. Note the plywood board to distribute the weight.

STEP FIVE

ROLLING THE FLOOR

Margin of Error: Not applicable

MOST COMMON MISTAKE

1. Omitting this step.

After you have finished laying the floor, or a section of the floor, go over the floor with a 100–150 pound floor roller rented from your supplier. If you can't get a roller, using a kitchen rolling pin with all your weight will work. This step must be done within four hours of when the adhesive was originally spread. This will insure proper adhering. Be sure to clean up any excess adhesive immediately.

Finally, replace your shoe molding. Be sure to nail this into the wall, not the

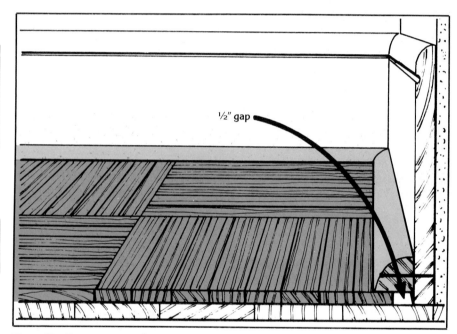

Figure 19. Expansion gap left at wall.

flooring, to allow the flooring to expand. Also, reducer strips may be needed where your new floor meets another flooring and is either higher or lower than this flooring. These reducer strips are the same color and material as your flooring and are available at the store where you bought the flooring. Also, if your flooring height has been raised by the new flooring, you may need to trim down your doors. Test the doors before scraping them across the floor and marring the floor. Do not walk on the floor for 24 hours after installing.

INSTALLING STRIP FLOORING

Until recently, laying a hardwood strip or plank flooring was a good bit more difficult than it is today. Strip flooring came only in a rather thick (¾") material that had to be nailed to the subflooring. This process took a special nailing gun and considerably more work than gluing. Though this flooring is still available and within the abilities of the novice do-it-yourselfer, the new thinner (⅜" or ⁵⁄₁₆"), prefinished floorings are much simpler. They not only require gluing instead of nailing, but also come prefinished so no sanding and finishing are required.

This type of flooring, like its cousin, the parquet flooring, comes in various colors and styles. Every style and color will affect the general aura of the room. Try to visit a room that has the style you are thinking of using, and then ask yourself if installing this style will give your room the atmosphere you want. The most important part of this decision is that the final effect of the flooring on the feel of the room be what you are attempting to achieve. To the degree you have done this, you have made a good design decision.

WHAT YOU WILL NEED

Time. Strip flooring can be put down by one person and will take about 10 to 15 work hours to complete.

Tools.

Carpenter's pencil	Respirator/face mask
Hammer	Eye protection
Circular saw	Pry bar and wood wedge
Utility knife	Extension cords (heavy duty)
Heavy duty shop vacuum	Chalkline and chalk
Fan(s)	Jigsaw
Tape measure	Notched trowel
Carpenter's square	150 lb. roller
Ear protectors	Handsaw

Materials. Materials required will depend on whether you need an underlayment, in which case you will need:

Leveling compound	6-penny ring shank nails
Particle board or luan mahogany plywood	

Otherwise, you will only need these items:

Straight edge board	Plywood
Mastic or adhesive	Reducer strip
Tongue-and-groove planking (glue down)	Adhesive cleaning solvent
	Rags

STEP ONE

PREPPING AND REPAIRING THE FLOOR

Margin of Error: Within ³⁄₁₆" of level

MOST COMMON MISTAKES

1. Installing over a badly damaged, damp, or sloping floor.

2. Not correcting problems before applying floor.

This step is exactly the same as covered under parquet flooring.

STEP TWO

PLANNING THE FLOOR

There are a few planning guides that need to be understood before you begin.

1. Strip flooring installation traditionally begins at the most visible wall of the room.

2. Strip flooring is usually installed parallel with the long wall of the room, thereby perpendicular to the joists.

3. The last piece next to the most visible wall should be a full-size piece. If you are using random-width boards, this should be a wide board. The piece next to the wall across from this most visible wall can be a special-cut piece.

4. When installing flooring in adjacent rooms and halls perpendicular to the main room, you may want to turn the direction of the plank. However, avoid laying the flooring in the short direction of a long hallway, since this creates a "ladder" effect.

5. Work out of several cartons at once to assure a good blending of color.

6. Avoid boards that have a substantial "bow."

To assure that the most visible wall has a full-width board, and that the planks are installed straight, use a lay-out line. This is a line snapped on the floor with a chalkline approximately 30″–32″ from your most visible wall and running the direction in which the flooring will be laid. Its exact distance from the wall will depend on the width of the boards you are laying. Again, your object is to end at the most visible wall with a full-size plank. In the example that follows we are using both 3″ and 5″ planks, so eight planks will equal 32″ (four 3″ planks and four 5″ planks). We therefore measure out from the wall 32½″ at each end, mark this spot, and snap a chalkline there. The additional ½″ is for the needed expansion gap between the flooring and the wall. Then we must install a straight 2 × 4 as a straightedge to act as a guide when laying the floor. Be sure the straightedge is temporarily nailed to the subfloor perfectly straight and exactly on the layout line. This straightedge will determine the appearance of the entire flooring.

STEP THREE

APPLYING THE ADHESIVE

Margin of Error: Not applicable

MOST COMMON MISTAKES

1. Using wrong adhesives.

2. Applying when adhesive or room is too cold.

3. Using wrong trowel.

You will be applying the adhesive between the straightedge and the most visible wall 30″–32″ away. Never cover an area with adhesive that cannot be laid within four hours. Other than that, the adhesive is applied the same as discussed under parquet flooring.

STEP FOUR

LAYING THE PLANKS

Margin of Error: Exact

MOST COMMON MISTAKES

1. Not wiping off excess glue.

2. Not laying full-size piece next to visible wall.

3. Not achieving a tight fit between boards.

4. Using bowed boards.

5. Not leaving ½″ expansion gap between all walls and flooring.

Your first row of flooring will be laid tightly up against the straightedge. Install it so that the tongue is against the straightedge. If you are using random-width boards, be sure the piece next to the wall is the wider piece.

Be sure this first piece is a good, straight piece and installed *tight* up against the straightedge. This will assure a straight installation. If you are using flooring that has fake pegs, cut the end of the first plank in each row to be sure all the pegs do not line up next to a wall. Also, be sure that there are always at least 5″ between the ends of the planks in all adjacent rows. Leave a ½″ expansion gap between all walls and the flooring.

As you lay the planks, use a hammer or mallet and a scrap piece of flooring to force the planks tightly together and assure a snug fit (see Figure 23). Remember, be sure the adhesive has properly set up to a sticky feel before you apply it. Don't slide the planks into place, because this will cause adhesive to ooze between the boards. Rather, insert the tongue into the groove and adjust into final position. Should any adhesive get on the planks, wipe it off immediately with a rag wet with solvent. (Never apply the solvent directly to the plank, since it could affect the finish.)

Figure 20. After the floor is completed, use a 150-lb. roller for proper adhesion.

Work toward the visible wall until that section is completed. You can use a pry bar against the wall to force the last piece snug up against its adjacent course.

Avoid kneeling or walking on the newly laid planks. Use a clean piece of plywood as a kneeling board to spread your weight out. Be sure there is no excess glue on the planks before placing the plywood on top.

As you get each section covered, go over it with a 150-lb. floor roller rented from your supplier.

After you have done your original area, remove the straightedge and lay another section, as described above. Your final piece, across from your most visible wall, may need to be specially cut to fit.

After you have completed the floor, install the baseboards and any needed reducer strips, as described under parquet flooring.

TOOLS AND MATERIALS CHECKLIST

Tools For All Hardwood Floor Projects

Carpenter's pencil Circular saw
Hammer Utility knife

Heavy duty shop Eye protection
  vacuum Pry bar and wood
Fan(s) wedge
Tape measure Extension cords
Carpenter's (heavy duty)
  square Nail belt
Ear protectors 3-pronged
Respirator/face adapter (if
  mask needed)

Tools For Repairs

Variable-speed Chisel
  drill Putty knife
Drill bit stop Pry bar
Drill bits Caulking gun
Nail set Screwdriver

Materials For Repairs

Graphite (tube) Subflooring
Wood dough adhesive
8-penny finishing 2 × 4, 2 × 6, or
  nails 2 × 8 for
3/16 round head bridging
  wood screws Rags
3/4 inch
  hardwood
  flooring strips

Tools for Refinishing

Putty knife Paint tray and
Drum sander with roller
  wrenches Lamb's wool mop
Edge or disc Orbital sander
  sander Floor buffer
Paint scraper or
  block sander
Nail set

Materials for Refinishing

Duct tape Wood stain
Plastic sheets Wood sealer
Coarse-grit Polyurethane
  sandpaper Paint stick or coat
Medium-grit hanger
  sandpaper # 2 steel wool
Fine-grit machine discs
  sandpaper and pads
Tack cloth

Tools for Parquet Floors

Chalkline and Toothed trowel
  chalk 150-lb. roller
Jig saw Handsaw

Materials for Parquet Floors

Leveling Mastic or
  compound adhesive
Particle board or Parquet tiles
  luan mahogany Plywood
  plywood Reducer strip
6-penny ring Adhesive cleaning
  shank nails solvent

Tools for Plank Flooring

Chalkline and Toothed trowel
  chalk 150-lb. roller
Jig saw Handsaw

Materials for Plank Flooring

Leveling Tongue-and-
  compound groove
Particle board or planking (glue
  luan mahogany down)
  plywood Plywood
6-penny ring Reducer strip
  shank nails Adhesive cleaning
Straightedge solvent
  board
Mastic or
  adhesive

Figure 21. Planning floor installation by installing straightedge at proper distance.

CHAPTER EIGHT

Furniture Refinishing
Bringing Out the Best of the Wood

WHAT YOU WILL BE DOING

Many who want to refinish a piece of their furniture are put off by the amount of work involved. Others are oftentimes too impatient to complete the job and end up with something they either are dissatisfied with or no longer like well enough to go back and do it right. Still others are fearful of ruining a cherished table or chair.

Refinishing furniture does not have to be painful. It can even be fun. But you must first have the right attitude and realize that a thorough job cannot be completed in one day.

New materials and products for refinishing wood are frequently introduced on the market. It helps to consult your local home center or hardware store personnel for suggestions concerning the particular item you will be working on. The suggestions in this chapter are meant to serve as an overview of basic techniques. I cover two different procedures of stripping: one for items having multiple layers of paint and/or old finish; the other for stripping unpainted furniture.

A few tips on furniture repair will be covered; because, usually, every piece requiring refinishing needs some repair as well. This step should always be taken care of prior to the final staining and sealing of your furniture.

Finishing can be achieved in a variety of ways from antiquing and custom painting to the use of a simple hand-rubbed oil on bare wood. I cover only the stripping, staining, and finishing processes in this chapter, but I try to include a variety of materials for you to choose from.

BEFORE YOU BEGIN

SAFETY

Because of the caustic chemicals involved in refinishing furniture, great care must be taken to follow safe-use practices.

1. Always use the proper tool for the job at hand.

2. When working with chemicals, remember that they are flammable. Do not smoke. Extinguish any pilot lights or open flames in the vicinity.

3. Wear durable rubber or neophrene gloves, safety goggles, and long sleeves when stripping wood, to protect against splatters and chemical burns, especially to eyes.

4. Chemical strippers produce vapors which are harmful if inhaled. Provide for proper ventilation with a window fan, or do the work outside.

5. Seal all heating and air-conditioning ducts and electrical outlets when sanding indoors. Wood dust can ignite. If your project involves a lot of sanding, the basement would be a poor choice. The ventilation is inadequate, and wood dust can ruin a furnace or washing machine motor.

6. Take care in storing oily rags, which can spontaneously combust.

7. Wear ear protectors when using power tools, since some operate at noise levels that can damage hearing.

8. Always unplug your sander when changing the sandpaper.

9. Individuals with pulmonary disorders or weakness should consult with a physician before using chemical strippers.

WHAT YOU WILL NEED

Time. Time will depend on the size and complexity of your project. Be sure to allow plenty of time to complete the stripping in one day, and remember to allow for drying times for any finishes you apply.

Tools. Tools required for refinishing furniture are not very specialized. Most of them should be found in your home toolbox.

Natural bristle brushes (preferable to synthetic ones, which can melt when they come in contact with harsh chemicals)	Screwdrivers
	Wood chisels
	Files
	Syringe or putty knife
Steel wool (0000–3)	Sanding shapes
Old paint brushes	Sanding block
Paint scraper	Orbital sander
Plastic buckets	Electric drill
Putty knife	Lamb's wool pad for drill
Brass bristle brushes	Vacuum cleaner
Screwdrivers	Rubber mallet
Durable rubber gloves	Various clamps (appropriate to your project)
Safety goggles	
Canvas and plastic drop cloths	Very sharp razor blade
Squeegee	Seam roller

Materials. The materials are somewhat specialized, although many of these you will have on hand, and all of them are readily available at home centers and hardware stores.

Denatured alcohol	Waxed paper
Cotton balls	Tack cloth
Clean dry rags	Plastic sheeting
Steel wool	Masking tape
Paper towels or rags	Lacquer thinner
Newspaper	Paraffin or linseed oil
Cardboard box	Latex wood filler
Cotton swabs	Mineral spirits
Toothpicks	Stain
Sandpaper (100–120 grit)	Sanding sealer
Carpenter's wood glue	Finishing sealer
Wood dough	Paste wax

10. Keep all chemical strippers and materials out of the reach of children and animals.

11. Most older paints contain lead, the particles of which are released by any means of stripping. The proper respirator with a cartridge designed to filter lead should be worn when stripping, sanding, or scraping. A dust mask is inadequate. Keep pregnant women and children out of the area. Wash work clothes separately from other laundry.

USEFUL TERMS

Camphored. Refers to edges or corners that are worn and/or rounded with use. This condition usually enhances the piece and adds value to it.

Lacquer. A clear varnish.

Mineral spirits. An inexpensive paint thinner which cleans brushes, thins paint, cleans furniture, and removes wax.

Paraffin. A wax applied to the edges of drawers and other movable parts to prevent sticking.

Penetrating resin. A finish which darkens and penetrates the surface of the wood. This type of finish is not easily removed.

Polyurethane. A clear, acrylic finish.

Tack cloth. A sticky cloth which picks up fine dust. It is used to wipe over wood before a stain or finish is applied.

Varnish. A resinous finish used to give a glossy surface to wood.

PERMITS AND CODES

No permits are needed when refinishing furniture. Codes do not apply here.

DESIGN

The design aspect of furniture refinishing rests in your choice of pieces to strip, repair and refinish. Choose carefully for value, planning the selection to enhance the individual rooms of your home.

MOST COMMON MISTAKES

The most common mistake in furniture refinishing is failure to read and follow manufacturers' instructions for chemicals being used. Other common mistakes are listed with each specific step.

Rub out water stains with steel wool and linseed oil

Figure 1. Be sure that you need to strip the old finish. Perhaps it can be restored without stripping.

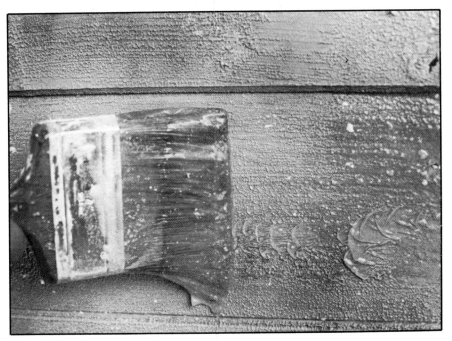

Figure 2. Brushing on a paint stripper.

135

Figure 3. Apply the stripper thoroughly to all areas.

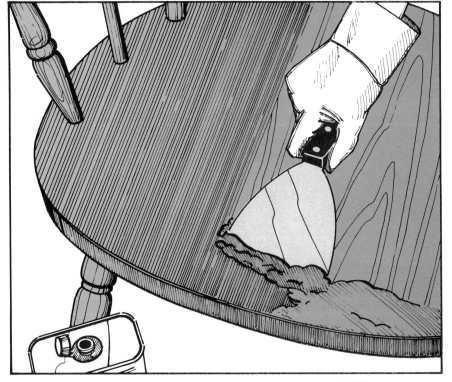

Figure 4. Wear rubber gloves when using chemical strippers to remove old finish.

STEP ONE

PREPARING THE SURFACE

Margin of Error: Not applicable

MOST COMMON MISTAKE

1. Not cleaning the surface thoroughly before refinishing.

Sometimes, if a piece of furniture is not too badly damaged, or if it is just worn, it is possible to patch up the original finish so that the authentic quality of the furniture can be saved.

Thoroughly clean the surface of the piece with a commercial wood cleaner, mineral spirits, or wax remover, to determine whether the present finish is salvageable. Then carefully look over the item to determine if a total refinishing job is necessary.

Determine which top finish was originally used. Begin by soaking a cotton ball with denatured alcohol. Apply this to an out-of-view area and let soak for ten minutes. If the finish dissolves, it is shellac. If not, apply a lacquer thinner with a brush to an out-of-view spot on the piece. If this method dissolves the finish, you know you are working with lacquer.

If neither of the above tests brings results, your piece has either a varnish or a synthetic top finish, both of which require a liquid stripper for removal.

Often surface blemishes, such as white spots and water rings, have not penetrated deeply. Use a 2/0 or 3/0 steel wool pad and a little paraffin or linseed oil to rub the spot. (Figure 1.) Rub with the grain of the wood. Once the spot is removed, wipe the surface with a dry rag and add a paste wax.

If the finish is merely worn out, you can sometimes overcoat with the same finish. (Follow the procedure outlined above to determine which finish to use.) Apply one coat and allow it to dry thoroughly. Then rub with a 2/0 or finer

0000–00 steel wool pad and wax with a paste wax. (Always test an inconspicuous spot before applying the finish to the entire piece.)

If the finish on the piece is in good condition, with only slightly damaged areas to be touched up, I recommend the reamalgamation technique. Use the appropriate solution tested in the procedure outlined above to dissolve the finish of the damaged area. Dip a natural bristle brush or fine steel wool into the solvent; then brush or gently rub it into the damaged area until the defect disappears. Apply more solvent to the area with long, light strokes — with the grain — to smooth the amalgamated finish. Once this is dry, remove any rough spots with 2/0 or 3/0 steel wool. Finish with a paste wax.

Figure 5. Use a wide broad knife to scrape off paint and stripper, but be careful not to scratch the wood.

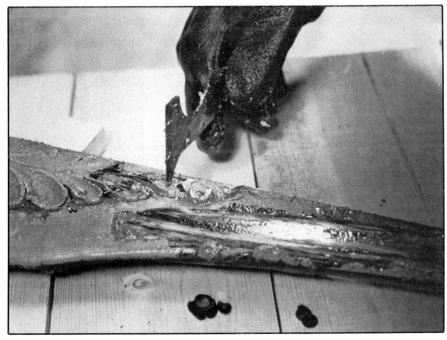

Figure 6. Using a scraping tool for hard-to-reach places.

STEP TWO

STRIPPING THE WOOD

Margin of Error: Remove paint and paint haze

MOST COMMON MISTAKES

1. Attempting to refinish a piece that is fully assembled. Break it down when you can for an easier, more thorough job.

2. Leaving the tops off of strippers while using. They evaporate quickly.

3. Failure to apply enough stripper to the surface of the work to keep it wet. As a result, it evaporates and dries out the wood. Never apply stripper in direct sunlight.

4. Not waiting the required amount of time for the stripper to work, thereby necessitating harsh scraping of the wood.

5. Spreading the stripping process over two or more days. Plan your time to complete the stripping in one day so you won't have to come back to paint that has had time to reharden.

6. Leaving some of the paint on the wood with the intention of sanding it off usually does more harm than good. Let the stripper do the work!

Unpainted Furniture

Unpainted furniture coated with only a stain, sealer, or varnish does not require a preliminary application of semi-paste stripper. Simply begin with the thin liquid stripper and follow the procedure outlined below under Painted Furniture. Use an old natural bristle brush and keep the surfaces wet with the stripper while working.

Painted Furniture

Furniture that has been painted can be stripped by hand. While it's more expensive than tank stripping (sometimes called "dipping"), the investment is a sound one. There is less chance of serious damage to the wood, and the wood is left a brighter color. This makes it easier to refinish it in a light or natural tone.

Most strippers have either a semi-paste or a thin liquid consistency, the premium agent of which is methylene chloride. When working with built-up layers of paint or varnish, begin with the semi-paste to remove 95 percent of the paint. Follow with a liquid stripper to complete the stripping. The optimum temperature for working with wood stripper is between 60 and 70 degrees.

You'll want to wear old clothes for this step. Also, durable rubber stripper gloves. Use goggles to protect your eyes from splatters. Set up a table in a place where you can work comfortably. If working indoors, protect your floors and any other furniture in the area. Cover the floor with a thick (at least 4 ml.) layer of plastic and add a canvas drop cloth on top of that. Open all the windows and provide further for adequate ventilation by installing a window fan exhausting outdoors. Have a respirator on hand and wear it if the fumes from the stripper are strong. These fumes are harmful if inhaled.

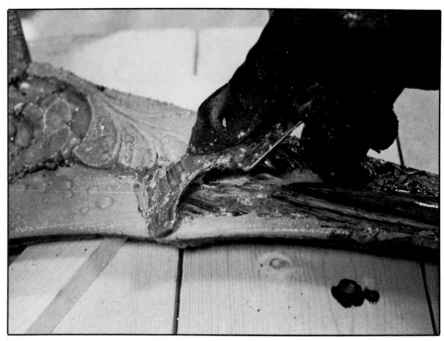

Figure 7. Getting to hard-to-reach places.

Figure 8. Brass-bristle brushes work well for removing paint and stripper.

Figure 9. Small bristle brushes for small areas.

To make the job more manageable, strip parts separately when you can. Remove mirrors from their frames prior to stripping, to avoid damaging the silvering, which would be costly to replace. By separating the drawers, doors, and other pieces, you can elevate them to a more comfortable working height.

Remove all hardware, hinges, and door handles and place them in a bucket of liquid stripper to soak. Cover the bucket to reduce evaporation of the stripper.

Pour a semi-paste stripper into another bucket to work from. I do not recommend working directly from the container, as stripper easily evaporates. The container should be kept sealed to avoid drying. Apply the paste to the surface of the wood, using an old natural bristle paint brush. (Natural bristles do not have the tendency to melt away in these harsh chemicals, as do synthetic bristles.)

Work from the top to the bottom, one section at a time. Spread the stripper liberally in one direction with the brush. Apply it thickly into the carved areas. Because stripper has a fairly fast evaporation rate, take care to keep the surface wet while the stripper is working.

Depending on the kind of stripper and the number of paint layers you need to remove, you can expect to wait from five to twenty minutes before scraping. (Read the manufacturer's instructions for application time.) The semi-paste is thick enough to cling to vertical and upside-down surfaces. It softens and lifts the paint up from the surface of the wood but does not discolor, raise the grain, or destroy the wood's natural patina.

It may take several applications to lift off all of the old finish. Practice and patience go a long way here. Always let the stripper do the work. If you labori-

Figure 10. Be sure to thoroughly clean off all the stripper.

Figure 11. A lamp can help you find any glossy areas that were missed during stripping.

ously try to scrape or chisel the paint off, the direct pressure to the scraper could cause it to gouge and damage the very wood you are trying to preserve.

When the stripper has done its work, use your scraper to lift and remove the residue. Consolidate the residue in an old cardboard box for easier clean-up. Scrapers are available with various curves and picks to make working with carvings and rounded legs less frustrating. Pipe cleaners and toothpicks are also useful. (A set of old dental tools is perfect for stripping intricate woodwork.)

Thin Liquid Stripper. Once 95 percent of the old finish is removed with the semi-paste, use another old natural bristle paint brush to apply the thin liquid stripper from another bucket. Again, keep the surfaces moist while you are working, to avoid drying out the wood. And wear your goggles for this step, since the liquid splatters much easier than does the paste.

When the liquid has had a few minutes to work (read the manufacturer's instructions for proper time frame), use a brass-bristled brush to work the solvent into the carvings and corners. Steel wool can be used for this step as well, but the brass brush is superior. The bristles don't break down and get caught in the grain like steel wool.

Keep two separate buckets of the liquid on hand — one to use over and over again while scrubbing and the other to use for a final rinse. Once the brass bristles have broken up the remaining paint, the old paint brush makes a great agitation tool to rinse the paint away.

The final rinse with the clean stripper is important. It will remove any film or "paint haze" caused by a little of the paint left in the previous bath of solvent. Never use a water rinse. It tends to raise the grain of the wood.

An unpainted squeegee works very well to clean off flat surfaces. A putty knife wrapped in a paper towel works well in corners and carvings.

After the final rinse, look over the piece carefully, making sure that all of the paint and finish have been removed. If there was a varnish coat underneath, look for any dark spots or "glazed" areas that are still slightly glossy. Work in a well-lit area, with at least 100-watt lighting, to detect any flaws. A high-intensity desk lamp could be useful here (Figure 11).

I do not recommend leaving even the slightest amount of paint or finish to sand off later. Sanding stain, finish, paint, or sealer is always a difficult job and can cause more harm than good.

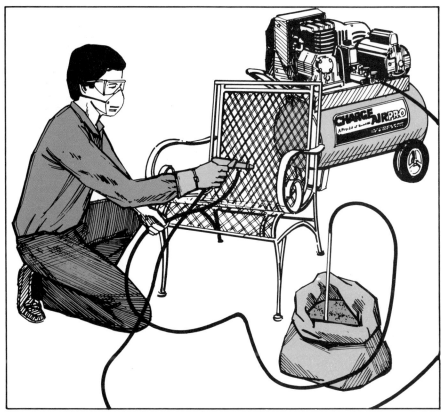

Figure 12. You can use a sandblaster to refinish metal furniture.

NOTE: For those of you interested in refinishing wrought iron or similar types of furnishings, I recommend you acquire a portable air compressor fitted with a sandblasting apparatus. This type of system will enable you to thoroughly strip (and simultaneously sand) an item of such complexity. The same air compressor, fitted with a paint spraying unit, is also the most economical and exacting method of recovering wrought iron.

TIP: Never use water as a final rinse, since it tends to raise the grain of the wood.

Figure 13. Use a putty knife to fill in cracks. Match the colors.

STEP THREE

MAKING REPAIRS

Margin of Error: Exact

MOST COMMON MISTAKE

1. Failing to make **all** necessary repairs before refinishing.

Although most of us look over our furniture carefully before beginning the stripping process to detect any repairs that may be needed, it is even more important to check again after stripping for conditions that may have been hidden under layers of old paint and varnish. Any repair that must be done on wood should be completed after stripping but before sanding and staining.

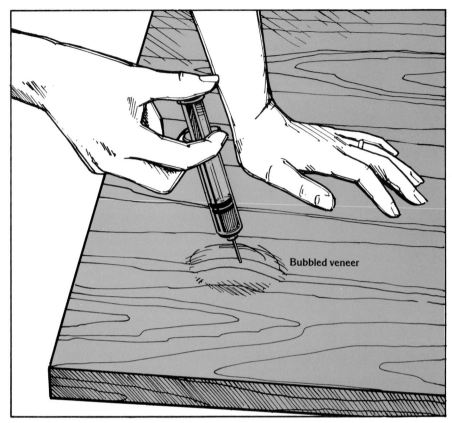

Figure 14. Using a syringe to squirt glue below bubbled veneer.

Figure 15. Repair veneer by gluing under the area and then applying weights.

Veneer

If you know that you will be working with veneer (thin, finished layers of wood), you don't want to allow the stripper to remain on the surface too long. It can seep into the cracks and lift the veneer by dissolving the adhesive.

Detect loose veneer edges by tapping your fingernail on it and listening for a change in sound. Before gluing, clean and scrape away the old glue and dirt at the contact points, being careful not to split the veneer more than it already is. Fill in the crack of the veneer with a small bit of carpenter's glue slipped in on the end of a putty knife. Or purchase an inexpensive (25 to 50 cents at a pharmacy) 20-gauge needle syringe, which slides under the veneer neatly and gently to apply a small amount of glue. Press down on the repair and wipe up any excess glue that oozes out of the crack. Cover the area with waxed paper and law a weight on it so that the surfaces are firmly pressed together while the glue is setting up (Figure 15).

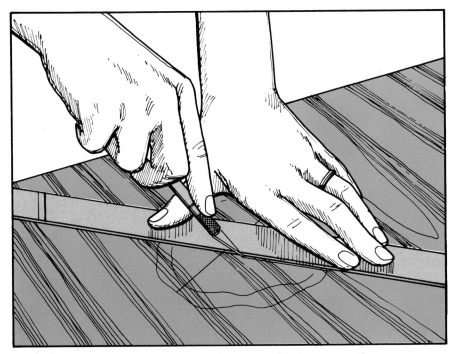

Figure 16. Using a small razor knife and a straightedge to make a crosscut on a bubble in the veneer.

of the clamp and the legs to prevent damage to the wood. (Figure 19.) Allow the glue to dry thoroughly before the final sanding and finishing phase.

Chips, Cracks, Nicks and Screw Holes

Any undesired holes or chips in the wood should be filled in with wood dough prior to sanding and finishing. Wipe a dab of the wood dough over and into the blemished area with your finger. Look for one that dries fairly quickly, can sand easily, and absorbs stain. Wood dough is also available in various wood colors.

To disguise the wood dough after sanding, simulate the wood grain with a sharp crayon, or use a fine artist brush with the matching color.

I recommend a latex wood filler for repair of splits and dents. It accepts stain and resists shrinkage.

When there are bubbles, cut into the veneer with a sharp razor blade using a steel rule for guidance. Make an "X" cut; neither cut should be with the grain of the wood (Figure 16). Then clean, fill, and weight down the surfaces, as outlined above. Use a seam roller to press the veneer in place.

Always allow ample time for the adhesive to set and dry before continuing the refinishing process.

Chairs

Here's a tip on checking the condition of wooden chairs. Kneel on the seat while holding on to the back of the chair. Then rock gently back and forth to detect any loose joints. Old and brittle glue is common with old chairs.

Dismantle any loose joints prior to stripping. Always use your hands or a rubber mallet to prevent denting and marring when dismantling furniture. (Figure 17.)

After stripping, sand the joint. Reassemble the leg and stretcher, adding carpenter's wood glue before inserting the stretcher into the hole. Clamp the legs together with a bar clamp. Place small scraps of wood between the jaws

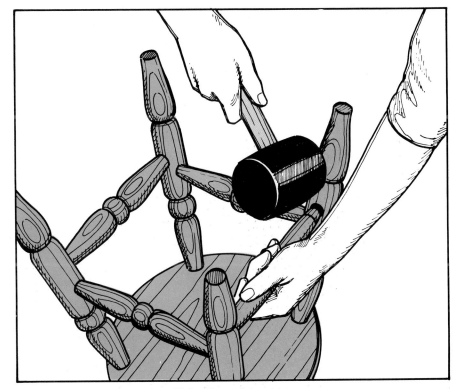

Figure 17. Dismantle by hand or with a rubber mallet.

143

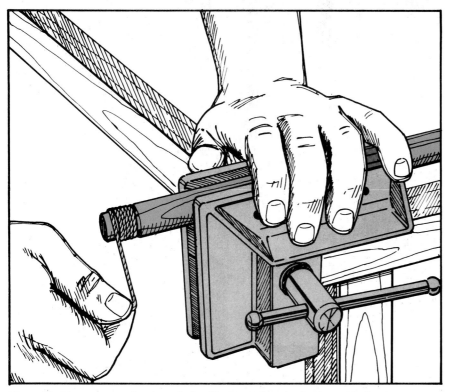

Figure 18. You can wrap a dowel or spindle with string to increase its size and make a loose fit snug. Coat with glue before fastening.

Wood scraps for padding

Figure 19. Large items can be clamped with bar clamps.

SANDING THE WOOD

Margin of Error: Sand enough to obtain desired finish yet not enough to gouge the wood or sand through the veneer

MOST COMMON MISTAKES

1. Sanding with an orbital sander that oscillates at less than 8,400 orbits per minute. This leaves swirl marks and scratches.

2. Refinishing requires time and patience. Plan enough time between steps to allow the glue to set and dry, the sanding to be thorough, and the finishes to dry properly. High humidity can more than double recommended drying time.

3. Gouging the wood with a belt sander or sanding discs in an electric drill.

Stripping closes the grain of the wood to the penetration of stain and finish. Sanding reopens the grain, evens out any discoloration that may have been left by a previous stain, and erases any scratches or blemishes in the surface.

Most of your furniture refinishing will require a sandpaper of 100 to 120 grits. Change the paper frequently. Once it begins to wear out it is no longer sanding, but polishing, which will close the grain again. To make your sandpaper last longer, use an old toothbrush to clean out the clogged sandpaper.

For all-purpose refinishing, the ideal tool is an orbital sander that oscillates at around 8,400 orbits per minute (Figure 24). This speed assures elimination of swirl marks and scratches in the wood.

Improving Your Home

Over the course of several years (and several home improvements and repairs), a house takes on the personality of its occupants. Whenever you undertake home improvements, try and keep that sense of personality consistent. As you walk from the outside of the house to the interior, bear in mind how the environments relate to each other. Progressing from the exterior of this converted schoolhouse to the interior foyer, you would not want too dramatic a change of style (you wouldn't want reflective mylar wallpaper in the entrance hall, for instance). Study your transitions from room to room and strive for a subtle and controlled change of environment.

When laying a vinyl floor, remember to consider the two crucial elements of design: color and pattern. Choose a color in the room that you want to emphasize. The pattern you select should be determined by the amount of space you are covering and the patterns already present in the room. A large, open space calls for a large, repeated pattern that will draw the room together. For smaller spaces, a more pleasing effect will be accomplished with a smaller pattern.

This combination living room/dining room (above) is drawn together gracefully with the use of the repeating floor pattern. The light pink floor accents the color scheme used throughout the room.

Contrasting patterns can be used to dramatic effect, as in this foyer, where the color *tones* are kept consistent between wall and floor. The square repeating floor pattern with the vertically striped wallpaper stands as a quiet background to the solid white loveseat.

Ceilings can exert a powerful influence over a room. With the new lightweight tiles and panels available you can install ceilings yourself.

The orderly tile ceiling in this formal dining room provides an interesting counterpoint to the dentil border and vertical styling of the woodwork.

A small and somewhat crowded room like this kitchen can be opened up remarkably just by raising the ceiling.

This handsome room addition accommodates a great deal of sunshine. In moderate climates, the use of well-insulated glass allows for plenty of sunshine with little heat loss at night.

Using sunlight wisely can save a significant amount on your heating and cooling bills. To stay warm, you'll want to let the sunlight in without letting warm air out. There are many ways to accomplish this task, from window insulator film to double- or triple-pane insulating glass. For comfort's sake, make sure all of your windows are energy-efficient.

As shown here, a simple and quite attractive approach to making your windows energy-efficient is the window quilt. The quilts can be purchased in numerous patterns, and when the shade is drawn the magnetic strips along the quilt's sides form an airtight seal.

The wallpaper used in this setting is extended to include the beams along the ceiling. The repetition of the border pattern adds a peculiar charm to the room.

When using home improvement material, give your imagination free rein. In the examples below, note the creative use of wallpaper and tile.

The tiles used on this kitchen floor are both attractive and easy to clean. With that in mind, why limit yourself to tiling the floor? The same tile used on the wall is both practical and beautiful.

Many contemporary wallpaper designs are no longer room specific. That is, the patterns are such that they can be used in kitchen, living room, bedroom, or bath. The small, simple, geometric patterns tend to work best on surfaces that are broken up into many small segments. On large expanses of wall they can be somewhat overwhelming.

This family workroom (left) is nicely unified by the wallpaper used here. A few years ago this deep-green color would have been thought of as too dark for a workroom. Today there is virtually no limit to the range of hue for wallpapering.

The contemporary wallpaper used in this country kitchen (lower left) gives the rural room a sense of modern sophistication.

The attractive lights in this kitchen are located to illuminate the principal work areas. The wooden ceiling adds warmth to the brilliant whiteness of the room.

Overhead lighting has a subtle but powerful effect on the ambience of a room. Traditional overhead lights, usually placed in the center of the ceiling, are largely being replaced by track lights and lights that give a more directed illumination.

This recessed wall system is made a focal point of the living room by the unusual track lighting system recessed into the ceiling.

The design of your sundeck can range from the simple to the ornate. Aside from the amount of money you have to spend, these are some key issues for you to consider: How will the deck be used? What will be placed on the deck? Should the railings be designed with planters or seats? How large should the deck be?

The simple design of this redwood deck allows for plenty of access from both the house and the yard. There are stairs near the house, but the deck is low enough to the ground that people can step right over the edge.

The arbor design overhead gives this deck the feeling of a room without blocking out wind or sun.

The multi-platform design of this deck actually looks more complicated than it really is. When combined with the tall wooden fence, this layout assures a great deal of privacy.

(I do not recommend a belt sander or sanding discs attached to a drill. These gouge the wood and leave obvious sanding marks.)

You need not press down on the sander — its own weight will do the work. Just keep the pressure equal and guide the sander in even sweeps, always sanding with the grain. When sanding veneers, remember that most are very thin ($\frac{1}{32}''$), so be careful.

Use a sanding block with 100 to 120 grit sandpaper for smaller areas. A rubber or padded sanding block has a little more give for odd areas. It also helps to have some different wood shapes (round, curved, etc.) available while you work. You can wrap the sandpaper around these when sanding curves or recessed molding (Figure 25). Remember to apply even pressure and sand with the grain whenever possible. Change the sandpaper frequently. And be sure to remove any glue that might have remained on the wood where you made repairs.

Where wood dough has been applied, take care to sand the surface flush so as not to leave a halo when you stain.

Once the sanding process is complete you will want to clean the piece and the surrounding area thoroughly. Vacuum up all the dust and go over the piece(s) you are refinishing with a tack cloth to pick up any remaining fine dust.

TIP: To check on the condition of wooden chairs, kneel on the seat while holding on to the back of the chair, then rock gently back and forth to detect any loose joints.

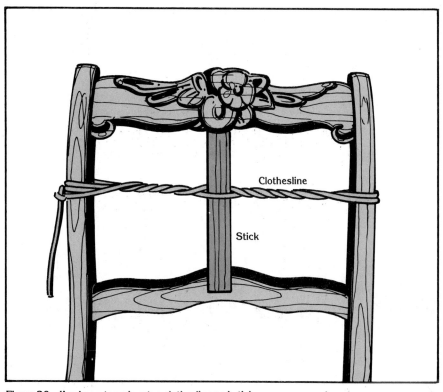

Figure 20. Used as a tourniquet, a clothesline and stick can serve as a clamp.

Clothesline

Stick

Figure 21. A hand screw won't mar the wood and can adjust to various angles.

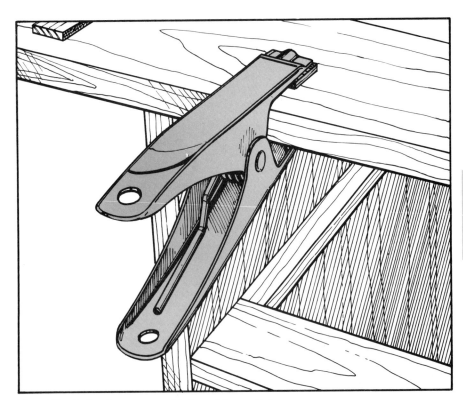

Figure 22. Spring clamps are useful when gluing small pieces.

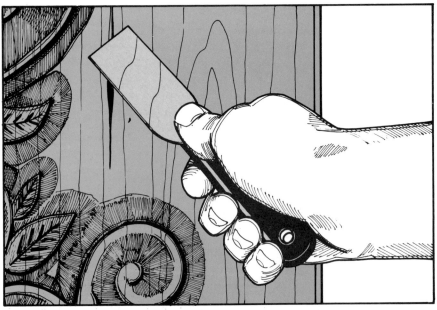

Figure 23. Fill splits with proper-colored wood filler.

STEP FIVE

STAINING

Margin of Error: Apply stain properly to create even coloration

MOST COMMON MISTAKE

1. Leaving the stain on too long — five minutes is a sufficient test time. You can always apply more.

It is your personal preference whether or not to stain. Many people prefer the natural colors of mahogany, cherry, rosewood, teak, oak, and maple. Staining is used to enrich the grain pattern of the wood or to darken the overall tone. Stains must always be applied prior to the finishing seal. Whether staining or just applying a clear finish, provide for adequate ventilation and lighting.

Take the time to test the stains and finishes on your wood. Species of wood react differently to stains and finishes. If it is a chest of drawers you are working with; test on the inside surfaces of the drawers. This will also seal against moisture and cut down on swelling and cracking.

TIP: To find out what wood will look like without stain but just with a clear finish, wet a section of it with mineral spirits. It dries quickly without raising the grain.

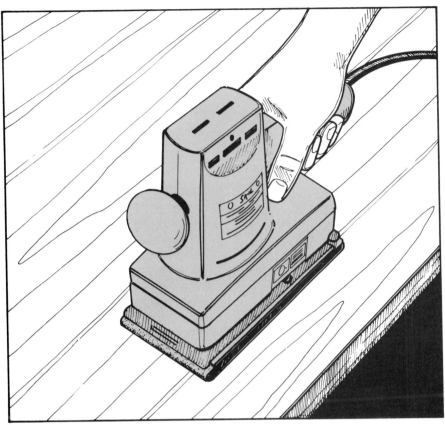

Figure 24. An orbital sander makes the job go much quicker.

control, leave the stain on no more than five minutes at a time. You can always add more.

Remove the excess stain with a clean rag. A good way to be sure you have removed all of the excess is to wipe it once again *across the grain* with another clean rag. If there are no streaks, it's clean.

Allow the stain to completely dry before continuing.

TIP: Once the brass bristles of your brushes have broken up the remaining paint, the old paint brush makes a great agitation tool to rinse the paint away.

You can find out what the wood will look like without a stain, just a clear finish, by wetting a section of it with mineral spirits. This dries quickly and does not raise the grain as water does.

Decide on a stain color by testing different shades on a portion of the piece that would not be seen — on the inside of a chair frame, under the seat, or inside a drawer. After choosing the stain, apply it evenly to the clean, dry wood. Use a natural bristle brush, which works the stain into carvings and corners easier than a rag.

Be sure you cover every inch of the raw wood. The longer you leave the stain on, the deeper it will penetrate and the darker the final color will be. For

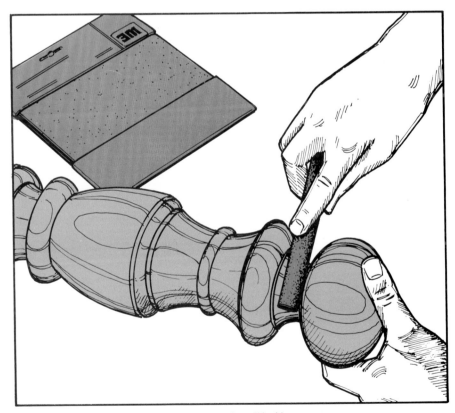

Figure 25. Using a dowel and sandpaper to sand small inside curves.

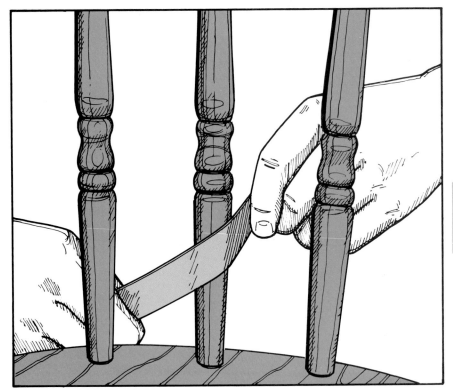

Figure 26. Strip sandpaper is handy for small curved areas.

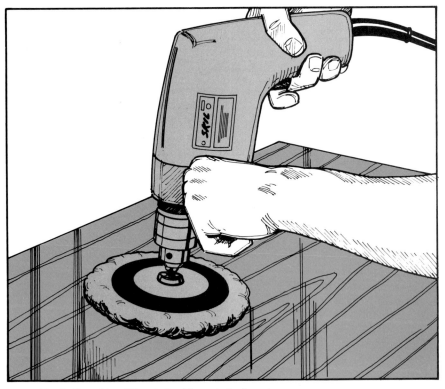

Figure 27. Buffing with a drill and a lamb's wool attachment.

STEP SIX

APPLYING THE SEALER

Margin of Error: Not applicable

MOST COMMON MISTAKE

1. Not letting the sealer dry before applying the next coat.

1. A sanding sealer should be applied after a stain. This is a transparent sealer put on the wood to firm up the fuzz of wood fibers which stick up after stripping and sanding. Sanding sealer was invented to solve the problem of shellac and varnish. It is also a solution to long drying times between varnish layers. (Apply one coat of sanding sealer and one coat of varnish.) Let the sealer dry overnight.

2. This sealer will make it easier to sand the wood smoother the next day, prior to applying the final finishing coat. Use an orbital sander (Figure 24) and the various sanding shapes (Figure 25) with a 220-grit sandpaper. The smoother the finish the longer it will last, because of less friction in cleaning and less places where dirt can lodge.

3. Go over the piece with a vacuum and tack cloth before continuing.

WARNING: Sanding sealer is not meant to be used before a polyurethane finish. Polyurethane will not adhere to the sealer and will peel off.

TIP: Do not use sanding sealer before using a polyurethane finish. The polyurethane will not adhere to the sealer and will peel off.

STEP SEVEN

APPLYING THE FINISH

Margin of Error: Properly apply finish to create desired effect and smooth finish

MOST COMMON MISTAKES

1. Neglecting to apply the finish smoothly, leaving streaks and ridges.

2. Not allowing the finish to dry sufficiently between coats.

3. Shaking or stirring a clear finish too fast, creating bubbles which show on the finished piece.

Finishes range from lacquers, varnishes, and polyurethanes to penetrating resins, catalytic sealers, and natural waxes. These come in various degrees of sheen from high gloss and semi-gloss or satin to a matte or dull finish. All have different manufacturer's application and drying instructions to follow.

Your chosen finish should be durable, waterproof, and good looking. One with a slow drying time will give you more control over any buildup or lap marks that could cause problems. These can occur with a quick-drying finish.

The hardeners in some finishes settle to the bottom, so it's important that you stir well, but slowly and gently so as not to create bubbles.

For easy application, work on a horizontal surface at a comfortable level as much as possible. Apply the finish with a natural bristle brush in a steady and smooth manner. Do not overload the applicator. It is better to return to your well frequently. Too much finish and an aggressive application can stir up bubbles, which can dry and pimple the surface.

When working into carvings and crevices, take care to apply a uniform coat with a minimum of runs. After the finish is applied, go over the work with a dry brush to even out the beaded areas and depressions. Follow the manufacturer's recommendation for the number of coats and drying time.

For a finishing touch, apply one or two coats of fine paste wax, to protect the finish and increase the luster. Buff thoroughly between wax coats with a lamb's wool buffing pad on your electric drill (Figure 27). Renew the finish from time to time. A wax finish is rich looking, but the wax can build up over time. Use a wax remover to take off the old wax. Then apply a new coat and buff again.

The final step is careful reassembly of the pieces and the cleaned hardware.

TIP: If working indoors, cover the floor with a thick (at least 4 ml.) layer of plastic and add a canvas drop cloth on top of that.

TOOLS AND MATERIALS CHECKLIST

Tools for Cleaning and Testing

Natural bristle brush	Steel wool (0000–3)

Materials for Cleaning and Testing

Denatured alcohol	Paraffin or linseed oil
Cotton balls	Clean dry rags
Lacquer thinner	Paste wax

Tools for Stripping

Old paint brushes	Durable rubber gloves
Paint scraper	Safety goggles
Plastic buckets	Canvas and plastic drop cloths
Putty knife	
Brass bristle brushes	
Screwdrivers	Squeegee

Materials for Stripping

Steel wool	Cardboard box
Paper towels or rags	Cotton swabs
	Toothpicks
Newspaper	

Tools for Repairs and Sanding

Screwdrivers	Vacuum cleaner
Wood chisels	Rubber mallet
Files	Various clamps (appropriate to your project)
Syringe or putty knife	
Sanding shapes	Very sharp razor blade
Sanding block	
Orbital sander	Seam roller

Materials for Repairs and Sanding

Sandpaper (100–120 grit)	Waxed paper
	Tack cloth
Carpenter's wood glue	Plastic sheeting
	Masking tape
Wood dough	Latex wood filler

Tools for Refinishing

Natural bristle brushes	Electric drill
Orbital sander	Lamb's wool pad for drill
Sanding blocks and shapes	

Materials for Refinishing

Mineral spirits	Sanding sealer
Stain	Sandpaper
Paper towels	Finishing sealer
Clean rags	Paste wax

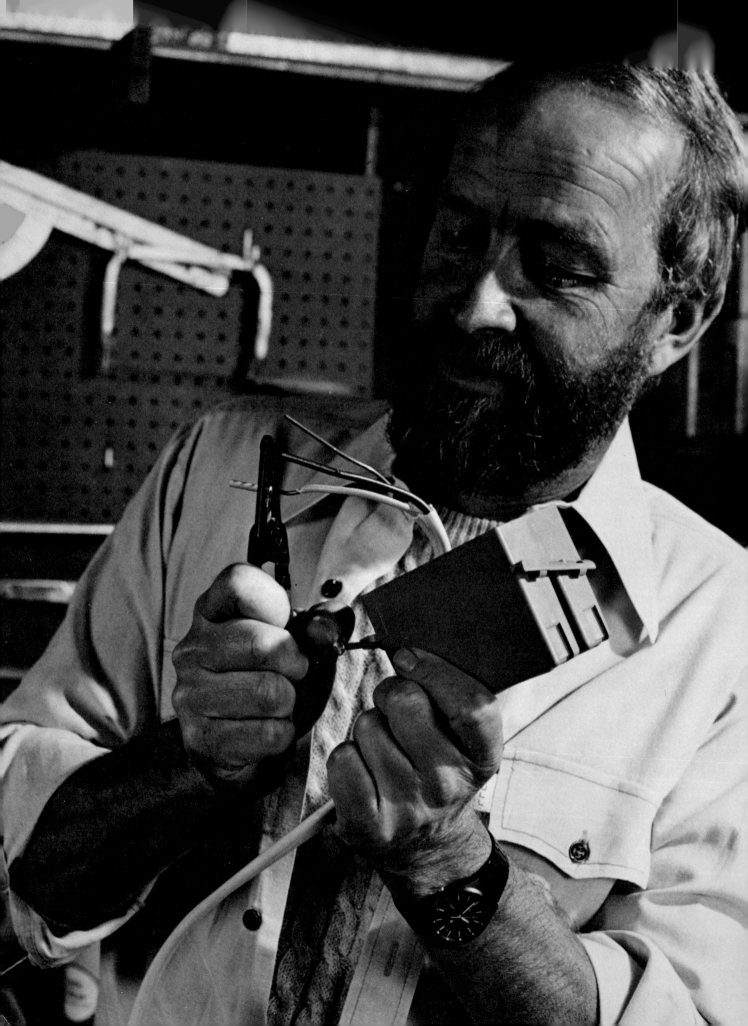

CHAPTER NINE

Electricity

Lights, Outlets, and the Essentials of Home Wiring

WHAT YOU WILL BE DOING

This chapter will help you discover how easy it is for you as a do-it-yourselfer to work with the 110/120 volt electrical system found in your own home. 110/120 volt is relatively simple to wire and connect and does not require a lot of special equipment or handling.

*Electricity can be an intimidating concept for many because of the potential danger. You can virtually eliminate that danger with a little knowledge and proper safety practices. However, regardless of how much knowledge you have, **never** become lax in dealing with an electrical system, or it can be deadly.*

*The information in this chapter is meant to give you an understanding of several common electrical situations that you might encounter. Because of the many options and variations in this area, it is not intended to be a complete guide to electrical work. **Never take chances with electrical work.** If you feel you need more information, consult an electrician or a more detailed reference book. If you plan any extensive electrical work, or to evaluate the condition of an older electrical system, I recommend you seek a professional.*

BEFORE YOU BEGIN

SAFETY

Safety is of utmost importance when working with electricity. Develop safe work habits and stick to them. Be very careful with electricity. It may be invisible, but it can be dangerous if not understood and respected.

1. Safety glasses or goggles should be worn whenever power tools are used, especially if you wear contact lenses.

2. Make sure the power is off at the breaker box before doing any electrical work.

3. Always work in a clean, dry area free from anything wet.

4. Wires should only be connected at accessible junction boxes. Never splice wires together and conceal them within a wall without a junction box.

5. Never attempt to strip wires with a knife. Aside from endangering your fingers, you will nick the wire metal, which will create an electrical hazard.

6. Ground fault circuit interrupter outlets should be used under damp conditions (basements, bathrooms, outdoors, etc.), as required by the National Electric Code.

7. Don't create fire hazards by overloading an outlet or an extension cord.

8. Avoid electrical shock by mapping and marking your switch and outlet boxes. Put the map on the door of the main power service panel.

9. Leave a warning message that you are working on the circuit at the service panel, and tape the circuit breaker in the off position. With a fuse box, take the fuse out.

10. Never change the size of a fuse or breaker in a circuit.

11. Be certain your connector is CO/ALR rated when you splice aluminum

Figure 1. Some typical tools needed for electrical work.

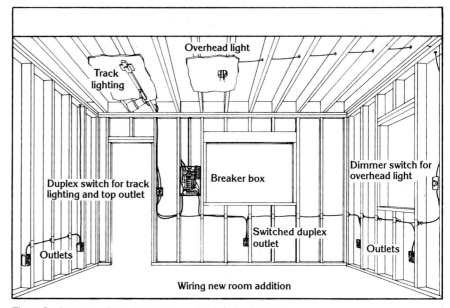

Figure 2. Anatomy of a typical electrical circuit for a new room.

wire. If it is marked CU/ALR, use only copper wire. Do not use aluminum wire with push terminals; use only copper or copper-clad aluminum wire.

12. Always correct the problem that caused a fuse or circuit breaker to blow *before* replacing the fuse or circuit breaker.

13. Replace wiring that shows signs of fraying or deterioration.

14. Avoid breaking your knuckles by bracing the powerful right-angle drill so that it cannot spin around if it gets stuck while drilling.

15. Before working with wires or electrical connections, check them with a voltage tester to be sure they are dead.

16. Plumbing and gas pipes are often used to ground electrical systems. Never touch them while working with electricity.

17. Don't use metal ladders with overhead electricity.

18. Use the proper protection, take precautions, and plan ahead. Never bypass safety to save money or to rush a project.

USEFUL TERMS

Ampere. Measures the number of electrically charged particles that flow past a given point on a circuit (per second).

Breaker box (breaker panel). Houses the circuit breakers or fuses; distributes power to various parts of your house.

Circuit. All wiring controlled by one fuse or circuit breaker.

Circuit breaker. Protective device for each circuit, which automatically cuts off power from the main breaker in the event of an overload or short. Only a regulated amount of current can pass through the breaker before it will "trip."

Fish tape. A long, flexible metal strip with a formed hook (to which you fasten the cable) or wire to pull through walls, raceway, or conduit.

Main breaker. Turns the power entering your home through the breaker box on or off. This is sometimes found in the breaker box, or it may be in a separate box and at another location.

Neutral bus bar. The bar to which the neutral wire is connected in the breaker box.

Roughing-in. Placement of outlets, switches and lights prior to actual electrical hook-up.

Volt. Measures the current pressure at receptacles and lights. Average household voltage is 120.

Watt. The rate at which an electrical device (light bulb, appliance, etc.) consumes energy. Watts = volts × amps.

WHAT YOU WILL NEED

Time.   The time needed will depend on the scope of the project.

Tools.   There are some special (although inexpensive) tools required for use with electricity.

Long-nose (needlenose) pliers	Wire stripper
Wire cutters	Colored tape
Electric drill	Voltage tester
Fish tape	Continuity tester
Cable stripper	Right-angle drill, which can be rented.

Other tools from your household toolbox include:

Tape measure	Combination square
Screwdriver	Utility light
Chalkline	Safety glasses or goggles
Hammer	Keyhole saw
Circular saw	Utility knife
Chisel	Pry bar
Hacksaw	

Materials.   Depending on the extent of wiring you will be undertaking, your list may include these materials:

Grounded receptacles	Track lights and fittings
Switches	Dimmer switch
Various junction boxes	Waterproof junction boxes
Nail guards	Ground fault interrupters
Wire nuts	Conduit
Horseshoe nails (electrical staples)	Cable
Push terminals	Silicon caulking
Breakers	

PERMITS AND CODES

Most states and municipalities use, and have additions to, the National Electric Code (NEC). Always consult the office of your local building inspector to determine what permits or special provisions must be met. All electrical work must pass local codes, no matter how small the job. Be sure to get the proper permits, and be certain that you are clear on how to do your work so that it will pass code. Local codes may differ, so don't rely on the information outlined here. It may not pass local code. Obtain a copy of local building codes by contacting the Building Inspectors' Association in your state capital, or check with the building inspector at your county court house or your city Building Department.

Some of the work may need to be done by a licensed electrical contractor. Never are inspectors more fearful of homeowners doing their own work than with electrical systems. The chances for electrocution, or a house fire resulting from faulty wiring, are great. Inspectors check electrical work very carefully. And they should. So be sure all work is done neatly, to code, and in the manner inspectors are used to seeing it done.

DESIGN

A successful wiring project requires a plan so that you know exactly where you want your outlets, switches, and fixtures to be placed.

Whether you are adding a room or rewiring an old one, don't skimp on the receptacles. Aside from it being dangerous to overload outlets with extension cords and adapters, it can be just plain frustrating to have dark corners where you most need the light. Code usually requires 12′ or less between outlets on the same wall. In this way, 6′ cord on an appliance or lamp can always reach an outlet without an extension cord. It will look better if you plan your outlets all to be at the same height. Again, this may be determined by local code.

If there are two entrances to the room, plan for a light switch at both doors. Place switches on the unhinged side of the door. Determine the most direct route for fixtures, and route them accordingly.

Draw a rough floor plan and note the location of all receptacles, switches, and fixtures. Such a plan will assist you in making up your materials list and in calculating the amount of cable you will need.

MOST COMMON MISTAKES

While it is easy to make mistakes when working with electricity, it is just as easy to avoid them. The single most important mistake to avoid is neglecting to turn off the power before beginning. Other mistakes include:

1. Not making a plan for the work being done.

2. Overloading circuits by plugging too many appliances into an outlet, or by using an inadequate extension cord. (See the section on the Breaker Box.)

3. Not labeling circuits at the service panel.

4. Not using UL approved materials.

5. Routing the wiring in an inefficient manner.

6. Mounting outlets and switches without assuring that they are flush with the final wall covering.

7. Not using the correct junction box for the wiring to be installed.

8. Not using weatherproof boxes for outdoor fixtures.

9. Neglecting to seal around holes drilled through exterior walls.

10. Forgetting to add nail guards where needed.

11. Not having your work inspected at critical points.

12. Neglecting to follow local code.

BASIC WIRING

STEP ONE

ROUGHING IN

Margin of Error: ¼"

Junction boxes for outlets, switches, and lights are "roughed in" before the fixtures themselves are installed.

TIP: If the box you wish to extend from has reached its capacity and you cannot find a second one from which to run the new cable, simply replace the box with a larger and deeper one.

STEP TWO

PLACING THE BOXES

Margin of Error: ¼"

Choose the correct junction boxes (where two or more wires are joined together) for your needs. Check your electrical code for local recommendations. They should be UL approved and have the right dimensions to hold the wiring, outlets, and connectors you will be using.

Use a ruler or other object of appropriate length (screwdriver) to rest the boxes on when establishing installation

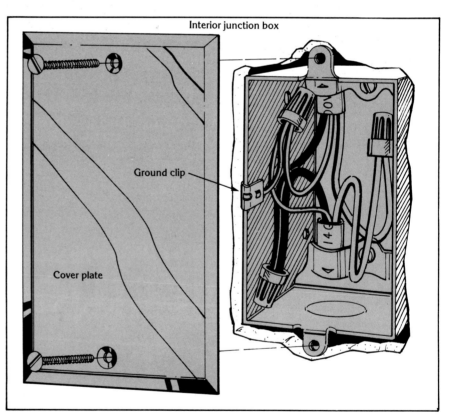

Figure 3. Use a junction box and blank face slate to join two lengths of wire.

Figure 4. Using a screwdriver to set a uniform height to the outlet boxes.

STEP THREE

PREPARING THE STUDS FOR WIRE

*Margin of Error: Exact — **Always** wire according to code — No room for error!*

Drilling with a right-angle drill and an auger bit is the most common way to run the wire through interior, uninsulated walls. Some of the larger drills have right-angle attachments, or you can rent a right-angle drill from a local tool rental establishment.

Drill your holes dead center in the studs. Brace yourself and the cumbersome drill so that it does not spin around if it binds.

Notching rather than drilling the studs works best when you have insulation you don't want to compress. To notch,

1. Use a chalkline to snap two lines 1″ apart across the studs. These will indicate the path the wire will follow.

2. Use a circular saw set to cut ½″ notches at those lines on each stud.

3. Then use a chisel to carefully remove those blocks.

4. After placing the cable, cover the notches with nail guards to prevent accidental nailing into the wire (Figure 5).

points (Figure 4). Assure that your boxes will be flush with final wall covering by holding a small piece of the covering (i.e., drywall or paneling material) between the box and wall stud while attaching the box. Check code for height at which to install switch boxes.

Remove the knockout(s) in each box in the direction of the most efficient route for the cable to run.

Figure 5. Be sure to install metal nail guards to protect wires from nails. Note notched stud.

STEP FOUR

INSTALLING THE WIRING

Margin of Error: ¼″

Local and national codes require wire that is insulated and is the most efficient size for the appropriate application. The most commonly used interior wiring is a 12- or 14-gauge NM (nonmetallic) sheathed cable, sometimes called "Romex." Within the cable are plastic-coated copper wires, colored for each function.

Hot wires, usually black (sometimes red or blue), carry the power. Neutral wires, usually white, return the power. Grounding wires of bare copper (sometimes green or green and yellow) provide a path to the ground when an electrical failure occurs.

Beginning at the breaker box, expose enough wiring to reach the breaker switch and neutral bus bar. Use a cable stripper to prevent cutting the plastic coating on the wires (Figure 7).

Knock out a box tab that will provide a direct route to the switch for the wiring. Knock out the tab at the junction box that provides the closest connection for each separate cable.

Pull the wire and secure with a cable connector. Make sure that only the uncut sheating is clamped at this opening.

Splice the cable back far enough to allow at least 6″ of lead wire to stick out of the face of the box.

Push the wire through each hole and roll the wire within the notches of the studs, keeping the wire smooth and free from kinks. Secure it with horseshoe nails at the notches. Local code will tell you how close to the junction box the first horseshoe nail must be (usually 8″), and how often the wire must be supported (usually every 4½′).

If, for any reason, you find that a wire does not reach from one junction box to another, do not tape two wires to-

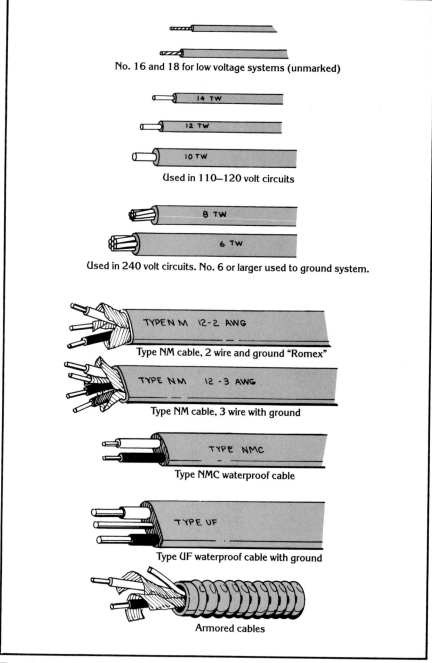

No. 16 and 18 for low voltage systems (unmarked)

14 TW

12 TW

10 TW

Used in 110–120 volt circuits

8 TW

6 TW

Used in 240 volt circuits. No. 6 or larger used to ground system.

TYPE NM 12-2 AWG
Type NM cable, 2 wire and ground "Romex"

TYPE NM 12-3 AWG
Type NM cable, 3 wire with ground

TYPE NMC
Type NMC waterproof cable

TYPE UF
Type UF waterproof cable with ground

Armored cables

Figure 6. Examples of various types of wire.

gether to make it longer. Separate wires should only be connected at junction boxes that will be placed in the wall. It is a good idea, and often required by code, to make these junction boxes accessible by placing a solid coverplate over a junction that will not make use of a receptacle. Try to play it safe and use a wire that is long enough to reach.

Provide at least 6″ of wire to spare at each end. Local code may vary on this length, so be sure to check. It is a good

idea to label both ends of each wire with colored tape so you can always determine where it leads.

Where there is less than 1¼″ between the face of the stud and the wiring, nail guards should be placed on the studs to protect the wire from any nails or screws that will attach the wall covering.

Now it is time to call in the inspector to check your work, before you complete the connections.

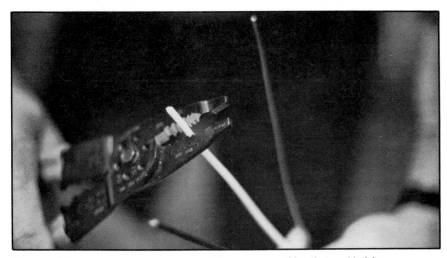

Figure 7. Using a wire stripper is mandatory. Do not use anything that could nick the wire.

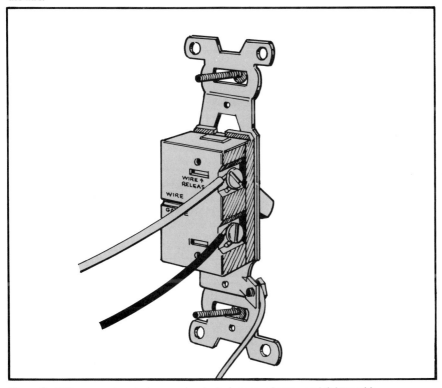

Figure 8. With a screw terminal, wrap wire clockwise around screw and tighten with a screwdriver.

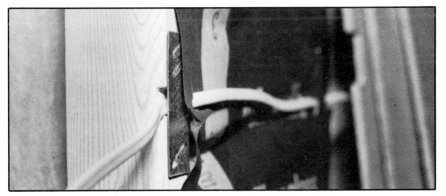

Figure 9. Be sure to cover wire with nail guards to protect them from nails.

STEP FIVE

PLACING THE TERMINALS FOR RECEPTACLES AND SWITCHES

Margin of Error: No room for error

Push terminals make connecting the wiring easy, but they should only be used for copper or copper-clade wire — never for aluminum. Strip away insulation to the length indicated on the strip gauge when you push the color-coded wires into the correct push terminal. The terminal automatically clamps down when the wire goes in, so the fit is nice and tight. To release, you need only insert a small screwdriver into the release slot.

If you choose to use a screw-type terminal, strip only enough insulation for the bare end to be wrapped three-quarters of the way around the screw. With long-nose pliers, make a loop on the bare end wire to hook clockwise around the terminal screw (Figure 8).

The white or neutral wire connects to the silver side of the outlet, and the black or hot wire connects to the brass side of the outlet. The bare grounding wire connects to the green screw in the bottom of the outlet. Bend wires and push switch or receptacle into the box and screw in place.

TIP: A dimmer switch installs just like any other switch. The only difference you may find on some of them is the presence of wire leads rather than screw terminals. Use wire nuts to fasten the two ends together, matching the color-coded wires.

Figure 10. Stripping away the sheathing to expose three inner wires.

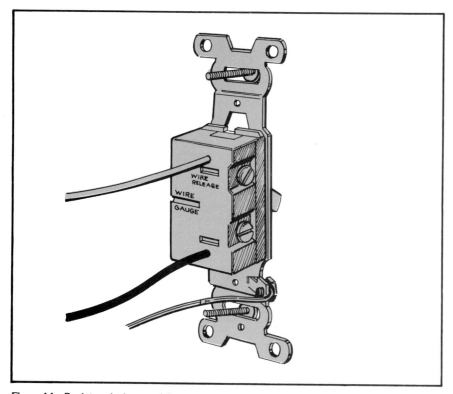

Figure 11. Push terminals are quicker and easier to use than the screw types.

STEP
SIX

CONNECTING THE WIRES

Margin of Error: Exact

Wire nuts are for making connections between wires of the same color. Wire nuts come in various sizes, distinguished by color, and may differ with each manufacturer. (Usually yellow, red, or grey will cover most household uses.) Always select the proper-size connector for the wires being used; these should only be used where the connection won't be pulled or strained in any way.

When making connections between solid wires using wire nuts, strip 1½" of insulation from the wires to be joined and hold them parallel. Twist these together securely with pliers. Then cut off the ends of the wires to fit the twist-on connector. Slip the wire nut over the bare ends of the wires, and twist the nut clockwise around the wires, pushing them hard into the nut.

A good safety precaution is to pull on each wire to assure that it is secure, then wrap electrical tape around the wire nut and the wires connected.

Simple wiring connections of two cables can be handled easily. More complex wiring, such as lights that involve switches, outlets that are switched, and junctions where the wiring is continued on to other receptacles, involves more wires. To simplify such arrangements, join wires by a method called "pigtailing." Local code may dictate use of pigtailing in your area.

Pigtailing

Pigtailing connects two or more wires together with another 6" pigtail wire that has been stripped ¾" on each end. The pigtail wire will be the wire you connect to the outlet or switch. This reduces the number of wires to be

---

TIP: Pull on each wire to assure that it is secure. Then, wrap electrical tape around the wire nut and the wires connected.

TIP: Use a voltage tester to check if electricity is present at the outlets.

connected at the receptacle. Below are some of the common uses of pigtailing.

NOTE: Always twist wires together securely before twisting on the wire nut.

Connecting wires at a duplex receptacle. Strip all wires ¾″ and then hold all of the wires of like color together with another 6″ wire of the same color. Twist the ends of the wires being connected with the pigtail wire tightly together (Figure 13). Then screw on a wire nut of the appropriate size. You can check the security of your connection by holding the wire nut and giving a good tug to each wire.

Now it is a simple matter to connect the pigtail portion of the connection to the terminal — black to brass, white to silver, and the bare grounding wire to the grounding screw. Once pigtailed, it is easier to bundle all of the wires together to fit them into the box. Then you can simply screw the duplex receptable (outlet) onto the electrical box with the screws provided.

Splitting a receptacle on a push terminal. Three cables (nine separate wires) come into the outlet box — one cable supplies power directly from the breaker box, another cable carries that power on to other receptacles or outlets, and the third cable comes from a wall-mounted switch so that half of that receptacle will be controlled by that switch. This type of connection, which divides an outlet, can only be done in a middle-of-the-run installation, not at a receptacle at the beginning or end. It is particularly used in bedrooms where you may want to control a lamp with a wall switch while still being able to plug in an alarm clock. Either the upper or the lower socket always remains hot, while the other is controlled by a switch.

The white wire within the cable that goes to the switch will be made hot, so it must be marked with black electrical tape at the outlet box, to distinguish it from the other neutral (white) wires. This same "hot white" wire should also be marked with black tape up at the switch.

Pigtail all of the same-colored wires together, as previously described, omit-

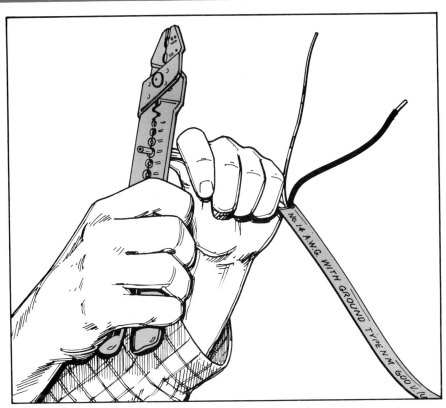

Figure 12. Using a wire stripper to remove insulation from wire ends.

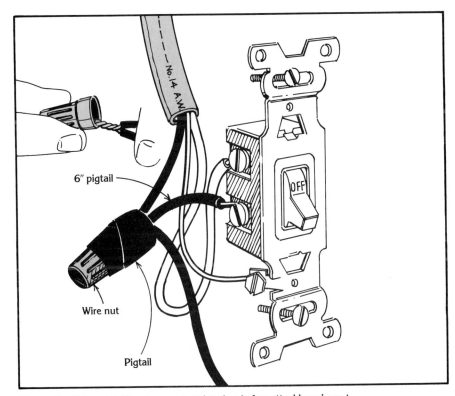

Figure 13. Using pigtailing, be sure to twist wires before attaching wire nut.

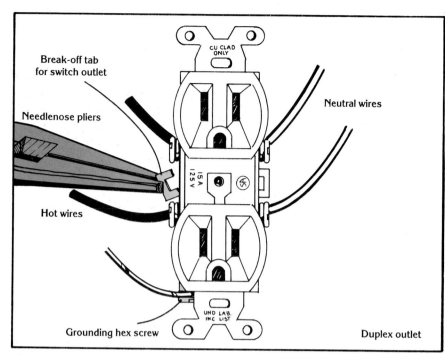

Break-off tab
for switch outlet

Needlenose pliers

Hot wires

Grounding hex screw

CU CLAD
ONLY

Neutral wires

15 A
125 V

UND LAB.
INC LIST

Duplex outlet

Figure 14. Typical wiring to split a receptacle to control one outlet by a wall switch.

rate grounding screws on the switches. *A switch should never be connected to neutral wires.* So join all of the white wires together with a wire nut and push them back into the box. Then pigtail the hot wires together.

Since a switch interrupts the flow of electrical current, it should only be connected to hot (black) wires; or, in this case, a white wire marked with black electrical tape designating it to be hot. On the first switch, push the hot pigtail wire into either push terminal, and push the color-coded hot wire that goes to the overhead light into the push terminal of this same switch. On the second switch, push the black hot wire, which was pigtailed to the other black wires at the outlet, and the white wire wrapped in black tape into the back of the switch. This white wire will be made hot when the switch is turned on and will take the electrical power to the controlled outlet.

ting the white wire that is marked with black tape.

Hook up the pigtail ground wire to the ground screw on the receptacle, and the pigtail neutral wire to the silver side. (If it is a metal box, use two ground pigtail wires — one grounded to the receptacle and the second to connect onto the box grounding screw.) The hot pigtail wire goes into the permanently hot (lower) side. The white wire marked with black tape goes into the hot outlet side — upper or lower, depending on which socket you wish to control with the switch.

Breaking the tab on the hot side linking the two brass terminals of the outlet will allow half of the receptacle to work off of a switch, while the other half receives continuous power. (See Figure 14.)

Wiring two push terminal switches. If your box and your switches are plastic, connect all grounding wires with a wire nut and push into box. When using metal boxes, pigtail all of the bare ground wires together with *three* separate pigtail wires. Then connect one pigtail wire to the grounding screw in the box, and the other two to the sepa-

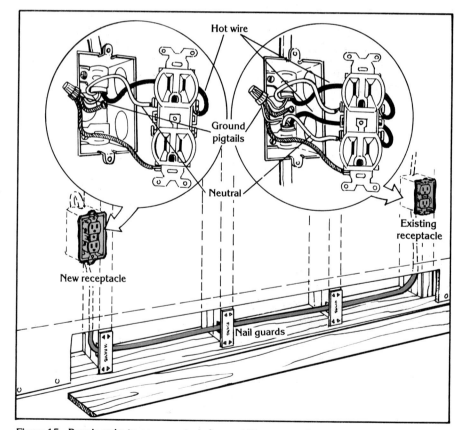

Hot wire

Ground
pigtails

Neutral

New receptacle

Existing
receptacle

Nail guards

Figure 15. Running wire to new receptacle from existing receptacle.

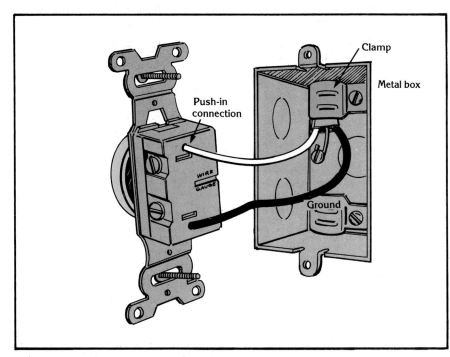

Figure 16. Wiring for a dimmer switch.

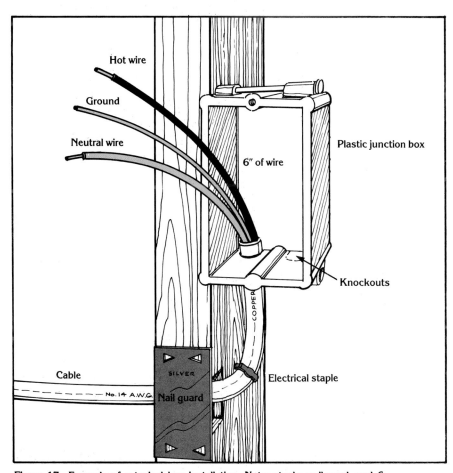

Figure 17. Example of a typical box installation. Note: staple, nailguard, and 6 inches of stripped wire.

STEP SEVEN

HANGING LIGHT FIXTURES AND RECEPTACLES

Margin of Error: No room for error

When you did the "roughing in," the electrical box was attached to the attic or second floor joist so that the plate is flush with the finished ceiling material. At this point you are ready to complete your wiring.

Pull the electrical wire through the cutout and box and strip it, just as you would for the outlets. Attach a surface-mounted hanging light with the attachment strap that is screwed to the electrical box. Connect the wires together, black to black, white to white, and ground to ground, using the wire nuts as previously described. Push the wires up inside the electrical box. Then it is a simple matter to attach the coverplate of the hanging light or the plate of the receptacle with the provided screws.

Track Lighting

Track lighting may be connected by adding a new ceiling box or by using an adapter cord that reaches to an existing receptacle. In a new addition, you may find placing a ceiling box more advantageous, since you need not hide the cord.

Screw the mounting bracket into the electrical box. Push the wires of the electrical connector through the slot in the track connector; then through the slot in the box adapter. Now attach the wires to those in the box, matching colored wires and using the appropriate screw nuts. Push the wires up into the electrical box. Attach the two-piece mounting assembly to the box tabs. (See Figure 19.)

Hold a ruler flat against the ceiling (or wall) so that one edge of the ruler is lined up with the center slot on the track connector. Using the ruler as your

161

guide, draw a line along the ceiling (or wall) from this slot, as long as necessary, to where the track will end. Make marks at even intervals on the penciled line to indicate the attachment positions of the clips that will hold the track. Hold the clips in position, mark and drill pilot holes in the ceiling (or wall) at these points, and screw the clips in place. Partially insert the side screws into the clips. Then push the track wires firmly into the electrical connector and slide the track into the track connector. Tighten the side screws of the clips to hold the track in place. The connector cover will then easily snap in place to cover the wires.

OUTDOOR WIRING

Outdoor wiring is essential for many uses outside the home — for security lights, porch and yard lamps, and tool operation, to name a few.

Basically, wiring fixtures suited for exterior use is the same as wiring indoor fixtures. However, exterior moisture-proof coated wires and boxes must be used. If possible, choose an outdoor outlet location that is convenient to get to, as well as close to, an indoor receptacle. This will simplify the installation.

Outside outlets (or those in the bathroom, or garage) must also include ground fault interrupters. GFIs measure the amount of power the hot wire brings in and the neutral wire returns. If there is a 5 milliamp difference or more, due to excessive moisture, the outlet automatically shuts off. This reduces your chances of shock in wet or high-moisture areas. A GFI is usually a type of circuit breaker that is installed in the breaker box, whereupon you then use a normal outlet or an exterior light, the circuit of which is attached into a GFI breaker. However, GFIs also come built directly into the receptacle. The circuit of that receptacle can then be attached to a standard breaker or fuse.

Drill a hole through the existing wall to take the power outside. Even though you want to be *near* the indoor receptacle, do not position the receptacles back to back. Run the cable or the conduit and install the appropriate junction box. Connect the wires as previously

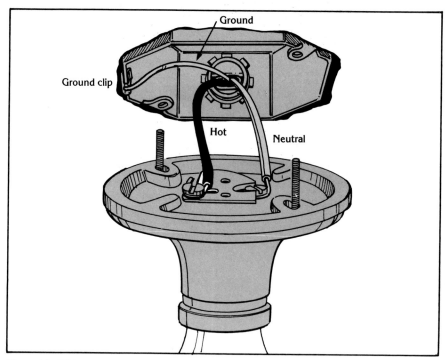

Figure 18. Wiring for a simple light fixture.

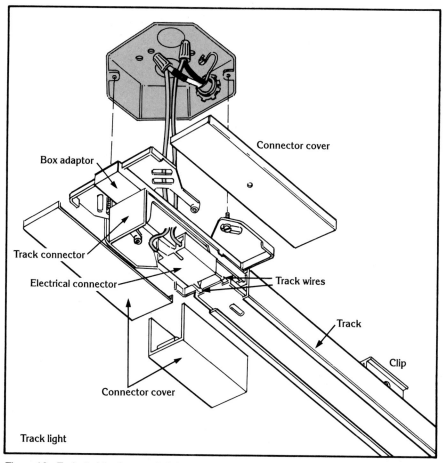

Figure 19. Typical wiring for a track light.

THE BREAKER BOX

All household members should know where the main power switch is located, in case of an emergency such as a fire or basement flooding. Even though it is not required, the most logical place for that main switch is at the main panel. Sometimes, however, the main switch is located in a separate box, even at a separate location. Some older homes have fused pull-outs; others have a lever that you pull to shut off the main power. In the latter case, you also have to pull that lever to change a fuse, which protects you as well. Still others have a circuit breaker switch or button. Whatever the set-up of your power panel, you will be able to operate the main switch without being exposed to live electricity.

Keep in mind how dangerous it is to work at the breaker box if the main switch is not turned off. The amount of electricity being brought into the house can easily kill. If you are unfamiliar with your box, or if you don't know where the main switch is located, have a professional explain how to work with your particular box.

Circuit breakers are protective devices that control the power going to a particular route of wiring. In case of an overload or a short on that circuit, the breaker trips and automatically shuts off power to that circuit.

Ground fault circuit breakers offer protection against more than just overloads. Many areas require these for outdoor wiring, or for rooms with outlets exposed to moisture, such as bathrooms and kitchens. Ground fault circuit breakers are also recommended for workshops and areas where power tools are in use.

Placing new breakers into the circuit box is an easy enough matter, providing you have room in the box to accept new breakers. If not, you will have to have an electrician install a new, larger circuit box or a secondary box.

Begin by turning off the power at the main circuit breaker switch. Remember, the box is still hot above the main breaker, so don't touch the wires above this disconnect. Again, be absolutely certain that this switch does indeed cut off the power into the circuit breaker box.

Bring the neutral and grounding wires into the box and attach them to the "neutral bus bar." Do this by sticking the stripped ends of the wires into any hole in the neutral bus bar and attaching them by tightening down the screw heads.

NOTE: Some boxes will have two bus bars, one for the ground wire, one for the neutral. Others will have only one bus bar for both neutral and ground.

Hook up the circuit breaker switch to the black hot wire by tightening the screw in the breaker over the wire, as previously described. Now it is a simple matter of snapping the breaker back into position in the box and turning the main switch back on. Then turn on the circuit switch that will feed electricity to this new circuit.

Use a voltage tester to check if electricity is present at the outlets. One prong is inserted into the hot side of the outlet and one into the neutral or ground side (Figure 21). If the wiring is right, the bulb will light up. (This device can also be used to test a faulty receptacle prior to replacement.) Be sure to touch only the insulated wire. Never touch any metal parts.

Call in the electrical inspector again for the final inspection.

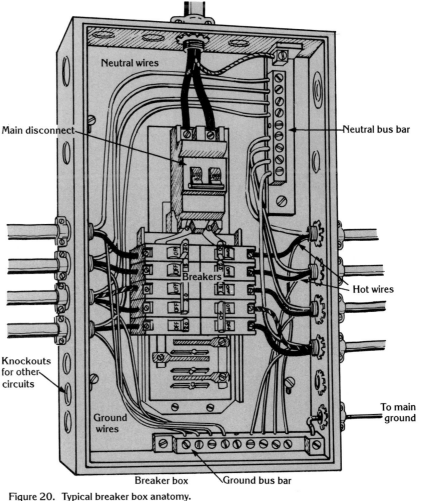

Figure 20. Typical breaker box anatomy.

described, matching the color-coded wires to the correct terminal. Be sure to seal around the holes with silicone sealant, once the conduit and/or wires have been put in place. If the circuit breaker box or fuse box is mounted outside, however, it will not be necessary to do this. Just run the wires directly from the box.

If you are adding exterior lights, many come with a special mounting strap which gets screwed to the box. Some have special threading so the light can be held to the wall.

EXTENDING WIRING IN OLDER HOMES

Many older homes are inadequately wired. Some older houses have only one 120-volt system (as opposed to today's standard of two systems which bring the household total up to 240 volts). If you have only two wires entering your house from a nearby utility pole (as opposed to the standard three wires), you probably only have 120-volt capacity. You'll have to call in the utility company and have an electrician up-grade your voltage system if you want to use many of today's modern appliances.

Before extending your wiring, make sure you understand the ampere capacity of the wiring you currently have in place. If you're extending a number 14 wire (which requires a 15-amp fuse), don't expect to operate a refrigerator and dishwasher both on this one line.

If you have any doubts or questions, or should you run into a situation not covered here, do not experiment. Consult with a licensed electrician for your own safety and that of your loved ones.

NOTE: Turn off the controlling breaker before beginning any electrical work. Tape over the breaker and leave a note on the breaker box that you are working on that circuit.

When extending wiring, always use the same size wire for a continuation of any wiring circuit, and make certain the circuit is grounded before you begin.

Locate the last outlet in the wiring run nearest to where you want your new outlet. Test this with a voltage tester or lamp, to be certain the outlet is not hot, before continuing.

Remove the plate, disconnect the outlet, and take the entire receptacle out of the wall.

NOTE: If the box you wish to extend from has reached its capacity, and you cannot find a second box from which to run the new cable, replace the box with a larger, deeper one. (See section on Roughing In under Basic Wiring above.)

This existing outlet will have wires connected to only two of the four terminal screws. The two unused screws will be your starting point for wiring to the new receptacle.

Pinpoint the new outlet's location by finding the nearest wall stud. Put the template where the new outlet will go (the same distance from the floor as the existing outlet) and trace around it. Use your utility knife or keyhole saw to cut out the hole for your new box. Attach the new junction box to the wall (as outlined above under Basic Wiring).

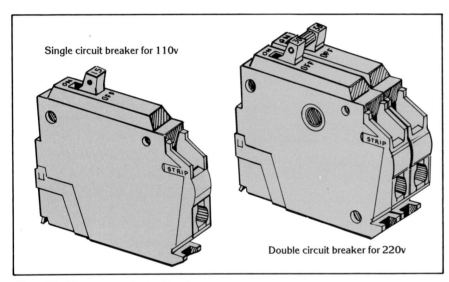

Single circuit breaker for 110v

Double circuit breaker for 220v

Figure 21. Two common types of breakers.

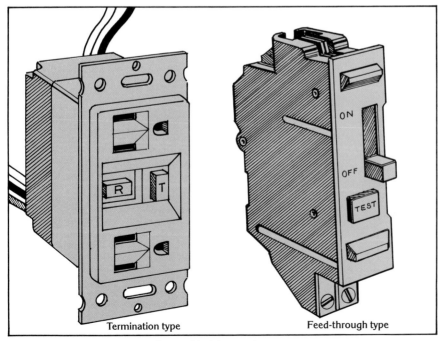

Termination type

Feed-through type

Figure 22. Two common types of ground fault interrupters.

Carefully remove the baseboard with a pry bar and wooden wedge. Cut out the drywall behind the baseboard with a jigsaw or drywall saw. Then notch the studs just above the sole plate. Use a fish tape to snag the wire and pull it through the existing outlet box and through the wall. Hook up the wires and push them back into the box. Run the wire along the grooves and install nail guards over the notches to protect the wires. Fish up the wire to the new outlet. Use push terminals to connect the two boxes, matching the colored wires to the correct terminal, as described in the sections on terminals and connections under Basic Wiring above.

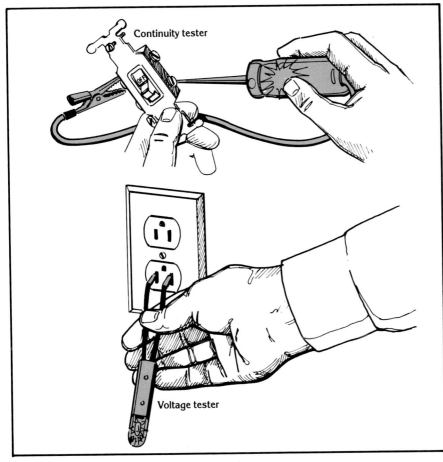

Figure 23. A continuity tester and a voltage tester in use.

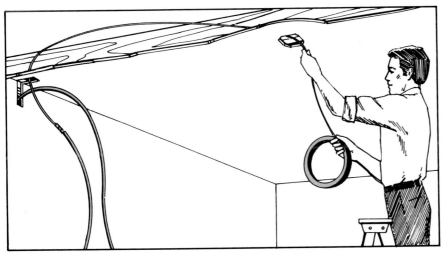

Figure 24. Using fish tape to run wire through existing ceilings and walls.

TOOLS AND MATERIALS CHECKLIST

Tools

Long-nose pliers	Fish tape
Wire cutters	Cable stripper
Electric drill	Wire stripper
Tape measure	Colored tape
Screwdriver	Voltage tester
Chalkline	Continuity tester
Hammer	Safety glasses or
Circular saw	goggles
Chisel	Keyhole saw
Hacksaw	Utility knife
Combination	Right-angle drill
square	Pry bar and wood
Utility light	wedge

Materials

Grounded	Push terminals
receptacles	Breakers
Switches	Track lights and
Rectangular	fittings
junction boxes	Dimmer switch
Octagonal or	Waterproof
circular	junction boxes
junction boxes	Ground fault
Square junction	interrupters
boxes	Conduit
Nail guards	Cable
Wire nuts	Silicon caulking
Horseshoe nails	

CHAPTER TEN

Weatherizing
Getting Ready for the Cold (and Hot)

WHAT YOU WILL BE DOING

Although insulation wraps your house in a nice warm blanket, heat or air conditioning can still leak out through seemingly inconsequential cracks. Often these "inconsequential" cracks can add up to as much as a 2-square foot hole!

Tracking down and sealing these leaks is not as difficult as it may seem. There are a number of ways to go about this. You can hire a "house doctor" to do an audit. You can contract for an energy audit (a scientific, thermographic audit, conducted by a professional firm, which produces a geographic picture of the leaks in your home). Usually, however, your local utility company will conduct an audit at your home free of charge. Just call and ask them about it. You may not get the detail in the free audit that you would in one you paid for, but it would still provide you with useful information and a place to begin. They may also suggest improvements that would make you eligible for energy tax credits. But, if your utility company doesn't answer your call, and if you're appalled at the cost of a professional, by following the guidelines presented in this chapter, you can do an effective weatherization audit yourself.

In this chapter you will not only learn where your home weatherization problems are, you'll learn how to correct them as well.

BEFORE YOU BEGIN

SAFETY

Although weatherstripping your home doesn't sound like a dangerous way to spend a weekend, simple carelessness can lead to some potentially harmful situations.

1. Wear gloves whenever working with fiberglass.

2. Wear safety glasses or goggles whenever hammering.

3. Provide for adequate ventilation when sealing your house weather tight. This eliminates unhealthy build-up of noxious fumes from various materials used in building the home.

4. Keep hot water temperatures set at less than 115 degrees. This eliminates scalding hazards, particularly where small children are concerned. It will save you money as well.

5. Do not extend insulation of gas hot water heater to the floor, thereby cutting off the air supply to the pilot light.

6. Do not tape or insulate too close to the duct on top of a gas heater.

USEFUL TERMS

Caulk. A flexible seal applied from pressurized applicator to seal cracks and gaps.

Countersinking. Sinking below the surface (as with the use of a nailset to countersink a finishing nail).

Door threshold (or saddle). The doorsill, a piece of wood or metal placed beneath the door.

Downspouts. The portion of rain gutter that drains from the roof to the ground.

Glazing compound. The type of caulk used to seal glass into panes.

Jalousie Window. Formed of horizontal glass slats.

Oakum. Loose, stringy, hemp fiber from old ropes which makes a useful caulk for deep cracks.

Soffits. The underside of an overhanging roof.

Window sash. The frame work for holding glass panes.

Weatherstripping. Materials added to movable parts of the home (doors, windows, etc.) to seal against air infiltration when closed.

Window film. A 6-ml. plastic covering (like a painter's drop cloth), stapled or adhered to the window in lieu of storm closures.

WHAT YOU WILL NEED

Time. The amount of time needed to properly weatherstrip your home will depend on the extent of work needed to be done. Most door and window caulking and weatherstripping applications can be accomplished in one weekend.

Tools. Weatherizing your home requires only the most basic tools. So any incurred expense will go directly into materials rather than additional tools. These are the necessary tools, found in any home toolbox.

Hacksaw with fine-toothed blade	Steel tape measure
Metal file	Scissors
Pry bar	Tack hammer
Circular saw	Tinsnips
Drill	Plane
Hammer	Putty knife
Nailset	Utility knife
Caulking gun	Hair dryer
Screwdrivers	

Since caulking is a major part of weatherstripping, acquisition of an air compressor with a caulking gun attachment would make this job go more smoothly and easily. If you do not have access to one, it can be rented.

Materials. The materials, of course, will depend on your assessment of your weatherization requirements. The following suggestions should cover most of your needs.

Threshold treatments	Fiberglass or oakum
Caulk	Window film
Finishing nails	Programmable thermostat
Wood dough	Masking tape
Sandpaper	Heating boosters
Stain	Insulating jacket for hot water heater
Sealer	Duct tape
Door-bottom seals	Plastic
Window glazing compound	Insulating fireplace baffle
Weatherstripping materials	Glass fireplace doors
Garage door weatherstripping	Foam pad inserts for outlets
Galvanized shingle nails	Pipe insulating tape

Once you have decided which materials best suit your situation (further reading this chapter will aid you in this decision), you'll want to make a complete list before you shop. Take measurements of all the cracks that need weatherstripping — doors and windows. Estimate the amount of caulking you will use. Note the number and sizes of openings you want to cover with window film. And jot down any specialty items, such as new thresholds, a programmable thermostat, or a water heater blanket.

PERMITS AND CODES

Most weatherizing tasks are simple enough not to require permits. However, I suggest you check with your local building inspector for a copy of the local building code and any permit requirements. If you are a frequent do-it-yourselfer, you will find it beneficial to keep a copy on hand for all your projects.

TIP: Never caulk the small openings in storm windows. They are there to allow moisture to escape and not condense on the glass.

MOST COMMON MISTAKES

1. Neglecting to do a *thorough* energy audit of your home.

2. Neglecting to insulate properly in conjunction with weatherization.

3. Applying caulk, sealants, and weatherstripping in temperatures too cold for the material being used.

4. Not providing for adequate ventilation and air circulation when making your home weather tight.

5. Sealing off the room that houses the thermostat control.

6. Neglecting to save receipts for materials and labor used in making your house more energy efficient. These come in handy for state and federal tax credits.

STEP ONE

THE WEATHERIZING AUDIT

Margin of Error: Not applicable

The first step in weatherizing your home is to gather information. Begin by checking each exterior door for the following most probable leaks:

1. Are there any noticeable cracks at areas where the door meets the frame?

2. Is there space at the joint between the frame and the interior and exterior walls of the house?

3. Is there a gap at the bottom of the door at the threshold?

4. Is there space between the base of the threshold and the floor underneath?

5. If your door has glass panes, are they properly glazed? Or is the glazing old and cracked or missing entirely?

6. Are any of the panes cracked or broken?

7. If the doors have existing weatherstripping, does it need replacement?

8. Does your home have adequate storm doors? And are they properly hung and caulked?

Taking the same approach to interior doors can't hurt either. Keeping them properly sealed helps reduce room-to-room infiltration and makes it possible to control more precisely the heating and cooling of individual rooms.

Next, take stock of all the windows:

1. Any moving parts that allow air to leak?

2. Gaps or flaws in construction around the frame?

3. Is the glazing compound around the glass old and cracked or missing entirely?

4. Are the seams around the window trim caulked?

Figure 1. Common areas around the home that are energy leakers.

Roof flashing, vents, and pipes

Vents and fans

Air conditioner
Heating and cooling ducts

Joints in gutters and downspouts

Where different materials meet

Windows and door frames

Between foundation and walls

169

5. If weatherstripping exists, is it in need of replacement?

6. Do the window panes that are cracked or broken need to be replaced?

7. Are the windows that are not covered with draperies, shades, or blinds offering insulative value?

8. Are storm windows installed? And are they properly fitted and caulked, to eliminate gaps where the window meets the framing?

Once you have covered all the conventional openings to your home, begin looking for other, not so obvious ones. Are there any air leaks around:

1. Foundation cracks or cracks in basement walls?

2. Separations between any two materials of the house construction, like an exterior chimney, and the house?

3. Utility pipes?

4. Phone and electric cable lines?

5. Mail slot?

6. Clothes dryer vent?

8. Outside light connections?

8. TV antenna entry?

9. Electrical outlets?

10. Cracks and splits in siding?

11. Gaps or loose mortar between block, bricks, or stone facing?

12. Air ducts for heating/cooling system?

13. Improper insulation around window air-conditioning units?

14. Leaking basement windows?

15. Exposed roofing nails?

16. Roof flashing?

17. Split or loose roof shingles?

18. Poor drainage around the house?

19. Damaged, blocked, or poorly connected downspouts?

20. Garage doors?

Figure 2. Caulk between door and window frames and the wall.

21. Adequate ventilation in any bathroom without a window to the outside?

22. Adequate ventilation in kitchen using a stove or range hood?

Simple Maintenance Tips

Energy leaks from your home in ways other than through openings. How do you rate on energy conservation?

1. Is your furnace properly cleaned and tuned for maximum efficiency? Is the air filter clean?

2. Have you checked your air-conditioning filter?

3. Have you checked the range filter?

4. Do you regularly look for dirty or blocked heating/cooling registers?

5. Do you set your thermostat too high in winter and too low in summer?

6. Do you turn your thermostat down when you are at work or otherwise out of the house?

7. Is the thermostat broken, worn, or dirty? Consider installing a programmable thermostat when you replace it.

8. Is your thermostat properly located? An improperly located thermostat (too near a heat or cold source or on an outside wall) can waste a lot of energy.

9. Do you seasonally check for leaks in heating and cooling ducts?

10. Is your hot water heater set at an efficient temperature?

11. Is the hot water heater malfunctioning in any way?

12. Are you lighting and heating or cooling unused or seldom used rooms?

13. Have you insulated your hot and cold water pipes and heating and air-conditioning ducts?

14. Do you turn the hot water heater off and extinguish other pilot lights when you go away on vacation?

STEP TWO

CAULKING

Margin of Error: Not applicable

Caulk is a material that forms a flexible seal to stop air and moisture infiltration. Some of the better types of caulk will last up to 20 years. Although these are more expensive, they will save you the time and expense of recaulking frequently.

Caulk is used on window and door frames, siding, corner joints, foundations, and almost any area in which you find a seam or crack.

Take another look at the weatherization audit you did at the beginning of this chapter. Most of the items checked off in the "not so obvious" category are prime targets for caulking.

There are many types of caulk for various uses, so check with your home center to find out what type will work best for your particular needs. Generally, you will apply caulk from a tube with a caulking gun or from a pressurized can. A standard cartridge of caulk will give you approximately 25 feet of ¼" bead. You can also purchase rope caulk which comes in a coil and is simply unwound and stuffed into cracks and crevices.

The trick to a good caulking job is learning to draw a good, even bead. This may take a little practice but it will work easier if you hold it at a consistent angle and draw the bead continuously rather than in a stop-and-start fashion. A trick here is to release the trigger before pulling the gun away to avoid excess caulk oozing out. Cut the nozzle with a sharp razor blade or utility knife to about a 45-degree angle. Then pierce the seal on the cartridge to allow the caulk to flow evenly.

Since caulking is a major element of weatherization, access to an air compressor would come in very handy. Fitted with a caulking gun attachment, the air compressor allows a smoother, almost effortless application in all areas needing caulk (see Figure 2).

Be sure the seam or crack you are filling is free from any built-up paint or old, deteriorated caulking. Use a putty knife or a large screwdriver to scrape the opening clean. There should be no moisture in the crack before applying the caulking, or it will be trapped inside once the caulk sets up.

If you are trying to cover both sides of a crack of seam with a single wide bead of caulk, make sure it adheres to both sides. The bead of caulk needs to be on the inside of the crack, so if the bead that you draw is on the surface of the material, use a putty knife to force it into the crack or seam and smooth it out. A little practice will give you the proper angle at which to hold the can or gun so that the caulk will be forced immediately into the crack as it comes out of the tube.

There are no practical alternatives to caulking. If you weatherstrip and caulk in addition to insulating your home, you will reduce your energy bill considerably.

The joint between the door frame and the exterior and interior walls can be as much as an eighth of an inch gap. This must be carefully and completely caulked to seal it against energy loss.

Figure 3. Using an air compressor to caulk.

In many of the older homes, there is a space between the windows that contains the weights for the older double-hung windows. This area is usually not insulated and can leak. Just like the doors, there is that fractional gap between the frame and the walls of the house. Caulking the outside of the window frame where it joins the overall structure of the house will halt this flow of air. (See Figure 4.)

NOTE: Never caulk the little openings in storm windows. They have a very specific purpose; that is, allowing moisture to escape and not condense on the glass.

Cracks in the foundation or basement walls can be terrific energy losers. You'll want to be certain the crack is very clean. Remove any loose mortar, dirt, and moisture. You may even want to go over it with a primer if the material is porous.

Smaller cracks can be sealed off with just a liberal bead of caulk, forced smoothly into the crack. Extra deep cracks should be stuffed with polyethylene foam, fiberglass, or oakum to within 1/2″ of the top surface. Then caulk over this to provide a seal.

If dissimilar materials meet — at sidewall and foundation, sidewalls and roof, chimney and house, or a porch and the house — a seal of caulk will reward you with lower energy bills.

Where utility pipes, vent pipes, exterior plumbing, and electrical or phone connections enter the house, caulk the separation. If any of these penetrate the ceiling below an unheated attic or the wall to a garage, caulk them as well.

On roofs or siding, repair areas around flashing with caulk or a sealant recommended for exterior metal. Seal flashing around roof stacks and vents, between roof valley flashing and shingles, and around roof additions and skylights. There are also types of adhesive caulking that will mend split or loose roofing shingles as well as splits or cracks in siding. (These are available in a variety of colors.) Exposed roofing nails should also get an application.

Keep all gutters, downspouts, soffits, and eaves clean and in good repair. Caulk them to prevent rot, decay, basement flooding, mildew, and dampness problems.

TIP: If you are not using your fireplace plug up the flue with insulating fireplace baffle (damper) to prevent warm air from drifting up and out of your home.

Figure 4. Window glazing in a cartridge.

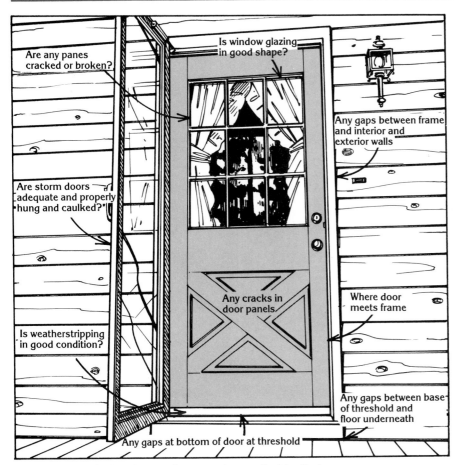

Figure 5. Areas of a door that are of concern when weatherizing the house.

Glazing

When reglazing, remove all old glazing compound from the window sash with a putty knife, chisel, or large screwdriver. On wood sash, pull out all glazier's points (triangular pieces of metal which hold the glass in place) with pliers. On metal sash, the spring clips or glazing strips will have to be removed. The sash should then be cleaned with a wire brush and primed with an appropriate primer to insure a good bond. Allow the primer time to dry before reinserting the points, clips, or strips and applying the glazing compound.

Glazing compound is a smooth, flexible material used to seal window panes in order to keep out air and moisture. You can also eliminate drafts and reduce condensation around windows by replacing the glazing compound that is cracked or missing.

Apply the new glazing compound according to the manufacturer's directions. It is usually applied directly from the container with a putty knife. However, special compounds are available in cartridges for application with a caulking gun. These eliminate much of the kneading and handling normally required when glazing. For best results, glazing compound should be painted.

Storm doors and windows go a long way in sealing up a house. These are specially fitted with heavy-duty weatherstripping and sealed glass inserts.

There are many do-it-yourself storm window and door kits available. If you do not wish to go to the expense of providing storms for all of your windows, there is an option available called window insulator film. This is a clear plastic film used with double-sided tape to shrink around your window, window grouping, or glass door. Application of window film is quite simple:

STEP THREE

WINDOW TREATMENTS

Margin of Error: Not applicable

Now on to the windows. Before we begin to discuss weatherstripping, let's go back to your weatherization audit. Did you find any cracked or broken panes? Any old or missing glazing compound? How about deteriorated weatherstripping that had been applied in years gone by? These items must be corrected before adding any new weatherstripping or it will all be a waste of time and money.

The cracked and broken windows are obvious. Replace them. Record accurate measurements and take them to your home center or glass shop.

Properly sized and placed, snug-fitting windows can save a significant amount on your heating and cooling bills. If it is necessary to replace windows, you may want to consider a different style which will allow for greater ventilation during warmer months. Casement windows offer almost 100% of their sash opening for ventilation, while double-hung and sliding types offer only 50%. And a well-placed sliding door will give up to three times the ventilation of an average window.

Energy efficient sash and frame windows with double-pane insulating glass have low infiltration rates and will easily pay for themselves in energy saved.

Figure 6. Use a blow dryer to shrink the film to a snug fit. This creates a very inexpensive storm window on the inside.

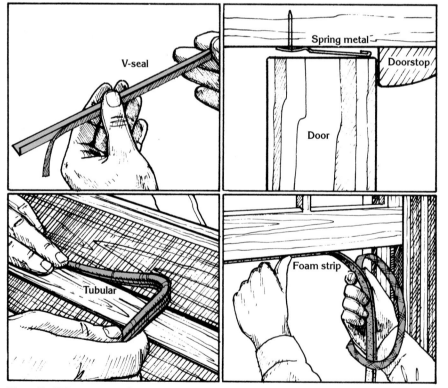

Figure 7. Different types of common weatherstripping.

1. Measure and cut the double-sided tape and apply it to clean outside edges or faces of the window molding.

2. Unfold the provided film and cut it to the size of the window (including trim), allowing two inches extra all around.

3. Start at the top and press the film securely to the tape. The film will have wrinkles.

4. Now shrink the film with a hair blow dryer set on the highest setting. Do not touch the film as you do this. (See Figure 6.) Just aim the hot air evenly over the entire covering. This takes the wrinkles out and leaves you with a clear "pane" to see through.

5. Trim the excess film with a sharp utility knife or scissors.)

This film reduces air leak by approximately 97%, thus reducing frost build-up on windows. The film and the tape can be removed at the end of the season.

Interior Window Coverings

Another area for refining your home energy management are window treatments — draperies, cornices, roller shades, venetians, roman shades, louvres, quilts, sunscreens, and even exterior awnings. These can offer greater energy savings at less cost than storm windows or double-paned glass. The combinations are almost endless. They can range from the simple sew-it-yourself, install-it-yourself window quilt systems up through complex, passive, solar gain controls intended to turn your house into an efficient heat pump. Of course, the latter are treatments for a professional. But there are many good-looking and energy-efficient offerings on the market which are inexpensive as well.

One type is that which can be sewn yourself or purchased inexpensively in the form of padded, quilt-like shades. With magnetic strips sewn into the sides of the shade, they effectively cling to magnetic strips installed on the window trim to form an airtight seal.

STEP FOUR

WEATHERSTRIPPING

Margin of Error: Not applicable

Weatherstripping products are numerous. Some are quite specialized. All are designed to seal some gap or space where energy is leaking away — most often around doors and windows. Modern materials and newer designs have resulted in a great number of effective, yet, inexpensive, easy-to-install products. Since there are so many choices, I recommend the following for ease of installation and durability. First, however, there are a couple of things to keep in mind when applying weatherstripping to doors and windows. They must be applied to a clean, dry surface and in temperatures above 20 degrees F.

If your door threshold (or saddle) is badly deteriorated, it may need to be completely removed and replaced before you add any new weatherizing effects to the doorway. A threshold seals the door at the bottom and is most effective when used in conjunction with a door shoe or door sweep gasket.

Wooden thresholds add warmth in appearance as well, but are a bit more costly than aluminum. Bronze and stainless steel are used but are considerably more expensive. Choose your threshold to match your floor. And take great care in measuring for a replacement. Both wood and aluminum are sold in different lengths for standard door widths.

TIP: When they are properly sized and placed, snug-fitting windows can save a significant amount on your heating and cooling bills.

Figure 8. Using a circular saw to cut out old threshold.

Cutting out threshold

Old threshold

Figure 9. Using a jig saw to notch and cut new threshold.

Notch threshold to fit around doorstops

New threshold

Replacing a Wooden Threshold

1. Check the clearance between the door and the trim pieces (such as the door stop) and remove if necessary.

2. Swing the door open as far as it will go. If necessary, carefully pry the trim loose with a pry bar and a wooden wedge so as not to damage either the trim or the frame.

3. You may need to use a circular saw or chisel to cut through the threshold to remove it from the doorway (see Figure 8). Take great care in this step that you don't cause damage to the interior floor and other trim.

4. Measure and cut the new wooden threshold to the proper length so that it will fit snugly.

5. Notch the threshold to fit properly around the stops.

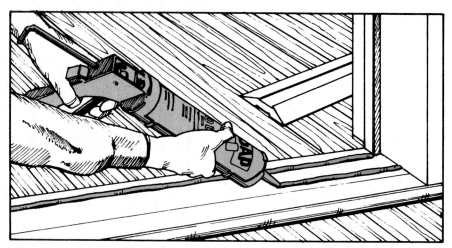

Figure 10. Applying caulk before installing new threshold.

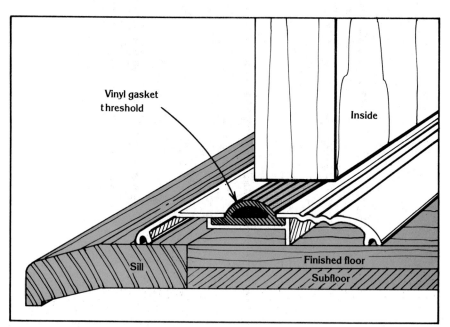

Figure 11. An aluminum threshold with a vinyl gasket.

6. After thoroughly cleaning the old material and dirt out of the doorway — this could mean scraping old caulk and even sanding the surface smooth — spread a generous amount of caulk on the bottom (see Figure 10). This will assure an airtight seal in that joint between the floor and the threshold.

7. Tap the new threshold gently into place with your hammer.

8. Drill some pilot holes slightly smaller than the finishing nails you will use to secure the threshold. Then nail the threshold into its permanent position.

9. Countersink the nails with a nailset and fill the holes with wood dough. Sand lightly when dry.

10. Apply a stain if you prefer, and a water repellant finish, or two coats of a penetrating sealer.

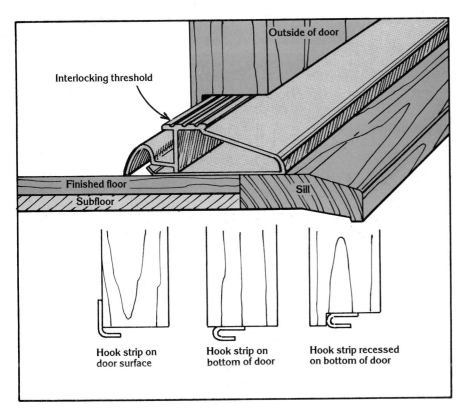

Figure 12. An interlocking threshold.

Aluminum and metal thresholds. This requires the same installation steps as the wooden threshold. The exception would be the use of a hacksaw with a fine-toothed blade to cut it to length and a metal file to smooth out the roughness. Pre-drill the screw holes in the floor to avoid splitting the sill and to ease screw installation.

You may decide on a vinyl gasket-type threshold, called a thermal threshold, as shown in Figure 11. Here a convex vinyl ridge across the top of the threshold presses against the bottom of the door for a tight seal against drafts.
Interlocking thresholds. Another type, less often used and recommended in cold climates, is the interlocking threshold shown in Figure 12. Although very effective when in good condition, the interlocking elements are difficult to install and easily damaged. Special tools are required, and complicated adjustments are frequently necessary.
Half thresholds. You'll find a half threshold necessary where two floors of different height come together. Half saddles are available in metal or can be made by adapting a wooden saddle. (See Figure 13.) You will need to know the difference in floor heights before purchasing this threshold.

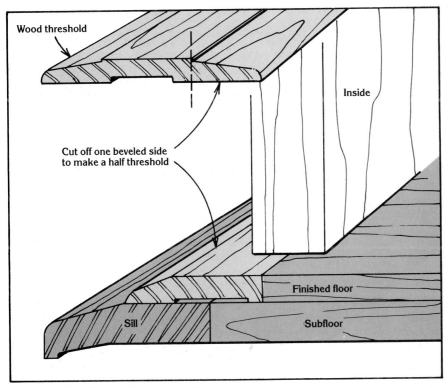

Figure 13. A half threshold for floors at different heights.

TIP: Never paint the tubular or bulb vinyl weatherstripping. Paint stiffens the vinyl and diminishes its sealing ability.

Door Bottom Seals

These products are used to close the gaps between the threshold and the bottom of the door. Usually, removal of the door is not required for door sweeps. You'll find these to be easiest to apply and inexpensive, thus the most popular. Again, measure carefully. These are sized for standard doors also. Look for products that have clear instructions and, if attached by screws, slotted screw holes for periodic adjustment.

The entry door seal is adhesive backed for ease of application. It is applied to the bottom of the interior side of the inward-swinging door.

A storm/entry door seal can be used for both interior and exterior applications and requires a drill and screwdriver for application. First cut it to fit. Remove the liner from the adhesive back and press it against the bottom of the door, positioning it for maximum contact with the floor. Drill pilot holes and secure the seal with screws.

Door Shoes

Door shoes (Figure 15) and automatic door bottoms will require removal of the door for application. For effectiveness, durability, and visibility, they rate about the same as the sweeps. If the clearance between door and threshold is between $\frac{1}{2}$ and $\frac{3}{16}$ of an inch, application should be no problem. Less than that, you'll need to trim some off the bottom of the door. More than $\frac{1}{2}$", you might as well look for another solution.

Installing the Door Shoe

1. Measure the door length to determine if the door needs to be trimmed after you install the new threshold. The door shoe should come with instructions specifying proper clearance. Once the shoe is installed, the door must be able to open and close easily, yet still tightly against all the frame elements.

2. Remove the door and lay it across a couple of sawhorses or on a sturdy worktable.

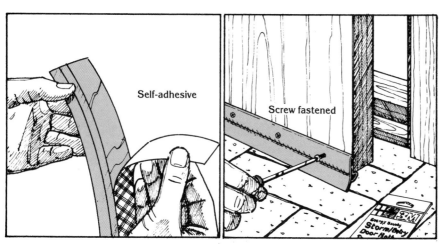

Figure 14. Applying door bottom seals.

TIP: A programmable thermostat eliminates excessive tampering with the setting and is easily installed.

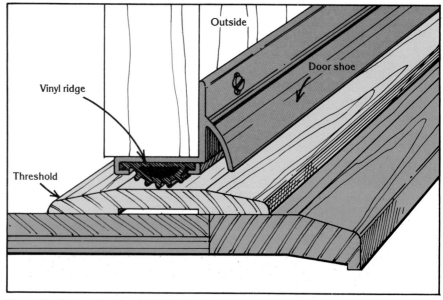

Figure 15. A door shoe threshold will require removal of the door.

3. Clamp a 2″ × 4″ or other straight-edge to the door bottom to act as a cutting guide. Then "saw" or "plane" the door as required.

4. Measure and cut the door shoe to the width of the door so that it clears the doorstops. For this you will need a hacksaw or a jigsaw with a jacksaw blade.

5. Attach the shoe to the bottom of the door with the screws provided.

6. Slip the vinyl bulb into place in the shoe and trim it to length with a utility knife.

7. Finally, rehang the door and check the fit.

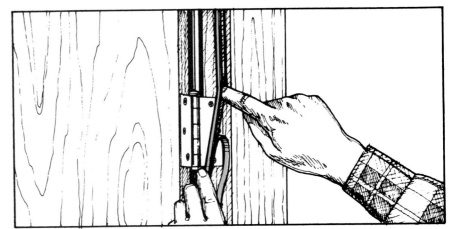

Figure 16. Use your finger or a screwdriver to crease the V-seal weatherstripping.

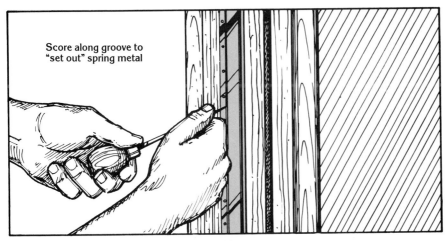

Score along groove to "set out" spring metal

Figure 17. An awl is used to score spring metal V-seal.

Automatic Door Bottoms

Automatic door bottoms work just the way they sound. When the door is closed, they automatically lower and when the door is opened they automatically raise up to clear the carpet or rug. These must be carefully installed so as not to cause too much tension on the spring mechanism.

That about covers the market for threshold treatments. Assess each doorway carefully and plan accordingly. Don't overlook those doors leading to unheated rooms, the basement, or the garage. They can drain off just as much energy as doors to the outside. If you

heat your garage, even periodically, it will be worthwhile to install a seal on that door as well. Special sweeps and shoes are made to keep rain out, in addition to sealing cold air gaps. If the weatherstripping does not come with its own fasteners, use galvanized shingle nails placed 3 inches apart.

Now let's get on with weatherstripping the gaps around those door and window frames. The best products for door treatments are of the V-seal variety or spring metal. Unlike windows, doors will be opened and closed frequently throughout the changing seasons. They require something sturdy enough to take constant use.

V-Seal

This self-adhesive, sticky-back type of weatherstripping is made of durable plastic. Easy to install as well as inexpensive, it will last a long time. V-seal should be installed in the seams around the door or window frame so that a tight seal is achieved when the door or window is closed.

Door application

1. Use a steel tape measure to measure the length of your frame on both sides of the door and across the top.

2. Cut the plastic V-seal to the appropriate length with scissors.

3. Remove a couple of inches of the paper liner and position it into place at the top of the door frame so that the bottom of the V-shape will point inward toward the house.

4. As you bring the plastic down, simultaneously pull off the paper backing and press it into place. (See Figure 16.) If you get it slightly out of line, simply pull it back up. The V-seal will adhere again when you press it back into position.

5. Run the V-seal all the way down to the bottom of the door frame. Do the same on the opposite side of the frame and at the top.

6. Now fold the plastic strip along its pre-scored center so that the V will protrude into the space you are trying to seal. Do this all the way around the door.

7. Be sure the door does not fit too tightly on the top or along the hinge side before installing the weatherstripping. You may need to plane and/or sand the surface a bit for a smoother fit.

Spring Metal

Although it is one of the more expensive weatherstripping materials, spring metal blends beautifully with the frame when the door is open and is virtually invisible when the door is closed. This one requires a bit more work to install, using a tack hammer and awl or screwdriver.

Spring metal on doors

1. Spring metal weatherstripping is installed on the door jamb next to the door stop. Measure along the sides and the top of the door jamb and cut the spring metal to the correct length with tinsnips.

2. Begin with the hinge side of the doorway, then do the latch side above and below the latch plate. Install the top piece last, miter-cutting the corners.

3. Position the spring metal so that the edge does not quite contact the stop.

4. Tack each strip at the ends to align it and stretch it flat against the jamb before nailing along its length.

5. Some manufacturers provide a strip to fit behind the strike plate. You can also trim a piece to fit.

6. When all the strips have been installed, run an awl or a screwdriver along the outside edge to spring the metal spring into position.

Now that we're ready to weatherstrip the windows, it is best to begin by discussing the different types of windows, in relation to the types of weatherstripping.

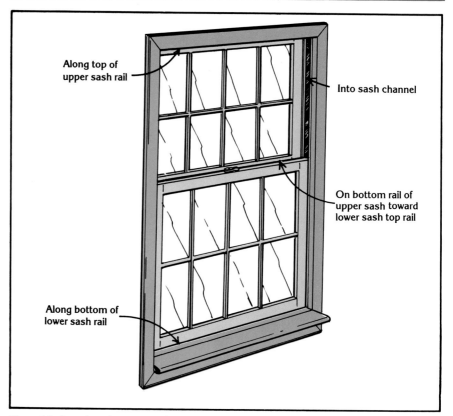

Figure 18. Location of the weatherstripping on a double-hung window.

Double-Hung Windows

V-seal and spring metal weatherstripping are most effective and durable on this type of window. Manufacturers require different fastening techniques. Some are pressure sensitive; others require tacking. For durability, the spring metal is the best. But the plastic V-types run a very close second.

A double-hung window is probably the most complicated to weatherstrip. But once you've done one, you can handle the others easily.

Application of V-seal or spring metal

1. As with any weatherstripping job, begin by cleaning the surfaces well of dirt, grease, and loose paint.

2. Measure from the base of the inner channel to 2 inches above the top rail of the upper sash. Cut four strips to that length for the inner and outer vertical sash channels. Scissors will easily cut the plastic, but you will need tinsnips for the metal.

3. Lower the top sash and slip the weatherstripping material down into the channel with the point of the "V" facing toward the house, or the springy part of the metal toward the outside.

4. Be sure you do not cover the pulleys and that the sash cords or chains can run free. This may require a bit of custom trimming.

5. Place weatherstrips full length along the top of the upper sash rail and along the bottom of the lower sash rail.

7. The mid-section of the window calls for some extra care. The strip for the bottom rail of the upper sash goes on the edge toward the lower sash top rail.

Keep in mind, if you are using spring metal, that the nail heads should be slightly countersunk so that they do not catch on the opposite rail when the window is opened.

Casement Windows and Awning Windows

These cannot normally be sealed by placing weatherstripping outside. The adhesive-backed foam weatherstripping works best on the interior frame where the sash makes contact. Self-adhesive foam rubber weatherstripping is easy to install, widely available, and quite inexpensive. Its major drawback is that it wears quickly and cannot be used where friction occurs, such as the sash channel of a double-hung window.

Sliding Windows

Weatherstripping for sliding metal windows is best installed by a professional glazier or weatherstripping contractor, since it is difficult to find anything on the market for home installation. Sliding wood windows are best insulated with V-seal or spring metal, but adhesive-backed foam or bulb vinyl can also be used effectively if you are closing windows down for the winter and do not plan to open them until warm weather returns. The tubular or bulb vinyl type is reusable season after season. This is especially good for sliding glass doors. Once you have cut it to the proper length, simply press the flanged protrusion into the gap to be sealed, either inside or out. Some types require nailing to secure it. Space the nails 4 to 6 inches apart. One thing the packages seldom tell you is that you should never paint the tubular or bulb vinyl weatherstripping. Because it is a highly visible choice, many people attempt to camouflage it with paint. Unfortunately, this stiffens the vinyl and diminishes its sealing ability.

If both sashes move, weatherstrip them as you would for a double-hung window. If only one sash is movable, use spring metal in the channel where the sash closes against the frame and bulb vinyl on the top, bottom, and where the sashes join.

Jalousie Windows

The design of these windows makes them nearly impossible to weatherstrip. A clear vinyl strip installed across the bottom of each pane is a partial solution, but these must be special ordered. I recommend a removable storm window.

TIP: During the winter wrap your window air conditioners in plastic and seal them with duct tape for better insulation.

STEP FIVE

ENERGY CONSERVATION

Margin of Error: Not applicable

Reduction in energy cost can be consciously obtained by making some of the necessary changes inside your home as you saw during your weatherization audit.

Appliance Adjustments

The thermostat. It does make a difference where your thermostat is located in your home. One located too near a heat or cold source, or on an outside wall, can give you unnecessary problems.

Keep in mind, while weatherizing the interior doors of your home, that you do not want to seal off the room with the thermostat. The purpose of tightening interior doors is to avoid heating or cooling unused rooms of the house.

Turning the thermostat down at night when you are sleeping; during the day when the house is unoccupied; only utilizing the heat or air conditioner in the morning and evening; are prime energy savers. By installing a programmable thermostat you can eliminate fooling around with the setting three or four times a day. This device is installed easily.

1. Turn the power off at the furnace or by removing the fuse or pulling the circuit breaker that runs the furnace fan.

2. Lift off the cover plate from the old thermostat. Carefully note on a piece of paper which numbered or lettered wire is connected to which wire on the existing thermostat and tag each one with masking tape.

3. Remove the thermostat and inspect the wiring. If it is discolored, or if the insulation is cracked, cut back the insulation to a solid material and rewrap the wire with electrical tape to within 1 inch of the end.

4. If the wiring leading from the thermostat to the furnace fan is not repairable, replace it. (See Chapter 9 for tips on working with electrical fixtures.)

5. Pull the wires through the opening of the new programmable thermostat wall plate and fasten the wires into place with the color-coded screws provided.

6. Screw the thermostat to the wall and install the cover plate.

Hot water heater. Turning down the hot water heater to a temperature of 110 degrees will generally supply you with adequate hot water. For those of you with small children, it will be an added comfort to know a mischievous child will not be scalded by this lower temperature. If a hotter temperature is needed, like on a dishwasher, you can get small water heating boosters. These are installed just before the appliance they are serving in the plumbing system. They work by heating just the water needed for immediate use.

Install an insulating jacket around the hot water heater to improve its heat retention capability (see Figure 20). This also will keep the heating element from working so hard to keep the water hot. If you have a gas hot water heater, be careful not to install the jacket too close to the floor. The pilot light needs to receive air.

When you leave your home for vacations or any extended leave of absence, turn off the pilot light to the hot water heater as well as any other pilot lights in the home. Check with your local gas company first about turning off and relighting gas pilot lights.

Tune-Ups and Maintenance

It pays to have your furnace and central air conditioner tuned up each year before the heating or cooling season. Although this is a job for a professional, you can take some measures to add to this efficiency.

Carefully examine all of the ducts and flues and seal any leaks with duct tape. These usually occur at a bend in the duct. Replace filters regularly on furnaces and air-conditioning units. Keep heating/cooling registers cleaned and free from blockage. Window air conditioners should be removed and cleaned in winter and/or have insulation added to seal the space between the air conditioner and the wall. Also wrap the air conditioner in plastic and seal it with duct tape (see Figure 21).

Fireplace flues allow warm air to drift right up and out of your home. Plug these effectively by installing a commercially available insulating fireplace baffle (damper). This must be custom fitted to your flue, usually by a professional. An option is to stuff the chimney flue with nonflammable material, if it

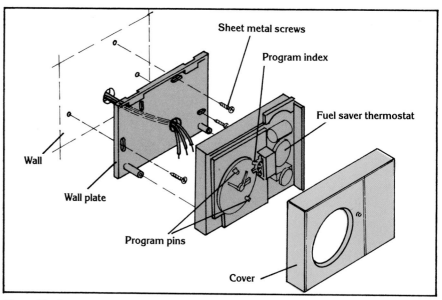

Figure 19. Components of a programmable thermostat. These are easily installed by the novice.

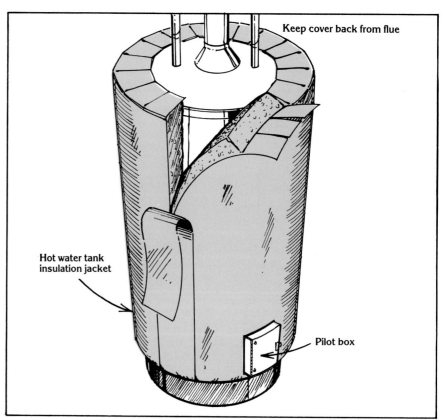

Figure 20. Insulating jacket for gas hot water heater.

Figure 21. Wrap plastic around air conditioner when not in use.

isn't going to be used. Glass fireplace doors work well for the occasionally used fireplace. They seal against the opening and provide excellent protection against infiltration.

There are kits available to help you seal off infiltration through electrical outlets. These are nonflammable foam pad inserts which fit right over the outlet under the plate. Cap the sockets when not in use.

Do not overwork your utilities. Insulating hot and cold water pipes as well as heating/cooling ducts can prevent sweating on hot days and freezing on cold days. Condensation can reduce the effectiveness of your subfloor insulation and cause many other moisture-related problems. Adhesive-backed,

foam pipe insulating tape keeps temperature extremes inside the pipe and eliminates the formation of condensation.

TOOLS AND MATERIALS CHECKLIST

Tools

Hacksaw with fine-toothed blade	Steel tape measure
Metal file	Scissors
Pry bar	Tack hammer
Circular saw	Tinsnips
Drill	Plane
Hammer	Putty knife
Nailset	Utility knife
Caulking gun	Hair dryer
Screwdrivers	Sawhorses or worktable

Materials

Caulk
Sealants
Window glazing compound
Replacement glass
Window film
Storm windows
Storm doors
Wooden threshold
Vinyl gasket threshold
Aluminum threshold
Thermal threshold
Interlocking threshold
Half threshold
Door bottom seal
Door shoe
Automatic door bottom
Finishing nails
Wood dough
Sandpaper
Stain
Sealer
V-Seal weatherstripping
Spring metal weatherstripping
Foam rubber weatherstripping
Bulb vinyl weatherstripping
Garage door weatherstripping
Galvanized shingle nails
Fiberglass or oakum
Programmable thermostat
Masking tape
Heating boosters
Insulating jacket for hot water heater
Duct tape
Plastic film
Insulating fireplace baffle
Glass fireplace doors
Foam pad inserts for outlets
Pipe insulating tape

TIP: Turning down the hot water heater to a temperature of 110° will supply you with adequate hot water without wasting energy.

CHAPTER ELEVEN

Insulation
Step Two in Getting Ready for the Cold (and Hot)

WHAT YOU WILL BE DOING

Heat naturally flows from a warmer area to a cooler one. It does this in only three ways: conduction, *where heat is transferred directly from mass to mass;* convection, *the movement of heated air from one space to another (hot air rises, heavier cool air sinks); and* radiation, *which simply means that any warm body gives off heat toward a cooler one.*

The function of insulation is to minimize the radiation and convection transfer of heat with a minimum of solid conduction so that our homes stay warmer in cool weather and cooler in warm weather.

In this chapter I discuss the merits and uses of various types of well-known insulations and inform you on how best to evaluate R-values.

R stands for "resistance to heat flow." The greater the R-value, the greater the insulative power. R-value requirements depend on factors such as local climate and the surface you are insulating (walls, ceiling, floor, etc.) and will be regulated by your local building code. I suggest you contact the office of your city or county building inspector for the requirements of your area. Each region of the country has different requirements for adequate amounts of insulation.

In most areas, as we discussed in the previous chapter, local utility companies will offer helpful suggestions on how to reduce your energy bills. Many will arrange to have an expert come to your home to point out areas that need to be insulated or weatherized. Often there is no charge for this service and it may even lead to low- or no-interest loan programs you may be eligible for. Also, state or federal tax credits may apply.

Check with your State Energy Commission, local power company, or local home center for the optimum R-value in your region.

BEFORE YOU BEGIN

SAFETY

Safe-use practices are important when you work with any type of insulation.

1. Dust mask and goggles are necessary for work with all types of insulation, or when sawing wood.

2. Fully cover your body, if possible — long sleeves, a hood, long pants, and gloves. Insulating materials are skin irritants.

3. Always use the correct tool for the job.

4. Be sure power tools are properly grounded.

5. Watch power cord placement so that it does not interfere with the tool's operation.

6. A hard hat should be worn, since roofing nails may be sticking through the sheathing.

7. If you are not allergic to tetanus shots, be sure yours is current. There are usually exposed, rusty nails in an old attic.

8. Keep the insulation clear (3″ or so) from objects that transfer heat, to reduce fire hazards, and install sheet metal baffles around recessed light fixtures, chimneys, and flues.

9. In older homes with possible frayed wires, do not allow the aluminum vapor barrier of batt insulation to come in contact with the wire, since it could short circuit.

10. Working in attics or other hot areas can cause loss of body salt by excessive sweating. Consider taking salt tablets.

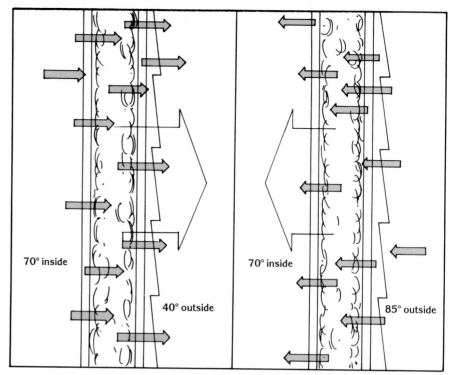

Figure 1. Illustration of how heat is transferred (and lost) through conduction.

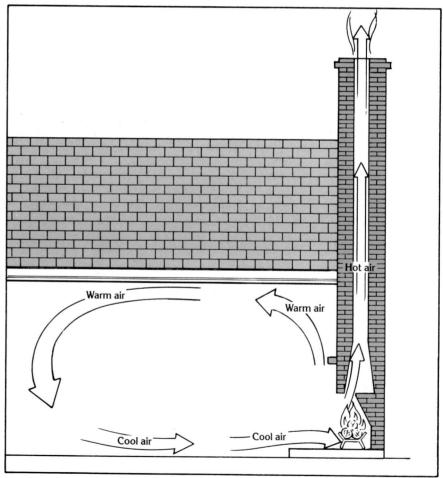

Figure 2. Illustration of convection.

11. When working outside on a roof, wear shoes or boots with rubber soles; stay clear of power lines; secure extension ladders with safety hooks that clamp over the ridge; and delay your work until the roof is free from dampness of rain, frost, snow, or dew.

12. When working high on the outside of the house, I suggest you rent scaffolding to provide a balanced, level working surface.

13. Do not step through attic floor joists onto the ceiling of the room below. It will give way.

14. Some types of insulation are flammable. Check with your local building department and fire department for special application precautions or restrictions.

USEFUL TERMS

Caulk. A pliable material, usually forced into a gap or crack with a gun or pressurized can, hardens into an effective seal against air and moisture infiltration.

Cellulose. Blown-in or loose, consists of rock wool, glass fiber, vermiculite, and/or perlite. Use this in floors, walls, and hard-to-reach places. This type of insulation is poured between joists or blown in with special equipment. It is best suited for use in irregular-shaped areas and is the best option for blowing into existing finished walls.

Fiberglass. Blankets or batts, a widely used insulator for walls, floors, ceilings, roofs, and attics. Fitted and stapled easily between studs, joists, and beams, I feel it is best suited for the do-it-yourselfer.

Flexi-vent. A waffle-like strip of plastic designed to allow air circulation to carry away moisture that could build up under insulation.

Foam. Extruded polystyrene, isocyanurate board, and fiberglass board. These rigid panels are used on unfinished walls, in new construction, or on basement and masonry walls or exterior surfaces. The panels are glued or cut to friction fit between studs, joists, or furring strips and must be covered with drywall or paneling for fire safety. They offer a high insulating value for a relatively thin material, but are highly flammable, and some chemically based sprays or foams may discharge poisonous films over a period of time. Be sure to use a closed-cell, waterproof rigid panel in exterior applications or in high-moisture areas.

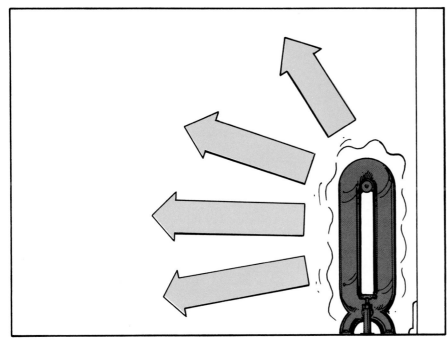

Figure 3. Illustration of radiant heat.

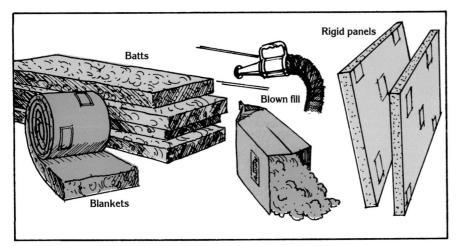

Figure 4. The most popular types of insulation.

TIP: Working in your attic is hot and tiring. Try to work early in the morning before it gets too hot. Carry a spray container of cold water to spray on yourself and your fogged-up goggles.

Furring. Strips of wood used to level out a surface prior to finishing.

Shims. Thin wedges of wood used to bring furring strips level with each other when used on an uneven wall.

Silicate compound. Made of glass and sand. It does not burn, release toxic fumes, nor attract vermin. It comes in lightweight, easy-to-handle bags and should be used in the same manner as loose fill or cellulose.

Vapor barrier. Most common is a 6 ml. sheet of plastic attached over insulation to eliminate moisture infiltration and deterioration of insulation.

WHAT YOU WILL NEED

Time. Time depends on the type of job being done. Allow yourself 3 to 4 person hours per 100 square feet when installing fiberglass batts and a vapor barrier in the attic. Allow yourself 4 to 6 person hours per 100 square feet when installing furring, insulation, and vapor barrier in your basement.

Tools. Most of the tools required for the installation of insulation are found in the home toolbox. Others can be rented reasonably from your local home center.

Dust mask
Goggles
Gloves
Pencil and paper
Trouble light
Extension cord
String
Steel tape measure
Circular saw
Utility knife
Staple gun and heavy-duty staples (An alternative tool would be an air

compressor with a stapling attachment.)
Hammer
Hole saw
Drill
Spackling knife
Circular saw
Ramset (rental)
Level
Caulking gun
Blowing machine (rental, if you choose to blow in your insulation)

Materials. As with any home project, the materials you will need depend on the type of insulation used and the extent of work being done. Your list will include many of the following:

2 × 4 boards
16 penny nails
Flexi-vent material
Duct tape
Fiberglass insulation
Vapor barrier (6 ml. visquine)
Cellulose
Spackling
Long, straight board
Rigid foam panels (regular or closed cell)
2" × 2" furring strips
Adhesive
Shim material
Vapor barrier (6 ml. visquine)
2" extruded foam panels
Construction adhesive (for exterior use and foam panels)

Tar paper
Sheet metal flashing
Drain pipe
Gravel
Tape
Plastic
Caulk
Waterproofing sealant
Closable vents
Drain tiles
Pipes
Sump pump
Soffit ventilation plugs
Sheet metal, louvred and screened vent
Continuous ridge vent
Wind turbine

PERMITS AND CODES

Codes for insulation requirements will vary in different parts of the country. A permit may be required in some areas if the work being done exceeds $100 in cost. Check with your local building inspector. Codes also will indicate required R-factors.

DESIGN

Choose the most effective insulation for a particular situation. I offer widely accepted suggestions but the climate, existing insulation, and design of your home will affect your decision.

MOST COMMON MISTAKES

Perhaps the most fundamental and often overlooked mistake do-it-yourselfers make when insulating is neglecting to find out the most efficient R-value for their area and insulating accordingly. Other common mistakes are listed below.

1. Not providing for good air circulation between the roof and the insulation.

2. Installing fiberglass batting with the paper side (vapor barrier) facing toward the outside instead of toward the heated area.

3. Omitting a vapor barrier, which prevents accumulation of moisture between the batting and the underside of the roof or wall.

4. Puncturing the vapor barrier unnecessarily, or neglecting to puncture the vapor barrier of the top batt when installing two layers.

5. Distorting, compressing, or squeezing the fiberglass batt insulation out of shape.

6. Using paper-faced batting against a heat source like a chimney, a heating duct, etc.

7. Neglecting to get into all of the small spaces and corners with the insulation.

8. Covering eaves' vents with insulation, thereby cutting off ventilation.

9. Making unnecessary trips up and down the attic stairs during installation. Assemble all tools and equipment in your work area prior to beginning the job.

10. Not using closed-cell (waterproof), rigid foam insulation panels on below-grade installations.

THE ATTIC

The attic is probably the greatest single heat loser in the home. The lighter heated air rises while the heavier cool air drops (convection). That's why your feet are usually cold or why your much-taller mate says it's too hot when you want to turn the heat up.

Adequate insulation in attics is imperative. Newer homes are generally well insulated — although it never hurts to check. But many older homes have little or no insulation. Oftentimes what there is has deteriorated or compressed beyond even minimal worth.

The most widely used insulation in the attic is fiberglass. Fiberglass commonly comes in 3½″ to 6″ thick rolls. It can be applied in double layers to increase it past 6″. It is available in widths to fit between 16″ or 24″ on center framing members. It comes in two forms, batt and blanket. Batt insulation is available in 4′ or 8′ lengths. Blanket insulation is available in lengths from 30 to 70 feet in standard manufacturer's thickness. I recommend blanket insulation. There are fewer gaps between pieces.

Fiberglass is available in foil-backed, paper-backed, and unfaced batts and blankets. Both the foil and paper act as vapor barriers. The foil, however, is only of value when used in conjunction with a ¾″ air space. Unfaced fiberglass is used in conditions of potential fire hazards and as the top layer of a two-layer application. Otherwise, paper-backed is used.

STEP ONE

PREPARATION

Margin of Error: Leave no gaps

Prior to actually installing the fiberglass, you need to do some preparatory work. The first thing to do is to decide how you want to utilize your attic space.

Have with you a pencil and paper, and a trouble light with an extension cord, before you go up to the attic. Carefully examine your attic space. Determine whether you will be using the space for living and therefore want to heat it or whether you prefer to insulate the main part of the house below the attic. Locate your insulation in such a way that it encloses the heated areas only.

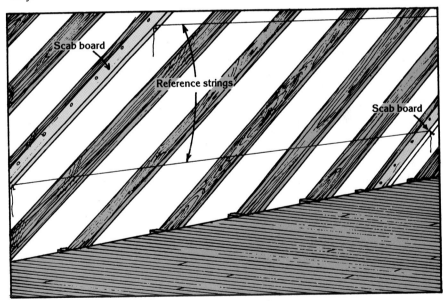

Figure 5. Scab boards are nailed to rafters to increase their depth so thicker insulation may be installed.

If you wish to finish and heat the attic space, look closely at the rafters, checking them for depth and uniformity. They must be adequate to house the depth of batting needed for your area. Furring out the rafters to the proper depth will also give you a point of attachment for the vapor barrier and a structure capable of supporting finish-

---

ing material like drywall or paneling.

Some rafter systems are not deep enough for fiberglass batting, for an attached vapor barrier, or to support a finished wall of paneling or gypsum board. Attaching scabbed-on boards to the existing rafters will extend them out and increase their depth (Figure 5). You need to be sure these new boards attached to the rafters all come out to exactly the same level, because you need to attach your finishing material to an even surface. To do this, nail up a set of reference strings on two scab boards, one on each end of the attic roof, as shown in Figure 5. Stretch the strings across the face of the rafters to show you the proper depth to align the scabbed-on 2 × 4 or 2 × 6 boards.

Jot down the required lengths of the boards. Measure and mark the boards with a steel tape measure and cut them to length with a circular saw. Cut all the boards at one time. Make the cuts in the attic if possible, to avoid unneces-sary trips up and down the stairs.

Position each board against the rafter and align it with the string. Nail it firmly into the rafter, using 16d nails every 16″. Continue this process until the entire rafter system is scabbed out to accommodate the insulation. Be sure all scab boards come right to the reference strings.

STEP TWO

VENTILATING THE ATTIC

Margin of Error: Not applicable

Ventilation in the attic is of the utmost importance. If the attic isn't properly ventilated, moisture can be trapped, causing a great deal of deterioration in the insulation as well as in the wood structure. Insulation loses its R-value as it takes on moisture. Also, built-up heat is not vented in the summer and the attic becomes super-heated. Few attics in older homes are properly vented.

Soffit ventilation allows air to travel from outside the house into the attic space rafters and out the gable wall vents, or through ridge ventilation at the peak of the roof. Soffit ventilation plugs are screened and louvred so air can pass through but insects cannot. To install these vents, simply drill a hole with a hole saw between each rafter all the way around the outside roof overhang of the house. Push in the soffit ventilation plugs. On the gable wall, near the peak, you may want to install a sheet metal, louvred, screened vent to let the air out as it moves toward the top of the attic.

Another option is the continuous ridge vent, which is screened and available in 10′ lengths. This is designed to be installed along the entire ridge of the house, letting air out but keeping rain from getting in. These ridge vents can be difficult to retrofit in existing homes, but they are recommended in new construction and can be considered when reroofing.

The wind turbine is a most effective ventilation piece, also installed near the roof peak. The wind or air rising through the turbine turns the vanes in the turbine and gets the air moving near the top of the house, drawing moisture out.

To install a wind turbine, find a good

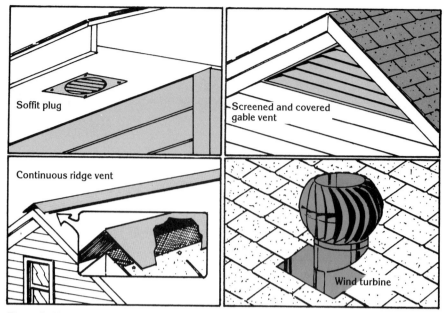

Figure 6. Key places where a house should be ventilated.

location near the peak and between rafters. Remove enough of the roof shingles, tiles, gravel, or other roofing material down to the tar paper. You will need to expose an area slightly larger than the flange of the wind turbine. Place the flange in position, and mark the flange opening on the tar paper with a piece of chalk or colored pencil.

Drill a starter hole using a hole saw or a 1″ drill bit or larger. Once the hole is started, you can use a reciprocating saw to complete cutting the entire flange area. Be certain the blade is long enough and suitable for cutting tar paper and sheathing. You may want to keep a few extra blades on hand, since the long, narrow reciprocating blade

Figure 7. Stapling up styrofoam waffle boards to allow for proper ventilation behind the insulation.

tends to break easily. Wear safety glasses or goggles when sawing.

Next, use a caulking gun to apply a generous amount of roofing asphalt cement on the outside perimeter of the opening to serve as a sealer. Now you can nail the base of the turbine to the roof with roofing nails. Roll some tar paper over the flange to create a double seal, and carefully replace the shingles to cover the tar-papered flange. Be sure the turbine is properly interwoven with the shingles. Then, simply install the wind turbine into the base and you're in business with a very fine ventilator. Be sure you install the turbine properly or there can be leaks. It is essential that the flange and the shingles are installed in the proper overlapping fashion. Also, you may want to consider calling in a professional when installing a turbine in a flat or nearly flat roof, since leaks are more likely to occur with these.

Complete your preparation by attaching flexi-vent material (a waffle-like strip of plastic) between the rafters and against the roof sheathing (Figure 7.) This is designed to allow air circulation to carry away moisture that would build up between the roof and the new insulation. Butt these strips right up next to each other and against the roof itself.

STEP THREE

INSULATING THE RAFTERS

Margin of Error: Fill entire cavity and plug holes exactly

Working on your knees in an attic for long periods of time can be very hot and tiring. You will be covered from head to toe in clothing and gear. Plan for a few breaks in your work schedule, and try to work early in the morning before it gets too hot. It may help to add a spray container of cold water to your toolbox — to spray yourself and your fogged-up goggles. You might even consider taking salt tablets. Check with your doctor to see if they might be necessary.

Begin by measuring the length of each space. Cut each piece of insulation an inch or two longer than needed, to assure a snug fit. Use your straight-edge to compress the insulation before cutting. Use a very sharp utility knife to assure a good straight cut across the fi-

berglass batt. Staple it to the rafters or scabbed-on boards with a staple gun so that the paper backing is toward the interior of the room, to act as a vapor barrier. Use ⅜″ heavy-duty staples every six inches. Attach the insulation to the rafter scab board by the paper flange so as not to compress the fiberglass. Make sure the paper flange and the staples lie flat against the board, to create an even surface for attaching the finished wall material. A time- and work-saving aid here would be an air compressor with a staple gun attachment. It can be rented, if you don't have access to one.

Where the spacing of the rafters is uneven, odd-angled, or not standard, you will need to cut the insulation to fit. Cut it 1″ wider than the necessary width, and tuck the fiberglass in to create a flange for stapling. Once the insulation is in place between all the rafters, I suggest you staple up a vapor barrier of 6 ml. visquine (a painter's drop cloth) over the insulation and across the face of the rafters. Although the paper or foil backing of the insulation is a vapor barrier, the added visquine covers completely, with no breaks. This assures that no moisture will form in the cavity. As you staple the vapor barrier to the rafters, draw it as airtight as possible. But be careful not to puncture the plastic unnecessarily as you put it in place. Should this occur, repair it with duct tape.

When installing insulation over wires, pipes, or fireblocking, it will be necessary to back cut the batt to fit over the obstacle, leaving the paper intact and the insulation uncompressed. (See Figure 8.)

TIP: When installing insulation, wear clothing that fully covers your body, and consider a tetanus booster and salt tablets.

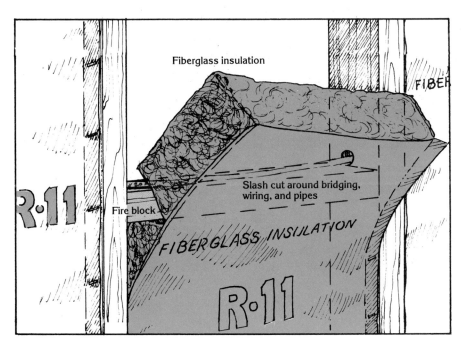

Figure 8. Back cutting insulation around fireblock is recommended.

STEP FOUR

INSULATING THE ATTIC FLOOR

Margin of Error: Fill all cavities and plugholes exactly

Placing the fiberglass insulation between the attic floor joists effectively insulates the lower portion of your home and avoids your using added energy to heat unused attic space. Use this method if you don't plan to convert your attic into living space.

Begin by unrolling the insulation, paper face down, toward the heated area of the house, between the joists, starting in a corner. Use a stick to tuck it into the corner, but be careful not to compress the fiberglass. If there are soffit vents, leave a space at the eaves for air circulation.

The greatest concern comes with infiltration of the heat from the rooms below up through any cracks that may occur around the insulation. Therefore, be very careful about the way you install the insulation around any obstacles in the joist space. These include plumbing, piping, heater ducts, chimney stacks, or the bridging (Figure 10). Cut the insulation to fit snugly around the object.

NOTE: Unfaced fiberglass must be used when working around heat sources like a chimney, flue, or heating duct. The paper facing on most insulation is flammable. A 2″ air space between the chimney and the insulation is recommended. With prefabricated flues and chimneys, check the manufacturer's recommendation.

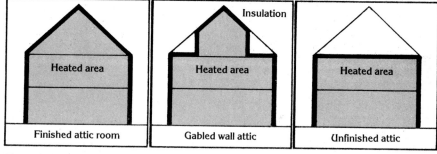

Figure 9. Note that insulation is replaced to contain the heat in the heated areas only.

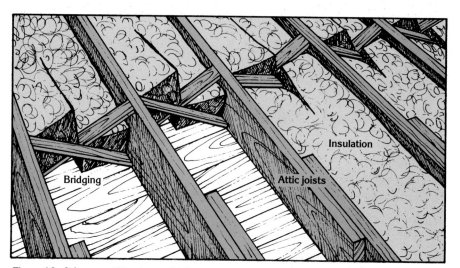

Figure 10. It is a good idea to cut the insulation to fit around any floor bridging, as shown.

Figure 11. Be sure pieces are joined closely together.

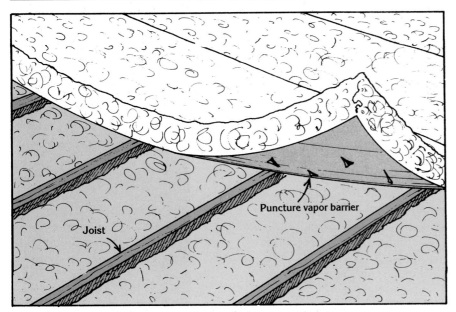

Figure 12. When installing two layers of batt insulation, be sure to puncture vapor barrier of upper layer so moisture is not trapped.

You can cover all electrical junction boxes (but not electrical fixture boxes) because they do not give off heat. Again, do not distort or compress the fiberglass. Leave about 3″ around recessed lighting fixtures for air to circulate and to keep the fixture cool. Wrap pipes separately to cut off air passage around them, and stuff scraps of fiberglass into small, hard-to-cover areas.

If one layer of fiberglass batting between floor joists does not meet the R-value you need, a second layer of fiberglass insulation can be added on top of, and at right angles to, the joists. There is less thermal loss with this method because the joists are covered as well. Your concern here is to avoid trapping

moisture between the two layers by having installed a vapor barrier between them. So, if possible, use unfaced insulation for this layer. If not, install the second layer with the paper face down and puncture the paper barrier on this second layer (Figure 12). Since you will have already taken care of any penetrating problems, your main concern with this second layer is that the batting fit good and snug, side by side and end to end. Start this second layer butted against the bottom of the rafters, beginning in a corner. Continue to install it end to end until you get to the center of the floor or near the stairwell. Then begin again at the opposite side and install to the center again, to avoid walking on and compressing the insulation over the joists. Install insulation on the opening hatch door to your attic as well.

Another method is to pour or blow in loose fill or cellulose insulation up to the joists for an even surface. Then unfaced or punctured batt insulation can be installed perpendicular to the joist system. A trouble light is needed to help you see that hard-to-reach places are being adequately filled with the cellulose. Blow in the cellulose to fill the joist spaces past the top of the wood framing, to achieve a higher R-value.

As you work back into corners and around eaves' vents, take care that you do not cover any ventilating areas.

A long straight board will help even out the cellulose (Figure 13). Drag it along the joists to push loose piles of insulation into the spaces between the joists.

After completing your insulation, you may find that your skin itches from fiberglass irritation. I've found that vinegar makes an effective rinse when I bathe or shower after working with fiberglass. It almost eliminates the itching, which comes from the small particles of glass left on the skin.

Figure 13. Using a board to level the blown-in or poured-in insulation.

THE WALLS

For new additions and remodeling projects, your choice of insulation will, no doubt, depend on personal preference, use of the space, and R-value necessary for your area. Fiberglass is most often used, although, in many areas, people are also installing rigid foam board on the outside of the frame underneath the siding, as well as fiberglass in the walls. Should you choose to use fiberglass, the principles for installing it in the walls are the same as for between the rafters. You will need a uniform surface to staple the insulation to and to apply a finishing material such as wallboard or paneling.

If your home is already built, your options for increasing the insulation in the walls are limited by the finished materials. It is to this situation I address the use of blown-in cellulose insulation as a way to avoid having to remove the siding or interior walls.

Usually this method will not give you as high an R-value as the same amount of fiberglass insulation. However, it is adequate for beefing up a poor situation in an existing home. Unfortunately, in time the insulation will settle toward the bottom of the wall, leaving uninsulated areas at the top where you need it the most.

STEP ONE

PREPARATION

Margin of Error: Exact

Calculate your needs carefully and discuss the possibilities with your dealer. Be sure the type you choose is properly treated with fireproofing. Having a professional do this work may be wise, but it can be done by the novice.

Blown-in cellulose has the advantage of being quick and easy. You won't need to carry a lot of tools and materials with you.

You can blow up to 100 feet away from where the machine is positioned. One person can load the machine in another part of the house or outside while another works in the area to be insulated. This eliminates the discomfort of cramped working quarters when insulating in tight places.

STEP TWO

BLOWING IN THE CELLULOSE

Margin of Error: Fill the cavities completely. Plug holes exactly

Blow cellulose into existing wall cavities between studs by cutting out a hole with a hole saw between each stud along the top outside wall. Blow in the cellulose until it begins to back up and out of the hole. Return the plug cut out by the hole saw into the hole and spackle over it. If the house is over five years old, fireblocking was probably installed between the studs. In this case, you will need to drill two holes between each stud — one above and one below the fireblocking (Figure 16). You can test this by drilling a hole at the top of the wall and inserting a stiff wire down into the hole to feel for any obstructions. Then drill below the obstruction as well.

For aluminum, plastic, steel, or any other similar outside surfaced homes that do not lend themselves to this method, blow the insulation in through holes in the interior wall surfaces. This will require a bit of patch and repair when it's done.

TIP: After you complete your insulation, your skin may itch from fiberglass irritation. I've found that vinegar makes an effective rinse when I bathe or shower after working with fiberglass. It almost eliminates the itching that comes from the small particles of glass left on the skin.

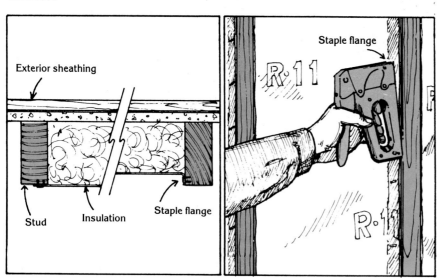

Figure 14. The flanges of the insulation can be stapled to the inside or front surface of a stud or rafter.

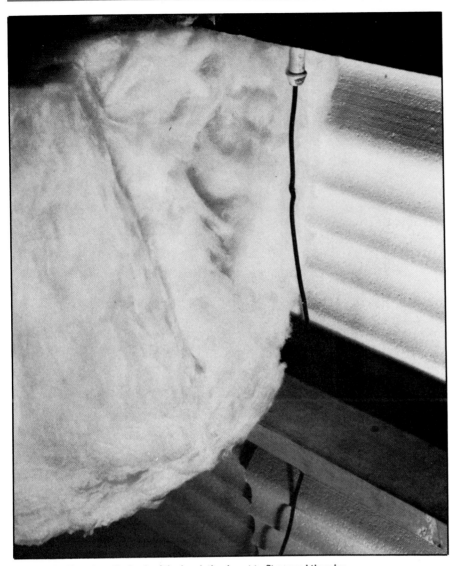

Figure 15. Note how the back of the insulation is cut to fit around the wire.

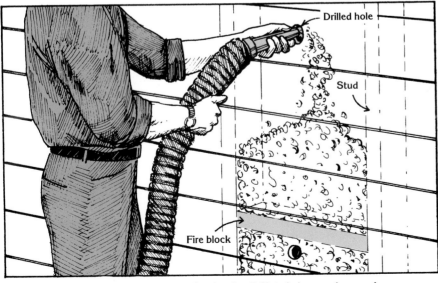

Figure 16. Blowing in insulation to an uninsulated wall. Note holes are above and below obstructions (fireblocks).

REPAIRING THE WALL

Margin of Error: Exact

To patch holes in a plaster wall, fill the hole with newspaper or wire mesh (metal lath). Cut the wire mesh to be 1″ larger than the hole all around. Tie a 5″ string through the center of the mesh and a pencil at the other end. Push the mesh through the hole and twist the pencil until it is tightly spanned against the wall. Apply spackling compound to within ¼″ of the surface. Allow it to dry completely; then cut the string to remove the pencil. Apply a second layer of spackling. Sand when it dries.

Holes in drywall can be repaired using a "hat patch" technique. After removing the damaged portion of drywall, undercut the edges for a good clean opening. Then tear off ½″–1″ of the paper around the perimeter of the hole so that only the bare gypsum is showing. Cut a piece of drywall to the exact shape and dimension as the area defined by the bare gypsum. Remove enough of the gypsum from this piece so that you are left with a plug (the size of the hole) with a paper "brim" that will cover the bare gypsum. Finish the patch by mudding the seam with drywall compound.

After the holes are filled in and dry, the wall must be smoothed. Use a hand sanding block or an orbital sander fitted with 120-grit sandpaper for a finish that is smooth, flat, and flush again.

There is no vapor barrier in place when blown-in cellulose is used. Even though it has been treated to resist moisture and deterioration, you may want to paint interior walls with an oil-based, non-breathing paint to act somewhat as a vapor barrier. Do not paint the exterior with a non-breathing paint or it will trap moisture in the wall.

THE BASEMENT

STEP ONE

PREPARATION

Margin of Error: ¼"

Before adding insulation to the basement walls or the crawl space foundation, and prior to refinishing a basement room, it is essential that you repair any leaks and solve any problems with dampness. Wait until it is thoroughly dry before you install the insulation, to be sure all problems have been eliminated. If you are unsure whether or not you have such a problem, tape a square-foot piece of plastic to the basement wall or floor. Leave it in place for a week. If condensation builds up under the plastic, you have a problem that needs to be solved.

The causes of such condensation can be extensive. Some of the most common are leaks and cracks in the concrete, and seepage, condensation, or drainage problems around the foundation. That may sound like a lot of work, but a systematic going over of each potential trouble spot will save you a great deal of time, trouble, and money later on.

Cracks can be caulked. Seepage can be lessened by painting waterproofing sealant on the interior walls.

I recommend installing closable vents for the crawl space. Open them in warm weather to air out the crawl space and close them in winter to prevent heat loss.

In low-ground areas where drainage is a problem, install drain tiles or pipes around the perimeter of the foundation. In some cases you may even need a sump pump to pump out excess water. Be sure the clothes dryer is properly vented outside.

For more information on caulking and sealing, see the preceding chapter

Figure 17. Installing insulation, using wires and nails for support. Note paper vapor barrier is toward heated side.

Figure 18. Installing the insulation between joists with chicken wire.

196

Figure 19. You can buy wire insulation supports that snap between the joists to support the insulation.

STEP TWO

INSTALLING RIGID FOAM INSULATION

Margin of Error: 1/4"

Interior application. Before beginning your installation, be sure to correct any moisture problems you may have on your basement walls. This can be as easy a job as painting a waterproofing on the inside of the wall, to as complex a job as having to install a drain tile system on the outside next to the foundation.

After correcting moisture problems, install 2″ × 2″ furring strips to the wall 16″ on center (Figure 20). Attach the furring strips with the appropriate adhesive, or a rented ramset if attaching to masonry walls. The furring will give you a firm, level surface to which you can attach drywall or paneling. The chapter on paneling will give you more in-depth instruction for attaching furring strips.

To even out the slight irregularities in masonry or old plaster, it is likely you will need some shim material to get the furring surfaces flush with each other. Put a level on the face of the furring strips and shim out as needed. (A shim is a thin wedge of wood which can be purchased inexpensively in packets at your home center or made yourself from scraps of wood.)

Measure and cut the foam to size with a utility knife or saw — to fit snugly between the furring strips. Then press the foam between the strips.

Staple a sheet of 6 ml. plastic as a vapor barrier over and at the top of the insulation. Do not staple it to the furring strips or puncture it unnecessarily. Gravity and the wall covering will hold it in place.

---

on Weatherization. Weatherization goes hand in hand with insulation, and many of the solutions overlap.

Insulating basement and crawl space sometimes calls for a different type of insulation than does insulating attic and walls of a home. In the first place, the basement and crawl space are more susceptible to moisture seepage, which can lead to problems like wet or damp surfaces, stained finishes, mildew, and so on. Water vapor moves easily through most materials used in construction, including brick and concrete block. A basement wall that is not adequately insulated with a moisture-resistant material will conduct warm moist air from the living space through to the cooler outer wall where it is likely to condense. If you are not heating the basement or crawl space, you will want

to insulate underneath the first floor. This is best done with fiberglass insulation installed between the joists with the vapor barrier *up* toward the heated area.

You may want to use a closed-cell, rigid foam panel or the reflective layered type of insulation in these areas if you plan to heat the space below the floor. In this case, you will be insulating the basement walls, not the floor.

Rigid foam panels can be used to insulate both interior and exterior walls. The closed-cell type is not as susceptible to moisture as are other types of insulation. Use only closed-cell types in below-grade application. It usually comes in 2′ × 8′ sheets and should be covered with a fire-resistant material, such as drywall, when exposed to the inside.

Exterior application. For exterior insulating projects, the tools remain the same, but with the addition of a shovel. You will need to add these to your materials list as well:

2″ extruded foam panels	Sheet metal flashing
Exterior adhesive	Drain pipe
Tar paper	Gravel

On the exterior side of basement walls, you will need to dig a trench — 2′ down all around the foundation exterior (deeper in a colder weather area with a deeper frost line). Check with your local building inspector to follow the local code.

Use at least 2″ extruded foam panels on the exterior, since they are denser and more efficient than regular foam and will hold up longer. Be sure they are the moisture-proof type. Place the panels right up against the concrete and butted closely against one another. Use an exterior adhesive to glue panels to the foundation wall.

To keep water from getting in between the foam panels and the exterior foundation walls, push sheet metal flashing up under the siding (Figure 21), and hammer it into place over the foam panels with galvanized nails.

If you have a drainage problem, this is a good time to install a drain pipe. In-

Figure 20. Using furring strips and shims to furr out for installing rigid insulation.

TIP: A time- and work-saving aid is an air compressor with a staple gun attachment. If you do not have access to one, it can be rented.

stall it at a slope and connect it to drainage outlets.

Back fill the previously excavated dirt to hold the foam panels in place around the foundation walls. Then plant grass seed or plants to prevent erosion. If you are installing a drain pipe, back fill with gravel, cover the gravel with tar paper, and cover the tar paper with the excavated dirt.

TOOLS AND MATERIALS CHECKLIST

Tools for Fiberglass

Dust mask	Circular saw
Goggles	Utility knife
Gloves	Staple gun and
Pencil and paper	heavy-duty
Trouble light	staples
Extension cord	Hammer
String	
Steel tape	
measure	

Materials for Fiberglass

Tetanus shot	16 penny nails
(optional)	Flexi-vent material
Clothing to fully	Duct tape
cover	Fiberglass
Salt tablets	insulation
(optional)	Vapor barrier (6
2 × 4 boards	ml. visquine)

Tools for Blown-In Cellulose

Hole saw	Blowing machine
Drill	(rental)
Trouble light	Spackling knife
Extension cord	

Materials for Blown-In Cellulose

Cellulose	Long, straight
Spackle	board

Tools for Rigid Foam Panels

Circular saw	Level
Ramset (rental)	Utility knife

Materials for Rigid Foam Panels

Rigid foam panels	2″ extruded foam
(regular or	panels
closed cell)	Exterior adhesive
2″ × 2″ furring	Tar paper
strips	Sheet metal
Adhesive	flashing
Shim material	Drain pipe
Vapor barrier (6	Gravel
ml. visquine)	

Tools for Ventilation

Caulking gun	Drill
Hole saw	

Materials for Ventilation

Tape	Soffit ventilation
Plastic	plugs
Caulk	Sheet metal,
Waterproofing	louvred and
sealant	screened vent
Closable vents	Continuous ridge
Drain tiles	vent
Pipes	Wind turbine
Sump pump	

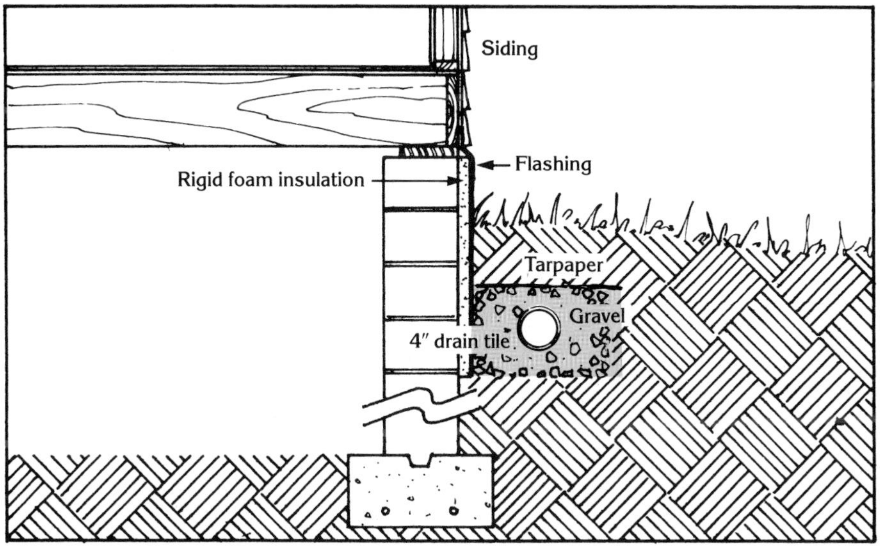

Figure 21. In basements that have moisture problems, or in areas with drainage problems, basement drain tiles can be retrofitted.

CHAPTER TWELVE

Home Security
A Do-It-Yourselfer's Prescription for Safety

WHAT YOU WILL BE DOING

For most of us, whether we live in the city, the suburbs, or the countryside, home security is an important issue. Every one of us has probably been touched by some sort of crime. And many of us feel the need to add an extra measure of protection to our homes, our possessions, and, more important, our loved ones.

There are no guarantees against crime; but, with a relatively small investment in time, energy, and money, we can implement certain home security measures to decrease the chance that our home will be broken into and increase the chance that stolen items are recovered.

It is easy to overlook these measures and feel secure — until something happens.

The purpose of this chapter is to introduce you to some common security measures you can implement around your home. You will also learn, in detail, how to install deadbolts and new entrance locks in exterior doors.

In addition to doors, I also discuss other issues of home security, including: safes and hiding places, windows, alarm systems, and fire security.

BEFORE YOU BEGIN

THE HOME SECURITY SURVEY

The place to start in implementing home security measures is a security survey done by a professional. Usually a local police force will send a security expert out to a home to walk the house and grounds with the owner. If this service is not available in your community, they may provide you with pamphlets or other materials that will allow you to do your own survey. Several books are on the market as well. Also, if you plan to have a professional install an alarm system, the company will often perform the survey. Be careful, because they might have a hidden agenda — to sell you a more expensive security system than you need.

To really do the survey correctly, you need to think like a burglar. Imagine that you want to break into your home without getting caught. Where would you enter? When? How? What do you think would give you away? A little imagination on your part will lead you to the following conclusions:

1. Your points of entry — doors and windows — are where you are most vulnerable.

2. Burglars fear two things: being heard, and being seen.

Almost all home security is focused around these two facts, the mainstays in all burglary work.

A walk around your home, preferably with a professional, should quickly point out to you your weaknesses in home security. If you are like most of us, locking yourself out from time to time, you probably already know these points of vulnerability. You probably know as well just how easy it really is to break into most homes.

Windows are the most vulnerable point of entry. Your windows and screens may be equipped with the standard, older (sometimes newer) types of screens and window latches. These are often inadequate in deterring a burglar. The common window latch can be opened from the outside with a butter knife and just five seconds; the screens require a penknife and an additional five seconds.

Many doors are equipped with simple spring locks. These can be opened with a credit card or a knife. Even if they

make a list of all your vulnerable areas, especially those easily accessible from the ground, including the first floor, basement windows, and doors. Also check out second-floor entry points that are quickly accessible with the use of a ladder.

Ask yourself, What would make my house a house a burglar would not want to hit? (Park the Jaguar in the back; the VW in the front.) Are there high bushes for burglars to hide in? Are there areas of the house that are well hidden? Is there inadequate lighting?

Figure 1. A security survey will reveal any vulnerable areas of the home.

are equipped with a more secure dead-bolt, if the frame of the door is not secure, a forceful shove can often break the wooden frame and trim around the door. Walk through your home and

Are there several vulnerable points of entry? Are there valuable items in plain view through first-floor windows?

If burglars believe they would be in full view of neighbors, you can be sure they will avoid your home. You may need to cut back some shrubs. If you live where there are no neighbors close by, noise from an alarm system is your best deterrent. At night, outdoor lighting is recommended.

Also, check to see if your exterior doors are hollow core or the more durable solid or metal doors. Do any trees offer easy access to second-story windows? Are sliding-glass or garage doors vulnerable? What type of windows do you have? Are they vulnerable? After you complete your security survey, you are ready to make some decisions concerning what security measures you want to implement. In the rest of this chapter I discuss ways of installing these measures yourself.

SAFETY

Safety will not be directly addressed in this chapter as home security is, in itself, safety. Keep in mind, however, the general safe use practices for any tool you will be employing when adding to your security.

USEFUL TERMS

Deadbolt. Consists of a one inch throw with a case-hardened insert that cannot be jimmied or cut.

Deadlocking latch. See deadbolt

Door lights. Window(s) immediately adjacent to a door.

Double cylinder lock. Lock for which a key is needed to unlock both inside and outside.

Hole saw. Drill accessory used in creating the space in which to insert the lockset into a door. Common sizes are from 1″ to 2½″.

Mortise. A notch or hole cut out specifically to fit a full mortise lock; it cannot be removed from the door by force.

Polycarbonate. Shatterproof plastic said to be up to 250 times as strong as regular glass.

Spade bit. Drill accessory used to create a hole in the door edge in which to insert the latch set.

Spring latch. A throw which has no hardened insert and so is easily jimmied with a credit card.

WHAT YOU WILL NEED

Time. Making your home secure is not something one can set a time limit for. The process will involve different amounts of time for everyone. Installation of a deadbolt or lockset can be accomplished by one person in 2 to 4 work hours.

Tools	**Materials**
Screwdrivers	Set pins for hinges
Wrenches	Tempered glass or polycarbonate
Hammer	Solid core wood or steel doors
Drill	3″ hinge screws

PERMITS AND CODES

Permits are not generally required when improving security around the home. However, some areas require a permit if more than $100.00 worth of work is being done. Replacement of doors and windows may fall into this category. Also, electrical work for exterior lighting and alarm systems will require permits and inspections.

In some areas code does not allow the uses of a double cylinder key lock. Check with the proper authority before installing this type.

DESIGN

Although design should not be given preference over safety when securing the home, it is understandable that you do not want to take away aesthetics of the home when making it secure. Alternatives are given in each section which will allow you to make your home secure without detracting from the visual continuity.

Tempered Glass. 4–5 times stronger than glass. Made by heating regular glass almost to the melting point then chilling it rapidly, causing a skin to form around the glass.

DOORS

Windows are easier to penetrate, so doors are not always the main entrance for a burglar. However, doors are usually their main exit.

Sixty percent of all home burglars enter through doors. The common key-in-knob lock can often be opened in a matter of seconds by a professional with a credit card or a screwdriver. There are simple ways to make this technique unusable.

First, let's talk about the door itself. There are many different types of entrance doors. Some are more secure than others. Many entrance doors include some sort of glass, or glass panel directly adjoining the door (door lights), that can be broken. Unless your lock key locks from the inside, a burglar can simply reach through the broken glass around to the inside and open the door. If the panel is large enough, he or she can simply crawl in.

If you have such a door, but do not want to replace it, consider replacing the glass panel with tempered glass. This glass is many times stronger than common plate glass and should deter any intruder. Many doors already have tempered glass, since local codes often

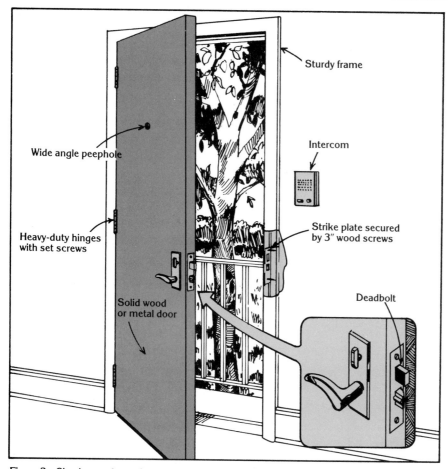

Figure 2. Check your doors thoroughly to be sure they are not vulnerable.

demand it. If not, take the exact measurements to a hardware store, home center, or glass company and order one. It may be relatively expensive. It has to be special ordered (it is too hard to be cut), but is well worth the cost. In any case, whenever a door has standard glass in it or near it, install a double cylinder lock so burglars cannot open the door by reaching through the opening after breaking the glass.

Study the door itself. Is it a sturdy, well-built door? Some newer homes use doors that have a hollow interior (hollow-core doors). These are very easy to break. You may want to consider replacing the door altogether with a new metal or solid-core door. Although replacing a door may seem intimidating, it is actually quite simple, even for the most novice of the do-it-yourselfers. You can buy these doors with the hinges and hardware pre-installed in all standard sizes. Simply remove the pins from the hinges of the

old door, remove the door, and slip the new door on and replace the hinges. If the hinges, handles, locks, or strikeplates do not match up, you will have to adjust for this.

Also note your hinges. If the hinges are exposed to the exterior of the home, you have a problem. Burglars can simply pop out the hinges and remove the door, *even when it is locked tight!* This, a burglar's dream, was some carpenter's mistake. If this is the case, reinstall the hinges so they are exposed to the inside. A better method is to replace them with hinges that use setscrews so that the pins cannot be removed. You can also buy kits that allow you to retrofit existing hinges with these setscrews so they too will be nonremovable. Burglars who succeed in penetrating your home, and who want to remove large items through the door, will not be able to remove the door if you are using a locking mechanism that locks from the inside as well

as from the outside *and* nonremovable hinges.

Even a high-quality metal or solid wood door with nonremovable hinges may be of little help if the frame around the door is not sturdy. The door can be penetrated with a good shove or use of a pry bar. The exposed frame around the door, the jamb, is made of 1"-thick wood which is easy to break through. However, this jamb is attached to a 2 × 4 framing member. If all hinge screws, strikeplate screws, and bolts penetrate into this thicker member, the door is more secure. Replace all these screws in the hinges and strikeplates with high-quality 3" screws which will penetrate deep into this frame (Figure 3). Also, use the longer deadbolts, so they will do the same.

You may want to consider replacing not only the door but the surrounding frame (jamb, trim, and molding) as well. Test to see if the frame is movable (if there is a gap between the frame and the wall stud). If it is, a burglar can simply push on the frame with a crowbar and pop the door open. Metal stripping can be installed around existing doors which will help make the door more secure. Though replacing both the frame *and* the door is somewhat complex, it is probably easier than you think. You can buy doors "prehung." This means that the door is hung in its new frame with all hardware and hinges in place. You take out the old door and frame and replace it with a new, more secure one. Depending on the type of siding and interior finish, this can be anywhere from a two-hour to a two-day job. Remember, it is not just the quality of the door itself you are concerned with, but the method in which it is attached in its frame.

A few other things to consider about doors are appropriate to mention here. Install a good door viewer or peephole that has a 180-degree viewing area, and use it. If you have sliding glass doors, check to see if they can be lifted off their tracks from the inside. If so, and to prevent this, screw some screws in up top that protrude into the track but do not obstruct the door from sliding (Figure 4). Also, install bars that can be fitted into the inside track so that the door cannot be moved when they are in place. These are available in any hardware or home center.

DEADBOLTS AND NEW ENTRANCE LOCKS

Regardless of the strength of your doors, an intruder can still gain entry if the locks you use are not adequate. Since there are several standard measurements for locking mechanisms, the bored holes on your door and frame may not always match the new lock to be installed. When possible, try to match the holes or enlarge existing holes. There is hardware available that aids in adaptation to existing holes. If all this fails, you will need to install a new door.

Four commonly used lock systems are described below and illustrated in Figure 5. I recommend installing the key-in-knob or the deadbolt for the best security and the most ease for the do-it-yourselfer.

1. **Key-in-knob locks.** These are the most common exterior door locks, but they can be easily jimmied. Better ones have a hardened steel pin with the beveled latch. This is called a deadlocking latch.

2. **Deadbolt locks.** These are an excellent way to add entrance security. Look for a bolt of at least one inch; a rotating steel pin within the bolt for hacksaw resistance; and a free-spinning brass cover over the outside cylinder which resists wrenches.

3. **Full mortise locks.** Almost always these have to be installed by a professional locksmith. They offer double-lock protection, including a deadbolt.

4. **Rim-mounted locks.** These are sometimes called "vertical deadbolts." They mount to the interior surface of the door and serve as a good second lock because of their ability to resist prying.

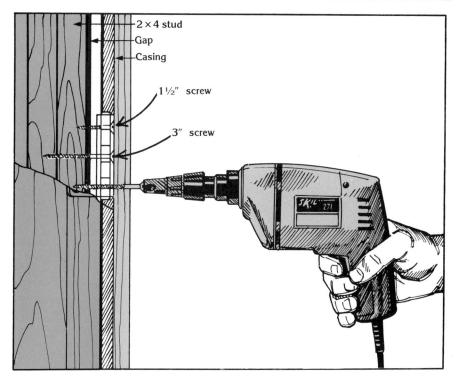

Figure 3. Note how longer 3″ screws penetrate into the studs.

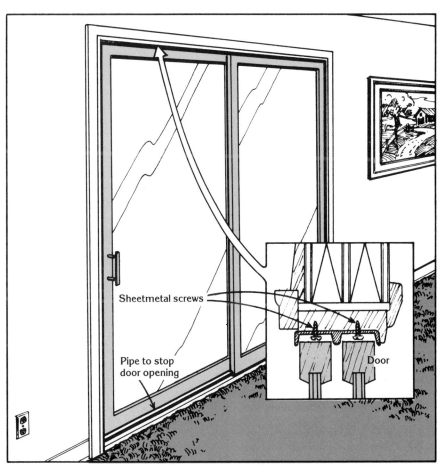

Figure 4. Screws inserted into the top track can prevent doors from being lifted off the track.

INSTALLING A DEADBOLT OR ENTRANCE LOCK

This is a rather simple project and should take no more than two to three hours and require only a few special tools. The main thing is to be sure of the exact location of the holes before you start to drill. If the hole is improperly drilled, it can ruin the door. Also, be sure that you use long (3″) screws for the strikeplate to penetrate deeply into the frame behind the jamb. Your main safety concern regards the use of your power drill. Always treat it respectfully.

NOTE: The method for installing the entrance lock is practically the same as that for installing a deadbolt. The differences are that a deadbolt is installed higher in the door and the two pieces of the mechanism attach slightly differently when installed from either side of the door. Otherwise, the techniques are the same.

WHAT YOU WILL NEED

Time. Although installing a new lock is a relatively easy project, because it requires great accuracy, allow yourself about half a day.

Tools

Hammer
Pencil
Tape measure
Sharp chisel (the width of the latch plate)
⅜″ drill
Electric screwdriver (optional)
Utility knife

Hole saw (size specified by manufacturer)
Spade bit (size specified by manufacturer)
Screwdriver
Allen wrench

Materials

Lock set

Figure 5. The four most common types of locks.

Rim lock
Mortise
Key in knob
Deadbolt

TIP: Metal stripping can be installed around existing doors to help make them more secure.

TIP: To create a clean, splinter-free hole, always drill from both sides of the door with your hole saw.

The most common mistakes in installing a deadbolt or entrance lock are covered under the individual steps below.

STEP ONE

CHOOSING THE PROPER LOCK SET

Margin of Error: Not applicable

MOST COMMON MISTAKE

1. Purchasing an inadequate lock system.

Before beginning, choose your hardware. I always recommend that you go with a nationally known brand. You can always trust their quality and reliability. This is not an area where you want to cut corners with a bargain brand.

There are several different styles and designs to choose from. If the design is a decorative feature, it is a matter of your own taste. However, you need to decide whether you want to use a double-cylinder, double-keyed lock or not. The advantage to using one is that you can lock the door on the way out and no one can open it from the outside *or* the inside without a key. This stops burglars from carrying things out your door. You may want to use an entrance lock that only key locks from the outside, combined with a deadbolt that has a key lock on both sides. This allows you to lock your entrance lock when you are home and not your deadbolt. In case of a fire, you will be able to exit quickly without fumbling for the key to open the deadbolt.

Also, latch bolts come in varying lengths. You probably want to choose the longest available. When it is needed (and hopefully it never will be), it will be worth the extra money.

STEP TWO

USING THE TEMPLATE

Margin of Error: Exact

MOST COMMON MISTAKES

1. Marking wrong location of hole.

2. Locating new latch at same level as previous strikeplate.

In the package with your entrance lock (or deadbolt) you will find a small paper template. This template is supplied in order to show you exactly where to locate the two holes you need to drill to install the system. You will need to drill a hole through the door face for the lock or deadbolt and one through the edge for the latch. These two holes must be coordinated so the mechanism will properly fit together. The template is your guide in doing this.

First, locate how high on the door you want to install the lock. For entrance locks it is usually 36″ above the floor. The main thing to watch for here is the location of the old strikeplate. If you will not reuse this strikeplate (and usually you will not), be sure you do not install the new strikeplate directly on top of the old. The chewed-up area of the frame at this point will not provide a good surface for the new strikeplate screws to bite into.

Instructions on the use of the template are usually provided in the package. Most of the time you simply bend the template and wrap it around the door so that one specified side is on the face of the door and the other side is on the edge. (See Figure 7.) Two holes are provided in the template, to make your marks on both the edge and the face. With a sharp instrument or nail, make marks in the doors at these two points. Check your work to be sure everything is as it should be. You don't want to scrap a good door because a hole was drilled off.

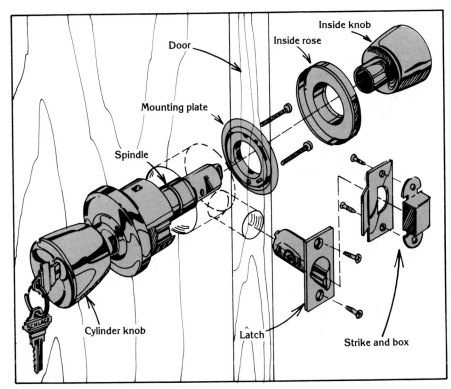

Figure 6. Components of a typical key-in-knob lock.

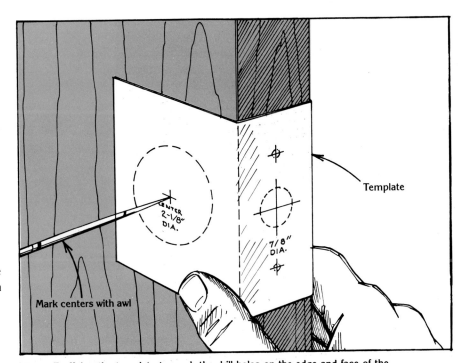

Figure 7. Using the template to mark the drill holes on the edge and face of the door.

STEP THREE

DRILLING THE HOLES

Margin of Error: Exact

MOST COMMON MISTAKES

1. Not drilling straight.

2. Drilling in wrong location.

3. Using wrong size bits.

4. Drilling all the way through both faces of the door in one pass.

5. Using dull drill bit.

6. Using small ¼" drill.

You are now ready to do your drilling. It is best to use a ⅜" drill to provide adequate power to cleanly drill through the solid door. Metal doors will most likely come pre-drilled. Use the size bits specified by the manufacturer (often 2⅛"). You will need a long spade bit to drill through the edge of the door for the hole for the latch. You will need a hole saw for the hole through the face for the lock itself or deadbolt.

It is important when drilling the larger lock hole through the door face to get a clean cut with no unsightly splinters. To do this, take a look at your hole saw. Note that the hole saw has a small pilot drill in the center. The function of this pilot drill is twofold. First, it allows you to exactly line up the center of the hole saw when you start to drill. Second, it will poke out the other side of the door *before* the actual hole saw penetrates all the way through. As soon as you see this pilot bit pop out the other side, immediately stop drilling. Remove the hole saw and start drilling again from the other side of the door. (See Figure

8.) This will create a clean, splinter-free hole. After the hole is drilled in the face, prepare to drill the latch hole in the edge. Never drill this hole first. *Always be sure you are holding the drill level as you drill to insure a straight hole.*

To drill the latch hole on the edge of the door, use the spade bit specified by the manufacturer. Drill this hole until it meets the larger hole you just drilled. Again, be sure you are drilling straight. (See Figure 9.)

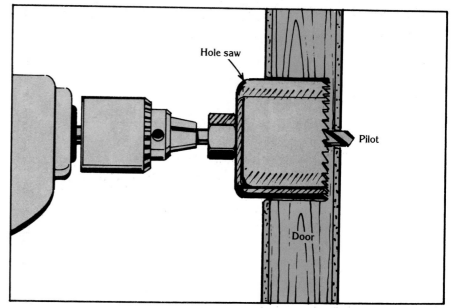

Figure 8. Using a hole saw to saw for large hole.

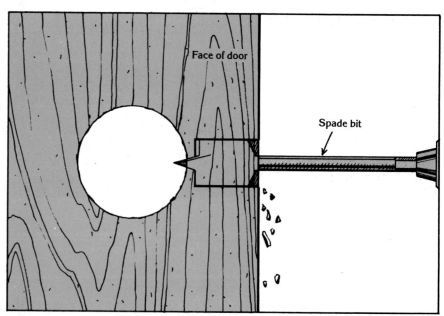

Figure 9. Using a spade bit for hole for the spring latch.

STEP FOUR

INSTALLING THE SPRING LATCH PLATE

Margin of Error: Exact

MOST COMMON MISTAKES

1. Chiseling the hole sloppily or too deep.

2. Not drilling pilot holes before inserting screws.

After both holes are drilled you are now ready to install the spring latch plate. This is a rather simple task and should come out perfectly if you take your time and do it accurately. You will need to mortise (inset) the plate into the edge of the door so that it is flush with the surface of the edge.

Place the plate so that the hole in the plate lines up exactly over the hole you drilled in the edge of the door. It is a good idea to actually install the spring latch itself in the door temporarily to be sure the plate is properly located.

Once you are sure the plate is properly placed, hold it snug against the edge of the door. With a sharp pencil or a utility knife, outline the plate on the door. Now you can chisel out this area to a depth equal to the thickness of the plate. (See Figure 10.) This will allow the plate to sit flush with the surface of the edge of the door. Use a sharp chisel the same width as the plate, if possible. Use light taps with a hammer so you won't gouge out too much wood and sink the plate too deeply. As always when chiseling, remember that the bevel part of the blade should be digging into the wood. This causes the chisel to always deflect out of the wood and not gouge too deep. Go slowly here to create a tight fit.

Figure 10. Chiseling out area for spring latch plate.

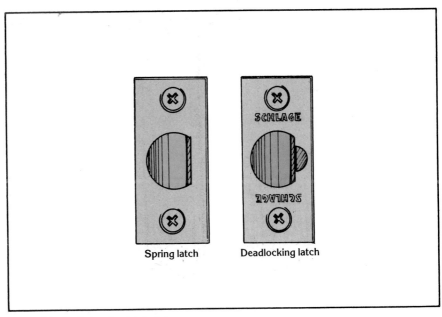

Figure 11. Typical spring latch plates.

When you are satisfied with the fit, you can install the plate with the two screws provided. In situations like this I always advise that you drill pilot holes first, then screw in the screws. A pilot hole is a hole drilled with a bit that is slightly thinner than the shank of the nail. This pilot hole assures that the screw will go in straight and not split the wood. After the pilot holes are drilled, hold the plate firmly against the door and install the screws.

209

With the cover plate and spring latch in place you can now install the lock mechanism. This comes in two pieces, each inserted from either side of the door. Needless to say, be sure the exterior section is pointing out. Slip in the exterior section, threading it through the latch piece, and then the interior. These two are joined together by two screws that insert through the interior section and screw into the exterior section, tightly sandwiching the door and firmly holding the lock in place. Now place the cover plate over the interior section. Finally, slip on the knob. There is usually a spring clip that you must press down to slip on the knob. When you release this clip, it fits into a groove.

TIP: Teach your entire family fire safety techniques.

STEP FIVE

INSTALLING THE STRIKEPLATE

Margin of Error: Exact

MOST COMMON MISTAKES

1. Not aligning strikeplate with spring latch.

2. Installing strikeplate in old hole formed by previous strikeplate.

3. Not using long screws.

After your entrance lock is in and properly functioning, you can install the strikeplate in the frame of the door. As I mentioned earlier, be sure that you are not installing this over the hole created by the previous strikeplate, or you will not have good wood to bite into. Of course, it is a little late to be thinking about this now, since the plate must align with the spring latch of the lock you just installed. Just be sure that this alignment is exact so the latch will easily insert into the plate and metal liner.

The strikeplate is often a three-part assembly made up of a strike frame reinforcer, metal liner, and finished strikeplate (Figure 12). The metal liner often requires a rather large hole. To create this hole you can usually drill two smaller holes and chisel this out to create one large hole. Locate the exact center of the strikeplate on the frame and drill two holes with a $7/8"$ bit, one $3/8"$ above this point and one $3/8"$ below (refer to manufacturer's instructions). After these two holes are drilled, forming a figure-eight pattern, chisel out the wood to create one hole that the metal sleeve can tightly fit into. Before installing the metal liner, install the rough strikeplate. Again, use two long (3") screws to penetrate into the wall frame. Be sure to drill pilot holes first. Next, insert the metal liner and then screw in the finished strikeplate. Test your lock. If it works smoothly and correctly, pat yourself on the back. If it doesn't, make the needed adjustments.

TIP: Do not install fire detectors near an air supply, open duct or vent as these may pull the smoke away from the detector. Also, avoid installing them near safe sources of heat or smoke where they will activate unnecessarily.

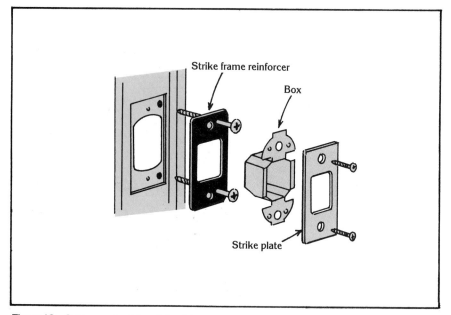

Figure 12. Components of the strikeplate.

SAFES AND HIDING PLACES

After you have taken all possible precautions to keep burglars from breaking into your home, you may want to consider taking some other precautions to keep them from locating valuables, if they do break in. This can be done by hiding valuables or placing them in safes so that, even if they are located, they cannot be removed. Nowadays there are some very simple hiding devices available that are inexpensive and clever. There are some mail order catalogues, for example, from which you can order a small container that looks like a head of lettuce, put your valuables in it, and place it in the refrigerator. Unless the burglar decides to make a salad or is aware of such new gimmicks, you're safe. Similar containers are available as soft drink cans and hollow books. You can buy hollow electrical outlet boxes as well. An imaginative tour of your home may reveal many other effective hiding places. Remember, burglars often don't have much time to search, so they usually grab what they see or can quickly find.

If you feel it's worth the effort, you can strengthen a closet to serve as a small vault (see Figure 13). This can be done simply by installing a metal or solid wood door and a couple of deadbolts. It is a good idea to line the interior with plywood, since drywall can be easily busted through. If you have an older home with wide (6"–12") baseboards, you can remove a section, hollow out the areas between the studs, put small valuables in, and tack the baseboard in place.

Many models and sizes of residential safes are available. Though somewhat more expensive than these other devices, they can be effective if properly installed. Smaller ones concreted into place are an excellent deterrent. But remember, a safe will only serve to alert a burglar to what's inside, so be sure it is well secured.

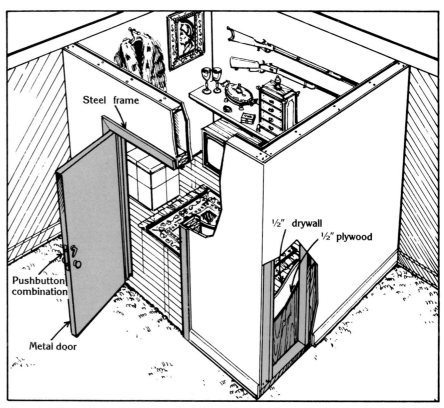

Figure 13. A closet can easily be converted into a vault.

Labels: Steel frame · Pushbutton combination · Metal door · ½" drywall · ½" plywood

WINDOWS

Windows are perhaps as popular as doors are as entry points for burglars. Unfortunately, they are much harder to secure than doors, because the glass can always be broken. There are several approaches you can take to reduce the threat of entry through your windows. Attaching them to a central alarm system is one of the best ways to do this. Also, the glass can be replaced with tempered glass or polycarbonate, but this is costly. Metal bars can be installed over the windows, but it doesn't enhance your view and can be a real life-threatening situation in case of fire. Unless you plan to use one of these techniques, perhaps the best way is to install security latches and other such devices onto your windows. These are inexpensive and easy to install and will usually deter burglars, unless they are willing to break the glass despite the noise.

You may think that the older type of locks on your windows are effective, but often this is not the case. These clasp locks can be opened with a butter knife inserted between the two windows. There are several different types of window locks on the market. All are relatively easy to install. Some locks even allow you to leave the window locked in a partially opened position, if you want to leave some of them open when you leave home. Battery-operated alarms are also available for windows.

Keyed locks for windows are sometimes used. These have one drawback in that, in case of fire, they are hard to open if you cannot find your key. Casement windows, which have cranks, can be secured by simply removing the handle. Leave it in an accessible place in case of fire. You may need to secure only the windows on the first floor, if you feel the second- and third-floor windows are not vulnerable.

Also, make note of air conditioners or fans installed in windows. Often these can be removed by a burglar. Be sure the units are bolted to the house in such a way that they cannot be removed from the outside. And be sure that the window cannot be raised.

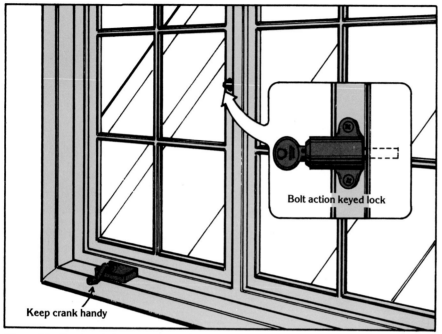

Keep crank handy

Bolt action keyed lock

Figure 14. Be sure windows are well secured.

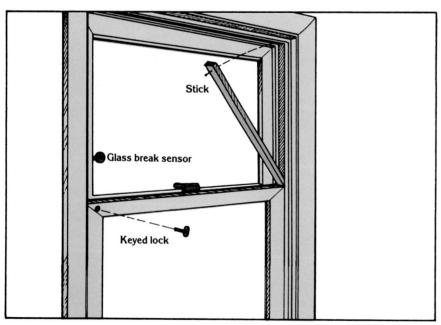

Stick

Glass break sensor

Keyed lock

Figure 15. Three ways of securing windows.

ALARM SYSTEMS

Modern electronics has improved our quality of life in many ways. For example, electronic alarms have become very popular within the last decade. Their popularity is well earned, since they are both effective and affordable. Be careful, however, to not put all of your faith into them. When combined with other safety measures discussed in this chapter, they will make your house relatively secure. But if you rely totally on alarm systems, you will be vulnerable.

Professional burglars know how to silence or incapacitate even the most complicated alarm systems. Remote alarms — alarms that ring only at the police station or at a private security office — often allow burglars time to get away before help arrives. Also, false alarms are becoming so common that a lot of alarms are ignored.

There are several different types of alarm systems on the market. Some of these are well suited to the do-it-yourselfer, while others are best left to a professional alarm company. You need to consider seriously your family's lifestyle when you choose an alarm system. Sensor detectors will not work if you have pets. If you have several children, or overnight guests or other visitors, alarm systems that demand you enter codes upon entering and leaving your home may not work. I remember visiting my sister and entering her house alone late one night. The soft buzzer went off on the alarm system, indicating that I had ten seconds to enter the code before the alarm would blast. I had forgotten the code and stood there helplessly in the hallway as the alarm woke my sister's family as well as all the neighbors. If the police's or security company's response time is too slow, you will need an alarm that rings at the house, thereby warning the neighbors.

As you review the different types of alarm systems, determine which one will work best for you. Be sure to buy a high-quality system. Hopefully, you will never need it, but, when you do, you will want it to work properly.

All systems have three basic components: the alarm itself, the sensor that senses the intrusion, and the control that causes the alarm to engage once the intrusion has occurred. These systems can be either battery operated or operated off the electrical currents in the house. The battery-operated units, though easy to install, often are not sophisticated enough to satisfy all your needs.

Self-Contained Alarm Systems

These have the alarm, control, and sensor all in one unit. They are mostly used in small houses, offices, or apartments where there are a limited number of doors and windows. Sometimes these are as simple as a cigarette box-size alarm that hangs on the door or chainguard and that activates in the case of an intrusion. Others can be plugged into any wall outlet and are activated with a simple motion detector. The more sophisticated models may work off a change in air pressure (as when a door or window is opened) or off of high-frequency sound waves. These units are less expensive and easier to install than some others. Their drawbacks are that burglars can quickly locate them (since the alarm is with the control). Also, the ones that work off of air pressure or sound waves can often give a false alarm resulting from noisy upstairs neighbors or high winds.

TIP: Replace externally exposed hinges with nonremovable hinges exposed only to the interior.

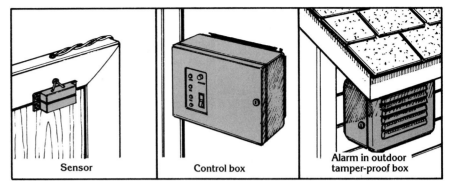

Figure 16. Three components of an alarm system.

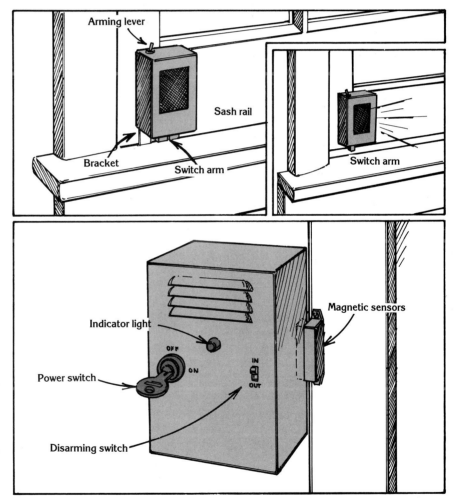

Figure 17. Typical self-contained alarms.

Figure 18. A rope ladder is a good idea for second-story bedrooms, especially if there is only one flight of stairs.

Alarm Systems with Separate Components

These units separate the sensor from the control and from the alarm and work well where you want to guard several rooms at once. Individual sensors (often a metallic tape with a current running through it) can be placed at the windows and doors, and the alarm and control hidden from the burglar. This makes it much more difficult for the burglar to dismantle the system.

These units often have several control stations around the house so that you can activate or deactivate all or part of your sensors. Some units even tell you which doors and windows are open or closed. They also have panic buttons that can be used when you think you hear someone prowling around outside. These systems are usually activated and deactivated by a code and can alarm at the house or the police station (or security office) or both. Also, some alarms can be wired to automatically dial a number and give a recorded message. You can change the number it dials and be reached wherever you are, in case the house is burning or you have been robbed. If you are installing an alarm, put decals on your doors that tell burglars your house is alarm equipped. They will probably go away.

FIRE SECURITY

Most of this chapter has been devoted to securing the valuables within the home. Here I explain ways to secure the home itself and its occupants against the threat of fire. This section of the chapter is much shorter than the sections on home security. Not because fire security is less important (in fact, it is much more important), but because fire alarm systems require no real do-it-yourself detailed information, as is the case with, for instance, installing deadbolts. You just screw the fire alarms to the walls at the right places.

Fire security is extremely important. To lose a valuable is one thing, but to lose a family member is something else all together. In the U.S., 750,000 homes burn each year, accounting for 10,000 deaths.

Fire safety begins with a thorough investigation of the home to locate possible trouble spots. It is a rare home that does not have a least one of the following possible fire safety problems:

Overloaded electrical circuit
Electrical cords running under carpet or rug
Frayed wires
Undersized electrical circuits
Defective appliances
Wrong-size fuses (oversized)
Stored flammable liquids
Stored pile of dirty, oily rags (possibility of spontaneous combustion)
Too many electrical appliances plugged into one outlet
Gas leaks
Accumulation of grease in stove
Accumulation of grease in range hood
Bare light bulbs (especially in closets)
Build-up of pitch in fireplace or wood stove chimney
Improperly installed fireplace or wood stove
Improper screen in front of open fireplace or wood stove
Outdoor barbeque grease build-up

Dry chemical extinguisher   Water extinguisher   Carbon dioxide extinguisher

Figure 19. Various types of fire extinguishers. The ABC type is a recommended multi-purpose type.

Children's access
to matches
Sloppy workshop
area
Smoking in bed

TV set left on all
night (can
overheat and
explode)

Christmas poses particular dangers:

Dry tree
Plastic tree that is
not fire
retardant
Burning candles

Tree placed near
heat source
Children playing
with candles

Visit your local fire department and get their pamphlets on fire safety. They may even offer a service in which they will visit your home for a security tour.

After you have evaluated all the possible problems and corrected them, you are ready to take some offensive, as opposed to defensive, tactics.

Plan fire escape routes. Be sure each bedroom is mapped out with at least two possible routes. Train the entire family in what to do in case of fire, especially children, and what the escape routes are. Remind them that most

deaths are caused by smoke inhalation, not the fire itself. Decide on a common meeting place outside or at a neighbor's, so you can quickly determine if anyone is missing and probably trapped inside. Tape the fire department number on all phones. Remind your family to forget about their possessions, just escape. Determine if any special fire escapes or rope ladders are needed from the second floor. Put a few fire extinguishers, the multi-purpose (ABC) types, around the house, especially in the kitchen. And, finally, conduct a fire drill.

Above all, install fire detectors. These simple devices are inexpensive and can be installed in just a few minutes. They can run off either household electricity or batteries. When you realize that the majority of fires occur at night, you see the wisdom of installing these detectors. Fire experts estimate that half the lives lost could have been saved with these detectors.

Install the detectors between the sleeping areas and the rest of the house. In multi-level homes, have at least one on each floor. In a two-story

house, install one on the ceiling at the bottom of the staircase. Put one at the bottom of the basement staircase as well. Be sure not to install them near an air supply, open duct, or vent. These may pull the smoke away from the detector. Also, avoid placing them near safe sources of heat or smoke where they will activate unnecessarily.

TOOLS AND MATERIALS CHECKLIST

Tools

Scribe or electric engraver	Utility knife
	Chisel
3/8" drill	Hammer
Key hole saw	Wood rasp
Spade bit	Pry bar
Pencil	Screwdrivers

Materials

Sheet metal	Bolt-action window locks
Tempered glass	
Acrylic	Lever-type sash locks
Polycarbonate	
Solid wood door	1/4" metal bar
Steel door	Hasp
3" flat head wood screws	Window bars
Setscrews	Simulated lettuce or soft drink can
Metal stripping	
Sheet metal screws	Hollow outlet boxes
Broom handle or iron pipe	Push-button combination deadbolt
Barrel bolt	
Deadbolt	Plywood
Key-in knob lock	Battery-operated alarm
Full-mortise lock	
Rim-mounted lock	Self-contained alarm
Padlock	Security program for home computer
Cardboard shim	
10-penny nails	Smoke detector
15/16" eyebolt	
Keyed window locks	

215

CHAPTER THIRTEEN

Sun Decks

How to Build a Redwood Beauty

WHAT YOU WILL BE DOING

In some ways deck building is a rather complex do-it-yourself project, but, since decks do not have to be leakproof or perfectly built, it is well within the scope of most novice builders. This book will provide you with the information you will need to do the work efficiently.

Deck building can be a demanding job both physically and mentally. It is, however, very rewarding. It moves quickly and will give you a pleasing living area for a small price.

Be sure you understand what you are doing before you proceed. The key things to remember in deck building are to be sure you have used all the proper materials and construction techniques, to fend off the decaying properties of water, and to be sure everything is level, plumb, and properly built.

BEFORE YOU BEGIN

SAFETY

Always understand, develop, and adhere to proper safety practices for each project. For deck construction, these include:

1. Always use the appropriate tool for the job.

2. Keep blades and bits sharp. A dull tool requires excessive force and can slip.

3. Safety goggles and glasses should be worn when using power tools, especially if you wear contacts.

4. Always unplug your power tools when making adjustments or changing attachments.

5. Be sure your tools are properly grounded.

6. Watch power cord placement so it does not interfere with the operation of the tool.

7. Wear ear protection when operating power tools, because some operate at a high noise level which can damage hearing.

8. Be careful that loose hair and clothing do not get caught in power tools.

9. Be careful when carrying long boards at the site.

10. Be careful to avoid back strain when lifting or digging.

11. Wear heavy-soled, sturdy work boots.

12. Bend from the knees when lifting large and heavy objects.

USEFUL TERMS

All-heart grades. Grades of wood which contain no knots or blemishes.

Band joists. Joists which form an attractive border or band around the framing joists.

Bow. The deviation from straight and true seen when looking at a board on its edge.

Construction common. A grade of redwood containing sapwood.

Crown. The highest point of a warped board, seen from the board's side.

Cup. The warp of a board seen from the board's end.

Girder. A support member of a deck floor framing system which rests upon the piers. The girder is in a position parallel to the ledger and supports the opposite end of the joists.

HDG (Hot dipped galvanized). A rustproof coated metal which is less expensive than aluminum or stainless steel.

Joists. A system of floor framing commonly using 2 × 6 or 2 × 8 lumber.

Ledger. A board of the same size as the joists, attached to a wall, to which the joists are perpendicularly attached.

Pier Holes. Holes dug to below frost line and filled with cement for a firm footing to raise foundation piers.

Plumb bob. A heavy object suspended on the end of a string for the purpose of establishing a true vertical line.

Toe nailing. Nailing at an angle which reduces chances of nails loosening under stress.

Torpedo level. A level 8 or 9 inches in length with vials to read level, plumb and 45 degrees.

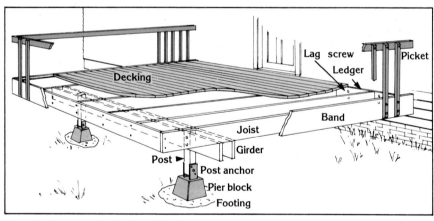

Figure 1. Components of a typical deck.

WHAT YOU WILL NEED

Time. A 12′ × 12′ deck with a simple foundation and railing can be completed by two people in 4 days (2 weekends). Figure on 64 to 85 work hours to completion, more for complex railing and foundation designs.

Tools. The tools you will need for your deck project are listed in the Tools and Materials Checklist at the end of the chapter. For most deck projects, common framing tools are needed. No specialized tools are necessary. You may want to consider using a pneumatic tool for nailing on the decking. It makes the process go quickly and easily.

Be sure to use high-quality tools that are capable of doing the job without strain. This is especially important in your choice of power tools.

Materials. Your choice of decking and fastener materials is very important. All materials must be chosen according to how well they resist decay and rust.

Fasteners. When choosing nails, bolts, screws and metal fasteners, use only hot dipped galvanized (HDG) fasteners. Double hot dipped is even better. These galvanized fasteners will not rust. Aluminum and stainless steel nails also will not rust, but HDG, more commonly used, is less expensive. Avoid electroplated galvanized (EG), since galvanized plating will often chip.

In recent years many types of galvanized metal fasteners have become common in deck construction. These simplify your project, while adding strength and quality to your construction, and are highly recommended. They can be used in many areas of deck construction, including the following attachments:

Joist to ledger (joist hanger)
Girder to post (post cap)
Joist to girder (right-angle bracket)

Post to rafter (rafter fastener)
Post to foundation (post anchors)

Wood. All wood used on the deck must be decay resistant. These woods include:

Redwood
Pressure-treated wood

Cedar
Cypress

Redwood is perhaps the most attractive and best wood to use, especially in exposed areas such as the decking and railing. It is decay resistant, dimensionally stable, and straight. Redwood is especially good for do-it-yourselfers because it is easy to saw and nail and has little or no pitch. It resists warping, checking, and cupping and is strong for its light weight. It comes in several grades. A construction common, which contains some sapwood, is ideal for the deck boards. The all-heart grades, which are more expensive, are used for luxury decks.

Pressure-treated wood is also commonly used. It is local evergreen treated to resist decay and is often green. If budget is a concern, you may want to use a pressure-treated frame with a redwood deck and railings.

Deck joists are usually 2 × 6, 2 × 8, or 2 × 10 stock. The decking boards are usually 2 × 4 and 2 × 6. 2 × 8 stock is too wide and will cup if used as a decking board.

PERMITS AND CODES

In most areas some sort of permit is required before you begin to build a deck. If the deck is not attached to the house, or if you live in a rural area, you may not need a permit. Before you start, check this out. It is never advisable to build without a permit where one is required.

The permit office will probably require a set of plans. These need not be elaborate, and you can draw them yourself, buy a set, or have a set prepared by a draftsperson or architect. The plans will specify the following (Figure 2):

A. Location of deck. They will want to be sure you are far enough away from neighboring property lines, utility easements, and gas, water, and sewer lines.

B. Space between railing pickets. Often the pickets can be placed with no more than a 6″ space between them.

C. Railing heights. If the deck is close to the ground, within, say, 30″, no railing may be required. If one is required, a minimum railing height of 36″–42″ is required.

D. Foundation piers. The local codes will regulate the size, spacing, number, and method of construction of your piers. They will also regulate the depth of your pier hole, depending on the frostline in the area.

E. The girder. The local codes will specify the size and location of the girder.

F. Joists. The code will specify the size and spacing of the joists. This will depend on the type of wood you will use. Joist charts are available at the code office for each type of wood.

G. Fasteners. Many codes will detail your nail or fastener schedules.

H. Decking. The plans will specify the size of deck boards and the type of wood used.

I. Posts. The plans will specify the size of the posts.

J. Earthquakes. In earthquake and hurricane areas there may be further requirements on how the piers are fastened to the foundations, the girders to the posts, and the joists to the girders. They may specify certain metal fasteners.

DESIGN

There is much to say about the design of a deck. My intention in this chapter is to provide you not with a thorough treatise on deck design but rather with a few parameters of design to consider. This is not to understate the importance of design. How well you are pleased with your handiwork and how much you will enjoy using it depend on design more than on construction. What follows are some key things to consider at this crucial stage. Your answers to these questions will largely dictate your design requirements.

1. At what time of day during each season of the year does the deck get sun and shade?

2. How much privacy will the deck give you from neighbors? Will this change when the trees lose their leaves?

3. What will be the deck's access from the house? To the yard?

4. How large should it be? And how much yard must be sacrificed?

5. How should the railings be designed? With planters? With seats?

6. Where should the stairs be placed?

7. Are there any utility lines overhead or below?

8. Should the deck be covered?

9. What will be placed on the deck? Bar-B-Q? Swing? Chairs and tables?

10. Will the deck block the light coming in any windows of the house?

11. How will the deck affect the rooms of the house?

12. How are the views?

13. How much money do you plan to spend?

MOST COMMON MISTAKES

Given the complexity of this project, the most common mistakes are listed at the beginning of each step. It is particularly important, when undertaking this challenging project, that you read through the entire chapter before picking up your tools and getting to work.

DETERMINING THE LEVEL AND LENGTH OF THE LEDGER

Margin of Error: 1/4"

MOST COMMON MISTAKES

1. Using badly bowed board.

2. Choosing wrong height or location.

3. Not using redwood, cedar, cypress, or pressure-treated stock.

4. Not following codes.

If you are attaching a deck to your existing home, you will probably use a ledger board. You bolt this board to the house and hang the deck on it, thereby attaching the deck securely to the house. If you plan a freestanding deck (not attached to the house), you do not use a ledger. In some areas a deck attached to a house will be taxed, but if it

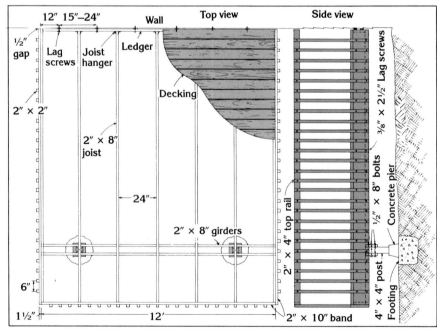

Figure 2. A typical set of deck plans.

is separated by even an inch or two it will not. In this chapter we consider the more common approach to attaching a deck to an existing home. If your deck is freestanding, everything discussed here will still apply, but the ledger is not bolted to the house. With freestanding decks, added bracing may be needed to stabilize the deck.

Before discussing the ledger itself, let's talk about its location. The location of the ledger will be determined by the desired level, or height, of the deck and its placement on the house. I assume you have already decided about the deck design and location, so let's look at the ledger's height and length.

The Level of the Ledger

The level, or height, of the ledger determines the height of the deck. Usually the top of the ledger will be $1\frac{1}{2}''$ below the final top surface of the deck (because $1\frac{1}{2}''$ decking boards will be nailed on top). Sometimes the deck joists, which support the decking or surface of the deck, are installed so that they sit on top of the ledger rather than hang from it, as shown in Figure 3. In that case the top of the ledger will be considerably lower than the final level of the deck (by the dimension of the joist width plus $1\frac{1}{2}''$). Before you install the ledger you will need to decide whether to hang the joists from the ledger or rest them on top. Whenever possible it is best to hang them from the ledger with joist hangers.

No matter what approach you use, you want to be sure the ledger is low enough so that, once the decking is installed, the level of the deck will be at least $1''$ below the level of the finished floor inside the house. This is necessary because you naturally want to step down from the house to the deck, rather than trip over it. Also, if the deck is higher than the floor, water runs from the deck to the house. If you never plan to put a door from the house to the deck, the height of the deck is not as important.

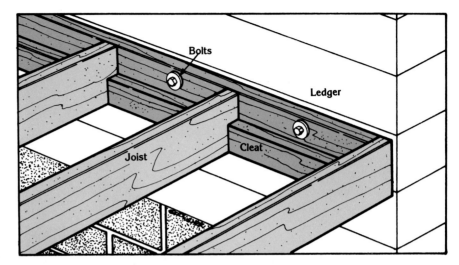

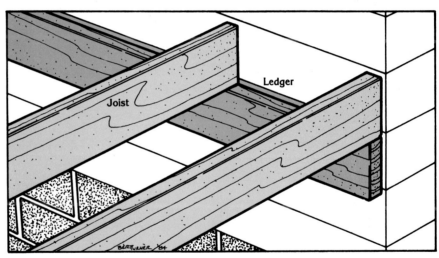

Figure 3. Joist can also be set on top of the ledger or notched and attached using a cleat. We will be hanging the joist with joist hangers.

Determine the level of the interior finished floor and transfer this level to the outside of the wall where the deck will be built. You can do this by measuring on the inside and outside from a common reference point, such as a windowsill. (Adjust your measurements if the sill slopes toward the outside.) If this is impossible, you may need to measure up from the foundation wall, accounting for the floor joist, subfloor, and finished flooring materials. Once you have determined this level, mark it on the exterior wall. This first mark will correspond to the level of the finished floor inside. Make a second mark a minimum of 2½″ below this initial mark. This will allow you to install 1½″ decking and still place the level of the deck 1″ below the level of the interior floor. You can place the top of the ledger anywhere below this second mark and be safe.

The Length of the Ledger

The length of the ledger equals the total length of the deck, less 3″. This 3″ is so that the joists at either end of the deck will overlap the ledger and be nailed to it. The joists are 1½″ thick, hence the 3″ reduction in length so that the finished deck will be the designated length. If possible, you will want to have the ledger be one long piece of stock. However, if the length is over 16′–18′, it may be hard to find a straight piece that long. In this case, two pieces will work. Always try to use pieces that are at least 6′–8′ long.

Location on the Wall

It is important that the ledger be securely attached. Place the ledger at a point on the wall where, once it is attached, the lag screws attaching the ledger will penetrate something solid such as wall studs or floor joists. Ledgers are often placed at the same level as the floor joists of the first floor, and

TIP: In areas of heavy rain or snow, place a metal flashing on top of each deck board before the deck boards are applied. The metal flashing helps keep water from getting trapped between the decking and the joists and causing rot.

this automatically solves the problem. In this case, the lag screws will penetrate the band joists.

If you are installing the ledger at some other level, see if there is anything solid behind the wall that the lag screws can be screwed into. If there is nothing, you may need to attach the ledger with bolts. First place some blocking behind the wall, to secure it.

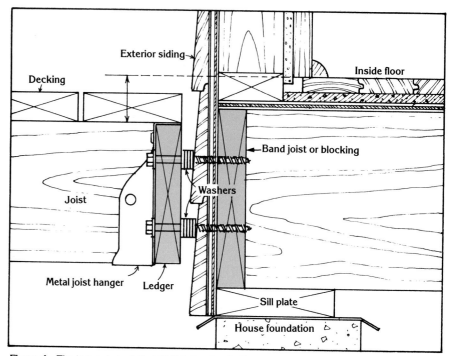

Figure 4. The ledger is installed 2½″ below level of interior finished floor. Be sure it is bolted or screwed into something solid (band joist).

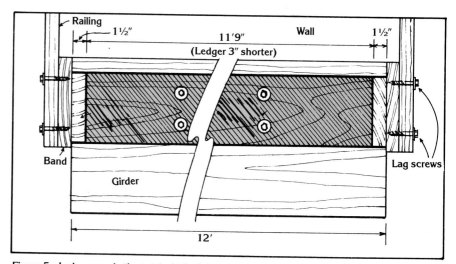

Figure 5. Ledger equals the total width of the deck less three inches if there is no band, or six inches if band is used.

Choosing the Ledger

When selecting a piece for the ledger, be sure it is straight with little bow (a curve in the board). If the ledger is curved, the deck will have a corresponding curve upward or downward. Some minor bow can be forced out as you apply it, but anything more than that (say, ½" of curve over 12' of board) will throw the deck off. Be sure the board, as with all decking materials, is of redwood, cedar, cypress, or pressure-treated lumber.

After you have decided on the final placement of the ledger, in regard to both its height and location on the wall, you are ready to install it. First, however, check to see if there are any obstructions, such as hose faucets, dryer vents, gas or water pipes, electrical wires, and so on. Any such obstructions may have to be relocated; or, sometimes, the ledger can break, leaving a gap where obstructions occur. Remember that everything below the ledger will be underneath the deck and therefore less accessible. You may need to call in an electrician or a plumber to rearrange some wires or pipes if you cannot do this yourself. Never play with the electrical or gas system unless you are confident that you know exactly what you are doing. Mark on the ground the location of any underground pipes or wires before you begin digging the foundation holes so that you can be sure that you will not be disturbing them. If you cannot locate any pipes or wires, dig slowly and be prepared to change the location of the foundation piers if necessary.

TIP: To help keep rain water running down the wall from flowing into the structure through the lag screw holes, squirt some silicon caulk in the holes before screwing in the lag screws.

STEP TWO

DRILLING THE HOLES FOR THE LEDGER

Margin of Error: ¼"

MOST COMMON MISTAKES

1. Using a badly bowed board.

2. Not using rustproof lag screws or bolts.

3. Not installing ledger at proper height or location.

4. Not caulking bolt holes before installing ledger.

5. Drilling holes where joists will be attached.

After you have decided on the placement of the ledger, in regard to both its height and its location on the wall, you are ready to install it.

Choose a good straight piece of ledger stock (usually the same size as the joists) and cut it to the proper length. Again, this is the total length of the deck less 3". Now you can drill holes in the ledger for the lag screws or bolts that will hold the ledger to the house. These holes are drilled with a bit that is ⅛" larger than the actual screws so that you will have a little play for adjustments. Usually the holes are in pairs, one on top of the other, every 30", or staggered singly every 15". Be sure that all holes are drilled at least 1" or more from the edge of the board for proper holding. You may want to check with the local code to see if there are any regulations concerning the location of these lag screws.

With the ledger resting on sawhorses, begin at one end and mark the lag screw locations. Always drill a pair of holes 12" in from either end. Drill all needed holes.

You are now ready to temporarily attach the ledger to the wall, mark the corresponding holes on the siding, remove the ledger, and drill the holes in the siding. If there is a slight bow in the

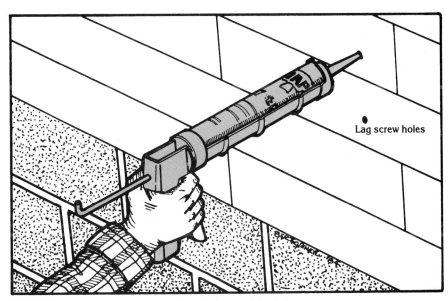
Lag screw holes

Figure 6. Squirt caulk into lag screw holes before applying ledger.

board, turn this toward the sky, since it is easier to push it down to get it straight.

Place the ledger's top edge at the mark you have located on the wall that represents the top of the ledger and nail one end temporarily in place. Then place a 4'–8' level on the board, get it exactly level, and temporarily nail in the other end. The ledger is now temporarily nailed in its proper place. Check once again to be sure it is exactly level before marking the holes. Then, with a felt-tipped pen or sharp pencil, mark the lag screw holes that were drilled in the ledger on the wall. Now remove the ledger.

You are now ready to drill the lag screw holes in the wall. *Do not use the same size bit* that you used on the ledger. Use a bit that is one size smaller than the shank of the lag screw. This will assure that the lag screw has a good bite into the wall. Drill all the holes, being sure to hold the drill straight so the lag screws will go in straight. Again be sure that you are drilling into solid wood, or use the blocking and bolt method described earlier.

After removing the ledger, as a precaution before you attach the ledger permanently to the wall, squirt some silicon caulk in the holes in the wall before screwing in the lag screws. This will help keep rainwater running down the wall from flowing into the structure through the lag screw holes.

TIP: Use a combination square and mark a perpendicular line across each joist so that you can place all your nails in a straight line.

STEP THREE

ATTACHING THE LEDGER PERMANENTLY TO THE WALL

Margin of Error: 1/4"

MOST COMMON MISTAKES

1. Not leaving a space between the wall and the ledger.

2. Not screwing ledger into something solid.

3. Not using rustproof lag screws.

4. Using galvanized washers with aluminum siding.

5. Not caulking holes before installing.

You probably think you are now ready to attach the ledger to the wall, but not quite yet. There is still one crucial detail you must attend to. The situation is as follows. If the ledger were attached directly against the wall, so that the back surface of the ledger was tight against the wall, rainwater running down the wall would get trapped between the wall and the back surface of the ledger. This would cause rotting. To avoid this you need to leave a small space (1/2"–

3/4"), so that water can continue to run to the ground.

The easiest way to do this is to install washers on the lag screws between the ledger and the wall. These washers should be hot dipped galvanized (HDG), which do not rust. Use aluminum washers if your wall is aluminum siding. Galvanized metal touching aluminum causes corrosion. These washers will leave an adequate gap. Also, if your siding is not flat but has different surface levels (beveled siding, aluminum siding, shingles, etc.), more or fewer washers can be installed on the top screws than on the lower ones, to compensate and cause the ledger to be installed true vertical.

After you have threaded the lag screws into the ledger, installed the proper number of washers on each screw, and squirted caulk into the holes, lift the ledger into place, tap the screws into the wall, and, with a socket or crescent wrench, tighten the screws. Be sure that the screws are biting solidly into the wall, especially the last 2". You are now ready to install the two edge joists and locate your pier holes.

If you are using pressure-treated lumber or a decay resistant lumber that is not all heart, we recommend that you paint a waterproofing on the cut ends of the ledger and all other exposed boards.

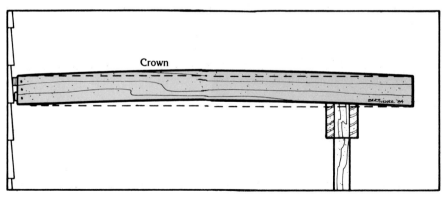

Figure 7. Always point crowns up.

STEP FOUR

ATTACHING THE TWO OUTER JOISTS

Margin of Error: ¼″

MOST COMMON MISTAKES

1. Joists not set at right angle from the wall.

2. Joists not placed level.

3. Joists not nailed to cover exposed ends of the ledger.

4. Not pointing the crown skyward.

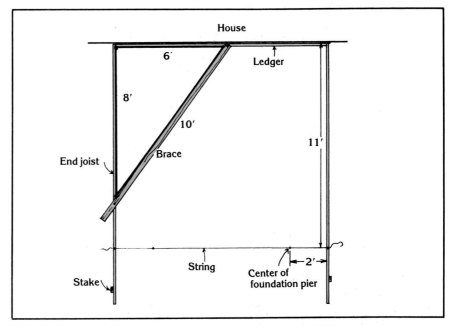

Figure 8. Use a 3—4—5 triangle to be sure two end joists are at right angles to ledger. Be exact.

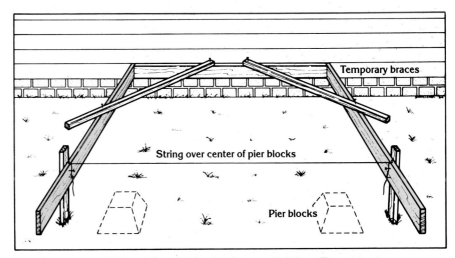

Figure 9. Two end joists are installed level and square to ledger. Then string is stretched exactly over centers of foundation supports.

Now that the ledger is permanently attached to the wall, you can install the two outermost joists at either end of the ledger. At this time these joists are being used as reference for locating the foundation pier holes. The outer joists are set in place, lines are drawn between them at the prescribed distance from the wall, and on these lines the location of the foundation pier holes are marked. These marks are then transferred down to the ground and the holes dug. The distance from the house to the supporting girder will depend on the size of your deck, the type of wood being used as joists, and the size and spacing of the joists.

This is a rather simple way of locating your pier holes. It usually works well, unless the lot slopes steeply. Some builders use other techniques, including setting up what is known as batterboards and layout lines. I think this method — using the two outer joists as references — is perhaps easiest for the do-it-yourselfer.

Choose two of your straightest joists to install at either end of the ledger. As you look down the joists you will notice that they have a small bow, or crown. Almost no piece of wood is ever perfectly straight.

Once installed, this crown should al-ways point up toward the sky. (See Figure 7.) This is called "crowning a joist." In time the bow will settle down if gravity is working with it. So be sure to crown your joists before installing. Don't worry about cutting the joists the proper length at this time. Let them run wild, since they will be cut when you apply the decking.

When you nail these outer joists to the ledger, do so with the joists cover-ing up the exposed end of the ledger.

Have one person nail the joist into the ledger using 3 or 4 16d (penny) HDG (double hot dipped galvanized)

TIP: You can apply waterproofing coats to redwood at twelve- to eighteen-month intervals to eliminate the darkening effect and preserve the beautiful buckskin color.

nails, while another person supports the other end of the joist in a more or less level position. After the end is nailed to the ledger, drive a temporary 2 × 4 stake into the ground that will hold the floating end level and at a right angle to the ledger. To do this, after one person has nailed the joist to the ledger and while the other person is supporting the other end, place a framing square at the intersection of the joist and the ledger. Once this is approximately 90 degrees, drive a stake in the ground to support the joist there, place a 4'–8' level on the joist to be sure it is level, and nail the joist to the stake. At this point none of these measurements are too accurate. The next step, using a 3–4–5 triangle, will insure the accuracy of your right angle. (See Figure 8.)

To insure this accuracy, use the old mathematical formula that states, in a right-angled triangle the sum of the squares of the sides equals the square of the hypotenuse. (In case you have forgotten your high school geometry, the hypotenuse is the side opposite the right angle.) For example, if the two sides of a triangle are 3 and 4 (feet, inches, miles, etc.) and the hypotenuse is 5, then the angle across from the hypotenuse is a true right angle (3 squared + 4 squared = 5 squared, or 9 + 16 = 25). This is also referred to as the 3–4–5 triangle. This remains accurate if you multiply each side by the same number, for example, 6–8–10, or even 300–400–500.

Back to our deck. Our goal is to assure that these two outside joists are at a true right angle to the ledger. Measure out along the ledger from the outside edge 8' and mark it. Measure along the joist 6' and mark. Now measure between these two marks. If it is 10' (we are using a 6–8–10 triangle) then you are at a true right angle. If not, readjust your stake and joist until it is exactly 10' between the marks. Once you have it exact, nail some temporary cross braces from the ledger to the joists at an angle to keep the joists in place. You should now have your two outer joists level, at true right angles from the ledger, and temporarily supported by stakes.

STEP FIVE

LOCATING THE FOUNDATION PIER HOLES

Margin of Error: 1"

MOST COMMON MISTAKES

1. Locating hole on top of underground pipe or wire.

2. Not checking plans for exact location of hole.

With the two outer joists in place you now have a clear outline of the edges of the deck. From this outline you can locate all your foundation pier holes. Check your plans to determine the exact locations. Say, for instance, your plans call for two holes, the centers of which are exactly 11' from the wall and 2' in from the outer edges of the sides of the deck. Then measure out along each of the two outer joists 11' from

the wall, mark the joists, drive nails at those points, and draw a string from joist to joist between the two nails. Now measure 2' from the outside edges of the joists along the string and mark the string. If there are decorative band joists to be added over the two side joists just installed (see Figure 1 at the beginning of the chapter showing deck components), be sure to allow for these in your measurements. These marks locate the centers of the two pier holes. You can now transfer these marks to the ground, using a plumb bob, and drive in two small stakes. Then mark out for the radius of the pier holes and begin digging.

NOTE: The location of the pier block holes is unique to each deck project. Code enforcement will have some say here, but design is also a factor. Piers are often inset from the sides of the deck to hide them from view. The supporting girder supported by these piers is often inset from the end of the deck a foot or two, because a cantilevered or overhanging deck has a nice visual appeal. In any case, be sure you know where you want the supports before you start to dig.

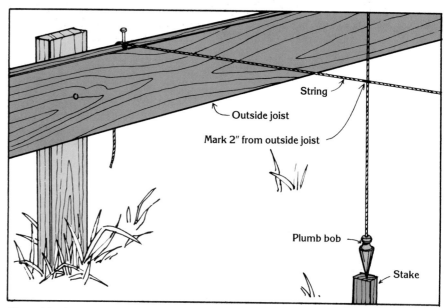

Figure 10. **Use a plumb bob to locate center of pier block holes.**

STEP SIX

DIGGING THE FOUNDATION HOLES

Margin of Error: 1"

MOST COMMON MISTAKES

1. Not digging deep enough for local codes and frost lines.

2. Not digging into stable, undisturbed soil.

3. Not squaring off walls at the bottom of the hole.

I won't insult you by trying to tell you how to dig a hole, but I need to say a few things about the hole before you start to dig. The size of the hole is important. The diameter is usually about 16", but check your local code. More importantly, the depth of the hole is often regulated by code. Distances of 12"–60" are the range, depending on the frost level in your area (the colder the climate, the deeper the hole).

Once you have determined the diameter and depth, simply dig your needed holes, being sure to dig good, straight (not sloping) walls. Dig until you hit stable undisturbed soil that will not settle. Never backfill a hole with loose dirt before pouring concrete. This compacts and causes settling.

TIP: Keep the concrete damp while hardening for a stronger pour. This can be done by sprinkling water on the pour as it dries or by laying wet cloths across the top.

STEP SEVEN

POURING THE FOOTINGS AND SETTING THE PIER BLOCKS

Margin of Error: ½"

MOST COMMON MISTAKES

1. Top of pier blocks not level.

2. Pier blocks not properly aligned.

3. Neglecting to use the metal connector where required.

Now you are ready to mix up some concrete, pour it in your hole, drop a pier block in the fresh concrete, level and align it, and continue.

A few words on mixing concrete. On small deck jobs I recommend that you simply buy the ready-mixed concrete with all needed ingredients in a bag, mix it with some water, and pour it in the hole. Purchase enough bags to fill your holes; you don't want to run short and have to rush back to the store to finish off a hole. You will be surprised how many bags a hole can require.

Mix the concrete in a wheelbarrow or pan with a cement hoe, and be sure to follow the instructions as to the proper mix. Pour the concrete in the hole within an inch or so of the top and smooth it out with a piece of 2×4 or a trowel until it is relatively level. You can now place the pier blocks.

Pier blocks serve as a transition from the posts supporting the girder to the concrete foundation footings. Although they can be built at the site, they are available at all home centers and hardware stores in a range of styles and sizes (Figure 11) and are therefore not worth the hassle of pouring them yourself. The most common type is simply a small truncated concrete pyramid on top of which the wooden post sits. The weight of the deck keeps the post in contact with the pier block. A version of this is a pier block that has a small piece of redwood or pressure-treated lumber embedded in the top so that the post can be toenailed to the block. Often metal fasteners are used in areas where there are earthquakes. They are embedded in the fresh concrete and the posts are bolted to them. This prevents the posts from shaking off the pier blocks in a quake.

After the hole has been filled with concrete, and the concrete leveled and smoothed, drop the pier block into the

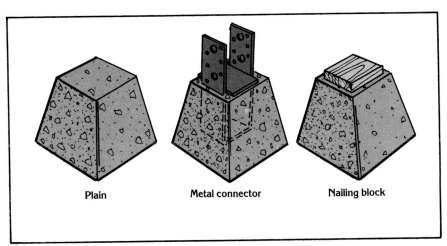

Figure 11. Three types of pier blocks. The one with the metal fastener is used in earthquake areas.

Plain Metal connector Nailing block

Sun Decks

fresh concrete and work it down until at least 3″–4″ of the base of the block are embedded. As you set the block, be sure of two things: that they are properly aligned and that they are level. It should be rather easy to check both. To check alignment, simply drop the plumb bob from the marks on your string to be sure the tip of the plumb bob is in the centers of the pier blocks. To check level, use a small torpedo level, placing it in both directions as well as diagonally across the top of the pier blocks until the tops are level. Tap and move the blocks around to make any needed adjustments. After your pier blocks are properly set, allow the concrete to harden (this can take anywhere from 2 to 24 hours). Then you can begin building the girders and posts. We recommend keeping the concrete damp while hardening for a stronger pour. You can do this by sprinkling water on the pour as it dries or by laying wet cloths across the top.

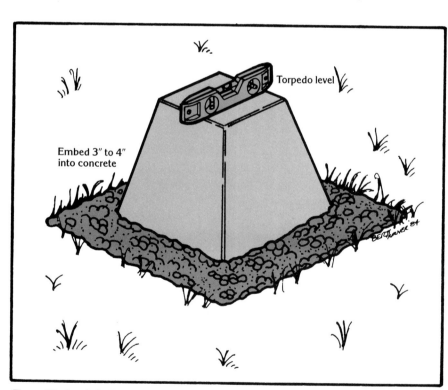

Figure 12. Level pier block using a small level.

STEP EIGHT

INSTALLING THE GIRDERS

Margin of Error: ¼″

MOST COMMON MISTAKES

1. Using badly bowed girder stock.

2. Girder not level.

Now you are ready to install your girders or beams. You may do this in one of two ways. One is to prebuild the girders/post system, bolt or nail the entire thing together, and then move it as one large piece into place. The other way is to build it piece by piece in place. If the posts and girders are not too long and heavy, we recommend the first procedure — putting it all together as one

piece and then moving it into place.

There are several different girder/post variations. As shown in Figure 13, the girder can rest on top of the posts attached with metal fasteners; or two girders can sandwich the posts and be bolted or nailed to them. As long as it passes your local code, either system will work. You may want to cost out the wood, since one system may be more cost effective than the other.

To build your girder/post system, first cut the wooden posts the proper height. In our case the posts' height is the same as the level of the bottom of the joists. Note that the bottoms of the joists rest on top of the girders and that the tops of the girders are at the same height as the tops of the posts.

To determine this post height, go back to your two outer joists and check to be sure they are still exactly level. Now move the string that is on top of the joists so that it is connected on the bottoms of the joists. The level of the bottom of the joists is the same level as the top of the posts you are about to cut. Now measure from the top of each pier block (or metal fastener) to the string, as shown in Figure 14, and cut posts corresponding to each of these measurements. It is that simple. But be sure you are accurate and that you make good straight cuts so the posts will sit smoothly on the pier blocks. To do this, you will need to mark around the circumference of the post, cut one side, and then rotate it and cut the sides adjacent to it. Finally make one more cut on the side opposite the first cut.

After the posts are cut, cut your pieces of girder stock the specified length. This will be the length of the ledger plus 3″. Try to use one continuous piece of girder stock for each piece, but if the deck is too long and that is not possible, be sure the two pieces meet at a post so they can both be attached there. Also be sure that all girder stock is extremely straight. Pick these pieces yourself at the store. If they are bowed, the entire deck will rise or fall, since the deck joists all sit on top of them. If there is a SMALL (½″ over 12′) bow, point it up toward the sky and it will settle down in time.

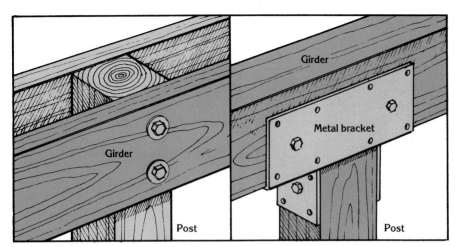

Figure 13. Two types of girders using 2″ and 4″ girder stock. Use metal fasteners to rest the girder on top of the post.

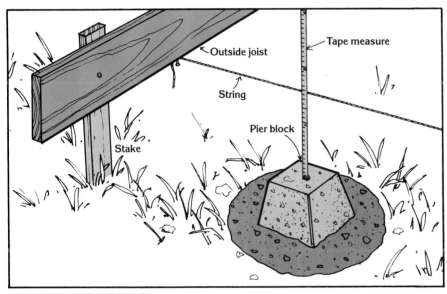

Figure 14. To determine height of post, measure from top of pier to top of post.

STEP NINE

LAYING OUT THE JOISTS ON THE LEDGER

Margin of Error: ¹/₄″

MOST COMMON MISTAKES

1. Nailing the joist hanger on the wrong side of the mark.

2. Improper layout.

After your girder is in place, you are now ready to install your remaining joists. To do this you need to make marks, called layout marks, on the ledger and girder that show where each joist will be located. This process is called a layout.

Usually joists are located so that their centers occur exactly every 16″, 24″, or 32″. This is called their "on-center" distance. The distance between joists depends on several important factors:

1. Size of the joists

2. Spacing of the joists

3. Length of span from ledger to girder

4. Type of wood used for joists

5. Any heavy loading, such as snow

This is one of the few crucial dimensions specified in deck building. If you undersize or overspace the joists, the decking can collapse or the building inspector can stop the project. Be sure you talk to a local retailer or building code office about the proper sizing for your joists and span. Joists placed 24″ on center are usually adequate.

After you have determined their spacing, the layout is rather simple. Starting from a nail nailed at the center of one of the two outer joists already installed, measure along the ledger, making a clear mark every 24″ (or 16″), as shown in Figure 15. These marks indicate the *center* of each joist. However, it is a good idea to make a second mark

With all your pieces cut you can now assemble posts and girders into one unit. Usually this is done with bolts, nails, or metal fasteners. I recommend using bolts. If you are resting the girder on top of the posts, use metal fasteners as shown in Figure 13. Be sure to always use hot dipped galvanized (HDG) fasteners, bolts, or nails so they will not rust. If you are bolting it together, drill your holes good and straight so the bolts will go through straight. Use a bit that is ⅛″ larger than the bolt, to allow for final adjustments.

Once the entire unit is assembled,

move it into place under your two outer joists. If you are assembling the pieces in place, the application is pretty much the same. Before toenailing the outer joists to the top of the girder, measure out from the wall to be sure the girder is the proper distance from the wall. Once you have ascertained this, check once again to be sure the joists are still at right angles from the ledger and still level. Once all this is checked, nail the joists into the girders with some 10d galvanized nails to use some special L-shaped metal fasteners.

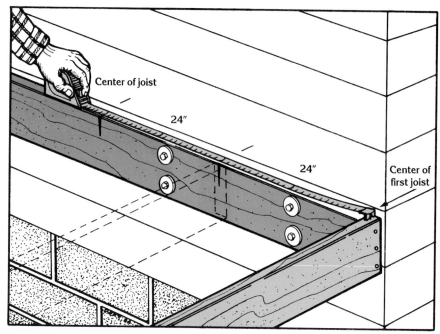

Figure 15. Hook tape at center of first joist and mark every 24″.

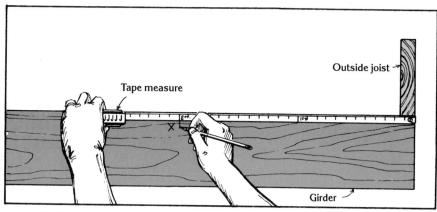

Figure 16. Mark joist locations on girder.

INSTALLING
THE REMAINING JOISTS

Margin of Error: ¹/₄″

MOST COMMON MISTAKES

1. Not crowning joists.

2. Placing joist on wrong side of layout mark.

It is now time to install the remaining joists. Again, this is rather simple. Some builders cut the joists to length before installing. I recommend you cut the joists after almost all your decking boards are in place. The reason for this will become clear later on. Now, simply insert the joists into the joist hangers as shown in Figure 18. Be sure, however, as you do this, that you crown each joist, pointing the bow skyward. Insert it in the hanger, nail the other (loose) side of the hanger tight up against the joist, and then nail hanger nails through the hanger into the joist and ledger. Then toenail the joist (using two 10d HDG nails) through the joist into the girder. Special HDG L-shaped fasteners can be used here instead of nails. This is especially recommended in earthquake areas.

NOTE: Some builders, especially in areas of heavy rain or snow, also place galvanized metal flashing on top of each joist before the deck boards are applied, as shown in Figure 19. This flashing helps keep water from getting trapped between the decking and the joists, causing rot. Inquire whether this is done in your area.

¾″ to either the left or right side of each of these first marks. This new mark locates one side of each joist rather than the middle; this makes it easier to locate the joist hangers on the ledger. Using a combination square, draw this new mark straight down across the ledger. Be sure it is a good, straight mark, since you will be nailing your joist hanger to this mark. Nail the hangers on flush with the edge of these new marks.

Do a similar layout on the girder, so that you know exactly where each joist crosses the girder. Again, draw new lines ¾″ to one side of the center line (the same as you did for the ledger) and then make an "X" so that you will know on which side of this line the

joists will finally sit (Figure 16).

After you have made all your marks, begin nailing the metal joist hangers on the ledger using the special stubby joist hanger nails provided with the hangers. Only nail on one side of the hanger, allowing the other side to float free until the joist is inserted. Nail on the one side so that the interior edge of the joist hanger is nailed along the line you drew to mark the side of the joist, as shown in Figure 17. Be sure as you go along that you are clear about which side of the mark the joist hanger and joist should be nailed to, to assure proper spacing. Even a seasoned professional can accidentally put the joist and joist hanger on the wrong side of the mark.

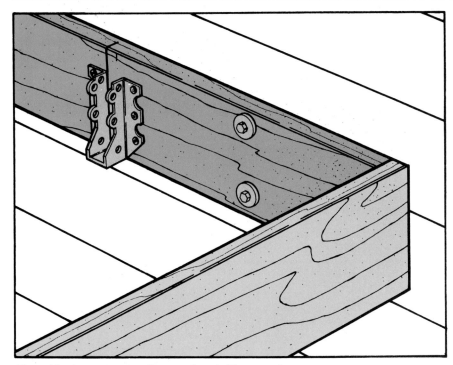

Figure 17. Attach one side of hanger aligned with new mark.

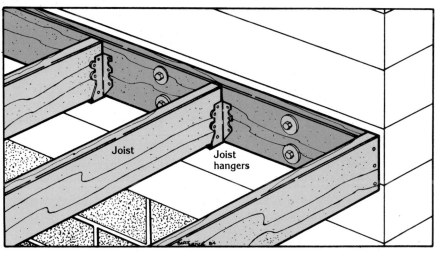

Figure 18. Joists are installed and nailed to joist hangers.

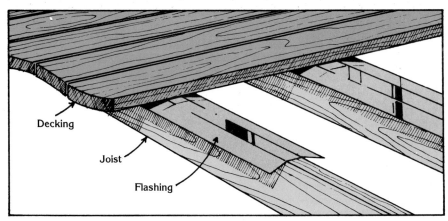

Figure 19. Flashing is sometimes installed over joist.

STEP ELEVEN

APPLYING THE DECK BOARDS

Margin of Error: ¼″

MOST COMMON MISTAKES

1. Not using enough nails.

2. Not leaving a gap between the deck boards.

3. Not forcing bow out of crooked boards.

You are now ready to start installing your deck boards. This part of the job goes quickly and easily and is rather exciting. You really start to see your deck coming together. You need to consider each board you apply since they all will be seen. Look at each piece and try to put the most attractive pieces in the high-visiblity areas. Also, look at each side of each board to see which side you want exposed. Check to see how badly bowed the boards are. If there are a few very bad pieces, reject them, because they will look crooked once the decking is down.

One advantage of redwood is its outstanding stability. In varying moisture conditions its shrinking or swelling is minimal. It resists warping, checking, and cupping better than other woods.

TIP: Hot dipped or double hot dipped galvanized (HDG) fasteners will not rust and are less expensive than aluminum and stainless steel nails.

Start your decking application from the wall and work toward the yard. Be sure that the first course you apply next to the wall is made of good, straight pieces, because this course is used as a guide and if it is crooked it affects all the other courses. Also be sure that you leave a gap between the first course and the wall, so that water can drain down the wall.

If possible, purchase boards that are long enough to span the entire width of the deck. If the deck is too wide, this may not be possible. Even if boards are available, any lengths over 14′ are often very crooked. If two pieces are needed, the pieces must always join directly over the center of a joist, to provide a nailing surface for each piece. Never join all the courses over the same joist, as it will look like a big suture running down the deck. Stagger the joints so that every other course joins over the same joists, as shown in Figure 20.

Finishing nails are not recommended for use in deck construction, rather use double HDG 16d nails. Stainless steel and aluminum nails work even better because they do not stain the wood, but these may be hard to find. Beware of electroplated nails, which often rust. Except with redwood, it is usually best to use three nails in a 2×8 and two nails in 2×4 and 2×6 boards, at each point where the board crosses a joist. On 2×4 and 2×6 redwood boards one nail per joist can be used. Alternate these nails from one side of the board to the other. This method counters any minor tendency to cup or pull. Two nails are used for boards 8″ or wider. All nails should penetrate $1\frac{1}{2}$″ into the joists.

I recommend you use a combination square and mark a true perpendicular line across each joist so that you can place all your nails in a straight line. It takes a little more time, but you will be surprised to see how much better it looks, once the deck is completed.

The process of nailing on the deck

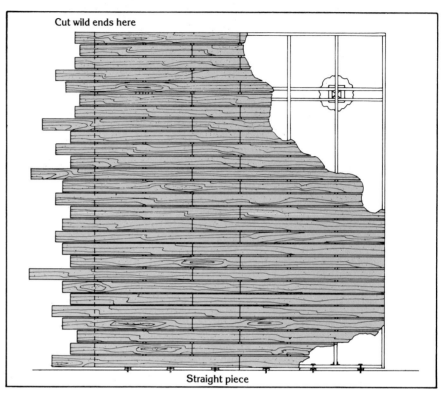

Figure 20. Remember to stagger the joists.

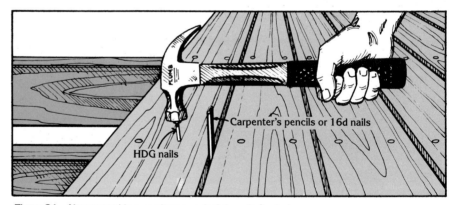

Figure 21. Always provide a gap between deck boards for drainage.

boards is rather straightforward, but there are a few things you need to know. First, be sure you always leave a gap between each course of deck boards. This allows water to drain off the deck. You can stick a flat carpenter's pencil or the shank of a 16d nail between the courses as they are applied; this should leave an adequate gap ($\frac{1}{8}$″–$\frac{1}{4}$″). (See Figure 21.)

No board is perfect, and many will have bows that need to be pulled out. This is done by forcing the bow out as you nail from one end to the other. This is why you never nail from both ends to the middle — you may trap the bow. Put in your spacer to create the needed gap and then force the board into place. It will usually straighten out if the board is not too badly bowed. Use a smooth-headed hammer and try not to scar the wood (though the first few rains will probably draw out most of the dents). Also, a pry bar can be used, as shown in Figure 22, to force the board straight.

Usually it is easiest to place the deck boards flush with the outside edge of one of the outer joists, let them "run wild" at the other end, and then cut this end all at once. The only other trick to applying the decking is to drill pilot holes when nailing near the end of a board. This involves areas such as where two deck boards join together in the center of a joist and both ends must be nailed to that joist. Usually you would split the wood if you tried to nail that close to the end of a board. To avoid this, use a cordless drill to drill a pilot hole, one slightly smaller than the shank of the nail (use HDG finishing nails for these end nailings), and then drive the nail into this. This will prevent splitting. (See Figure 23.)

Begin to lay the deck boards from

TIP: Paint the exposed ends of the joists and deck boards with a waterproofing for added protection.

---

the house end. Measure out from the wall every few courses to be sure all boards are equidistant from the wall as you progress. Continue until you are one course away from the end of the

joists. (See Step 12 for what to do then.) Also, stand up and look down on the deck to be sure you are not trapping any bows in the boards and that the deck, in general, looks good.

Figure 22. Use a pry bar to remove bow in deck board.

Pilot holes

Figure 23. Use a cordless drill to drill pilot hole to avoid board splitting.

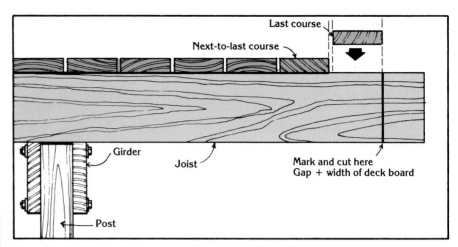

Figure 24. Cut joist to align last deck board with end of joist. This method assumes you are using a band.

STEP TWELVE

CUTTING THE ENDS OF THE JOISTS AND DECK BOARDS

Margin of Error: ¼″

MOST COMMON MISTAKE

1. Not cutting square ends.

As you begin to apply the last deck boards, a final adjustment can be made. What you are striving for is that the outer edge of the last course of decking boards be exactly flush with the ends of the joists. Some builders don't bother with this, but it adds a nice finished look. The only way to make this work out is to cut the joists after the next-to-the-last course but before the last course is nailed on. This way, you can tell exactly how things are going to work out. After the next-to-the-last course is in place, measure to the ends of the joists for their final cut. (See Figure 24.) The measurement is made from the outer edge of the next-to-the-last course to a point on the joists that

equals the gap between courses plus the width of a deck board (say, a ¼″ gap with a 5½″ board measures 5¾″).

Then mark the ends of the joists at this point and draw a line across them with a combination square. Now you can cut the joists at this point, install the final course of deck boards, and have a perfect fit. Be sure you make good, straight cuts so the band will fit on properly. After you have cut all the ends of the joists you can install your last course of deck boards. Again, be sure this is a good, straight course, since it will be more visible than the others.

After this last course is in place you can install the band joist (the piece that is installed across the ends of all the joists). Often this band joist is one size wider than the joist, to act as a curb for the decking.

Now you are ready to cut the "wild end" of the deck boards. To do this, make a mark at either end of the deck and pop a chalkline to get a perfectly straight cut. Cut off the wild ends of the decking boards to this line. (See Figure 25.) Be sure your marks are where you want them to be, remembering if you are designing in any cantilever over the joists. Set your saw to cut through the deck boards plus ¼″ and start cutting. Stop and check every now and then to be sure you are on line and not veering into or away from the joists.

It is a good idea to paint the exposed ends of the joists and deck boards with a waterproofing for added protection.

Figure 25. Popping line to cut wild ends.

STEP THIRTEEN

FACING THE DECK WITH BAND JOISTS

Margin of Error: ¹/₄"

MOST COMMON MISTAKE

1. Not measuring correctly to allow for mitered ends.

After you have cut the ends of the joists and the wild ends of the deck boards, you can apply the band joists. (See Figure 26.) Sometimes the band consists only of a piece at the end of the joists where you just made your final cut. Usually, however, for sake of appearance, the band covers all outer edges of the deck and is one size (2") wider than the joists so that it acts as a curb for the decking (Figure 1).

Also, the ends of the individual band pieces are miter cut so that there is no exposed end grain. This mitering process is not difficult but requires accurate measuring and cutting. When measuring, remember that the measurements taken off the deck refer to the inside cut of the miter, not the outside. Set your saw at the proper angle and cut. If the miter is not a 45-degree miter for a 90-degree right-angle joint, you may want to practice on some scrap pieces to be sure you have the correct angle set on the saw. Nail the bands to the joists with 16d nails.

STEP FOURTEEN

INSTALLING THE RAILINGS

Margin of Error: ¹/₄"

MOST COMMON MISTAKES

1. Pickets not plumb.

2. Top railing not level.

3. Pickets not evenly placed.

4. Pickets too far apart.

There are many different styles of railings for decks. Choose a style according to your budget, time, and energy, as well as to the overall look and use of the deck. Different styles do different things. You can incorporate planters, benches, tables, and stairs into your design. A book on deck design or a ride around the neighborhood will give you some inspiration.

I have chosen to teach a rather simple design but one that is often used. If you are building something different from this, many of the procedures outlined here will still apply. If you are copying a design from an existing deck, a close inspection of the deck with

sketchbook in hand should enable you to understand how the railing is put together. The main thing you want to be sure of in installing a railing is its stability. There is nothing worse than building the entire deck railing, only to discover later that it is weak and unstable, and then always worrying when a guest at your bar-b-que is going to make an unexpected visit onto your lawn.

There are usually codes that apply to deck railings. If the deck is more than a certain distance from the ground, often 30", a railing may be required. If the deck is closer to the ground, the railing may be optional. Also, the code will allow only a certain gap between the pickets, 6"–9", so that a child cannot slip through. The height of the railing is regulated, too — 36"–42". Be sure you check all of this before beginning.

The railing we are showing is constructed of 2 × 2 pickets with a 2 × 4 top railing. This is a simple yet attractive railing. Since we are not tying the railing into the foundation posts (which is often the case), stability is a concern. We provide this stability by bolting the bottom of the pickets to the band joists, using two HDG lag screws, and by tying the railing into the house at several places.

First, cut all the pickets. For aesthetic reasons we have put an angle cut on the top and bottom of each picket. After

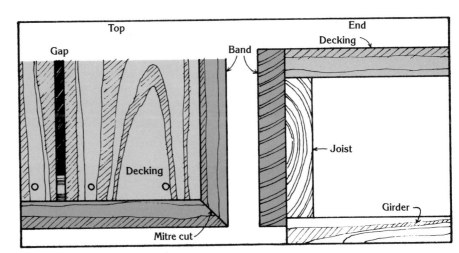

Figure 26. Facing the deck with band joists.

the pickets are cut, cut the 2×4 top rail. Try to use pieces that are long enough to span the entire length of each section. If the span is too long and two pieces are needed, you will need to join these two over a 2×4 picket for adequate bearing. Determine where this break should occur for the most balanced appearance. Also, where two sections of the deck come together, miter cut the top rail to cover any exposed end grain. This looks much better.

After all your pieces are cut, it is best to bolt the pickets to the top rail and then install the entire assembly onto the deck. Mark the top rail so that the pickets will be properly spaced. Then bolt the pickets to the rail using lag screws that are as long as possible without poking through the back side of the railing (about $2\frac{1}{2}$"). Be sure that your marks are correct and that the pickets are attached to the proper side of the marks. A picket that is off will show clearly, once installed. Also, at the bottom of each picket drill two holes that are one size smaller than the lag screws that will hold the pickets to the joists and band. Drill these holes so that they are as far apart as possible and yet at least $1\frac{1}{2}$" from the edge of the band and joists. You are now ready to install the entire assembly onto the deck. This is done by using two more lag screws at the base where the picket meets the joists and band. Again, use a $2\frac{1}{2}$" lag screw and, as always, be sure they are HDG, aluminum, or stainless steel so they will not rust. It is best to align the picket/railing assembly so that it is in its *exact* location and to nail a few pickets temporarily in place to hold it there. Then use a level to locate where each picket will meet the band and joists. By using the level at each picket, you can be sure that they will all be level and parallel to each other. Uneven pickets are easily noticed. It is imperative that the assembly be in its *exact* location before you start leveling the pickets. If you need to move the assembly, even slightly, after the pickets are attached at the bottom, the entire assembly will

look askew and will need to be redone. Once you have ascertained that it is in its exact location, and have leveled your pickets, hold the picket in place while you mark the location of the holes on the band and joists. Then drill these holes on the band and joists, again using a drill bit one size smaller than the shank of the lag screw. Then bolt the lag screws in, using a socket or crescent wrench. Do this around the entire deck until the railings are all in place. Where two railings intersect at their mitered cut railing top, drill pilot holes through one top railing into the other and then nail together with 10d HDG finishing nails, two from one direction and one from the other. Your railings should now be complete.

STEP FIFTEEN

WATERPROOFING THE DECK

Margin of Error: None

MOST COMMON MISTAKE

1. Not sealing the deck.

There is one final step that many builders take before completing the deck. This is to coat the deck with a water-repellant sealer. This not only protects the

Figure 27. A simple but sturdy railing design.

wood is smooth or rough sawn, a brush is recommended for application. Spraying is not recommended. Also note that "Shake and Shingle" paints, sprays, varnishes, or lacquers are not recommended for decks.

Bleaching agents can be applied that will give the decking a silvered weathered look. If no finish is applied to redwood, it will initially darken and then weather a driftwood grey.

TOOLS AND MATERIALS CHECKLIST

Tools

Framing hammer	Shovel
Torpedo level	Wheelbarrow or
4′ level	pan
Plumb bob	Cement hoe
Pencil	Trowel
Nail pouch	Pry bar
Safety goggles	Caulking gun
Ear plugs	Extension cords
First aid kit	Socket or
Framing square	crescent
Combination	wrench
square	Power saw
Tape measure	Handsaw
Sawhorses	

Figure 28. Waterproofing the deck.

Materials

Pier blocks	Post anchors
HDG nails	Railing stock
HDG lag bolts or	Flashing (if
screws	needed)
Decking	Ledger board
Girder stock	Band joists
Joist stock	Silicon caulk
Post stock	Water-repellant
Joist hangers	sealer
Joist hanger nails	Nylon string
Right-angle	Ready-mix
brackets	concrete
Post caps	

wood but also extends the life of the deck by preventing the costly effect of water damage. A clear water-repellant sealer can be painted on the deck that will keep the water from penetrating. A water repellant with a mildewcide will also help redwood keep its red color and not turn black with age. The California Redwood Association recommends applying the sealer to all pieces before construction, for a more complete coverage. This sealer serves well for a base coat for other finishes. If you apply the sealer to a redwood deck after it is completed, you can apply coats at 12- to 18-month intervals to eliminate the darkening effect and preserve the beautiful buckskin color.

If wood is left unsealed, it can rot, stain, and decay, often resulting in your having to replace the wood prematurely. Because of the enduring qualities of heart redwood, this is not as much of a problem with redwood as it is with other woods. The water repellant can be applied with a brush, roller, or spray and goes on quite easily because it is rather thin and, unlike paint, penetrates quickly.

Color or a bleached effect can be added to redwood and other woods by using decking stains and bleaches. Use a lightly pigmented, oil-based decking stain to show the wood grain or a heavily pigmented, heavy-bodied stain if you prefer an opaque effect. Whether the